ALIEN INTELLIGENCE

Stuart Holroyd

ALIEN INTELLIGENCE

Everest House
Publishers   New York

Contents

List of Illustrations   7

Introduction   9

Part I: Non-human 'Persons'
1 'They're Almost Human'   19
2 Computers and Artificial Intelligence   42
3 Aliens Among Us?   69

Part II: Non-physical 'Persons'
4 Vehicles of Vitality   97
5 Mind Beyond the End of Its Tether   125

Part III: Non-terrestrial 'Persons'
6 The Space People   149
7 The UFO Phenomenon   177
8 Supermind   205

Notes and References   227

Index   230

List of Illustrations

PLATES

1	Blaise Pascal	33
2	Cover of *Amazing Stories*	34
3	Illustration from *Amazing Stories*	51
4 & 5	Washoe using Ameslan	52
6	Lana activating a food dispenser	52
7	Peter the dolphin and Margaret Howe	61
8	Baron Wolfgang von Kempelen's chess automaton	61
9	Gray Walter's tortoises	62
10	The Hopkins Beast	62
11	Shakey	63
12	Shakey manoeuvres to push box off platform	63
13	Part of Charles Babbage's analytical engine	64
14	An experimental game of chess played against a computer	73
15	Magician invoking Paracelsus elementals	74
16a & b	Jack Webber in states of emanation of ectoplasm	91
17	Puzzling elements on a print of a photograph of Conan Doyle	92
18	Ectoplasmic materialisation of a face	92
19a	Representation of Oannes	101
19b	Assyrian fisherman thought to represent Oannes	102
20	Wall painting of Osiris	103
21	Stone figure of Quetzacoatl	104
22	Late Assyrian or New Babylonian Cylinder Seal	104
23	The Indian Vedic god Agni	104
24	The first incarnation of the Hindu god Vishnu	113
25	Ezekiel's vision of an angel	114
26	Hopi Indians in ceremonial dress	131
27	The Kachina ceremony of the Hopi	131
28	William Gerhardie	132
29a–e	The projection of the astral body	141–2
30a–f	The materialisation of Silverbell	143–4
31	The swaying of the astral body	153
32	Kirlian photographs of auras	154
33	Henry Sidgwick	171
34	Edmund Gurney	171

35 Frederic Myers   171
36 The corridors of a nest of termites   172
37 Three exposures of Sirius   172
38 'Flying-saucer nest'   181
39 A UFO photographed in North-Eastern Bohemia   181
40 Joe Simonton   182
41 Barney and Betty Hill   182
42 Artist's impression of the lunar Cyclops array   183
43 Three Arecibo type spherical antennas on the far side of the moon   183
44 'God creating the Universe', by William Blake   184

FIGURES

Washoe using Ameslan   27
Relative brain sizes of *homo sapiens*, dolphin and chimp   29
'The mightiest brain on the planet'   31
The crucifixion of Quetzacoatl   79
Moses encounters God on Mount Sinai   80
Ezekiel encounters beings from the skies   81
The strange creatures of popular fairy stories   84–5
Graph of the delaying radio echoes of Boötis   151
Total power levels radiated by TV transmitters 1940–85   158
Growth of man made radio signals 1860–1980   158
'It's not one of ours'   176
Sketch by Villas-Boas of the craft he saw   179
Vallée's map of France showing plots of UFO landings   186
Bright green creature spotted in Hopkinsville, Kentucky   188
Annual reports of UFO sightings 1815–1915   192
Monthly reports of UFO sightings 1956–61   192
Ceramic figure found in South America   199
Artist's impression of humanoids described by contactees   200–1

Introduction

Contemplation of the cosmic has strange effects on some people. Immanuel Kant, the great advocate and exponent of Pure Reason, concludes, by way of Newtonian physics, that the inhabitants of the outer planets of the solar system must have bodies of lighter material and therefore nimbler minds than inhabitants of the inner planets – and he suggested that sin was possible only on Earth because other beings were either too dumb or too evolved to be capable of it.

A century before Kant, another great thinker, Blaise Pascal, looked up to the heavens and uttered probably the best known of his *pensées*: 'The eternal silence of these infinite spaces frightens me.'

By way of contrast, here's a *pensée* by Yuri Gagarin, the Russian who in 1961 became the first man in Space: 'I felt like diving into this ocean and swimming to the horizon where earth and sky meet.'

Kant's whimsy, Pascal's existential fear, and Gagarin's boyish fascination are perhaps three typical reactions to awareness of the cosmic. Infinity and eternity are daunting concepts for a creature living on what is little more than a speck of galactic dust for a brief moment of time, with a hunger to know whether he is a freak or a paragon. Fear, fascination, and fantasy are three very human reactions to this situation.

What frightened Pascal was the thought of the ultimate aloneness and meaninglessness of human life. But his very next *pensée* was: 'How many kingdoms do not know us!'

Note that it is not a question, but an exclamation – or rather an anguished cry. In Pascal's day there was no foreseeable chance of ever establishing contact with any other cosmic civilisation, but since then the situation has changed. 'What do space flights promise mankind?' Gagarin asks, and he gives the answer: 'They will help us in revealing many secrets of nature which scientists the world over are striving to discover, to reply to the question which agitates us all: does life exist outside the Earth?'

Now this is a curious statement from a representative of a scientific, materialist culture: that the justification of one of the greatest resource-consuming projects that mankind has ever conceived lies in the possibility that it might answer 'a question which agitates us all'.

Anything that man gets agitated about, anything that engages and polarises his emotions – as the idea of the existence of alien life and intelligence does – is surely worth investigating.

I recently mentioned the title of this book to a friend, who laughed and said: 'There's no such thing.' If I were of that persuasion, there would, of course, be no book, but I understand his reaction. Man's religions, mythologies, and literature all testify to a longing for the existence of the alien, and the sceptic might well consider that whatever tenuous evidence there is in this direction must stem from that longing – that such evidence is mere wish-fulfilment fantasy.

We should, however, make a distinction between alien intelligence and intelligent aliens. My friend was taking the former term for the latter, but there is an important difference. That alien intelligence exists is indisputable, as the first two chapters of this book will show, and although whether intelligent aliens exist or not in some other part of the cosmos is another question, the demonstrable existence of such intelligence at least opens one's mind to the *idea* of the existence of intelligent aliens. It also diminishes the implausibility of such a notion.

Einstein is reported to have said of UFO sightings: 'These people have seen something. What they have seen I do not know and care less.' His attitude was surely uncommon. It was perhaps typical of the scientist, who has no means of scientifically getting to grips with the UFO problem, but to admit that people must have seen something and not to care what that something is does seem a rather severe renunciation of natural human curiosity and alien to the prescribed scientific method of truth-seeking.

Modern ethological studies have tended to narrow the gap between man and other mammalia, but man is endowed with an immense curiosity and passion for exploration that still sets him apart from other mammals.

Perhaps we should interpret Einstein's disclaimer as a renunciation of the UFO cult rather than as a repudiation of curiosity. No doubt the great man was plagued by people eager to tell him things about the universe that he did not know, and he may have been feeling tetchy when he uttered his dictum. But whatever the cause of it, it expressed an attitude of indifference that few people convinced of the authenticity of reports of things in the sky would share.

John Lilly, whose pioneer research on dolphin intelligence is discussed in the first chapter of this book, was trained in orthodox science, and when he conceived his project of investigating what he called the 'dolphin mind hypothesis', he found that his scientific peers regarded the hypothesis as on a par with that of the existence of God, spirits, or UFOs, and, as such, unworthy of serious scientific attention. This rejection promoted the following interesting reflections:

Modern science denies interest in the existence of such things as the spirit world, the direct influence of God on human minds, and extraterrestrial influence machines manipulated by other beings. Most of the phenomena described as happening within the minds of people can be explained by the projection of signals from within one's storage on to noise, and hence hearing or seeing what one wants to hear or see rather than some objectively existing 'spirit' or 'God'. . .

The existence theorem states: 'To prove the existence of a something one must first present evidence of that something and its existence acceptable to other minds.' The non-existence theorem states, 'as long as one assumes the non-existence of a something one will assume that the signals from the something either do not exist, are noise, are created in another human mind, or come from some mindless process in nature.' Therefore, if an unknown mind without a visible, detectable body sends signals, we ignore them, repress memories of having received them, attribute them to noise, or attribute them to a mindless but systematically varying source, or say that they are the results of faulty operation of the observer, i.e. projections from the observer's own mind.

What Lilly calls 'the non-existence theorem' is virtually a modern re-statement of the principle of 'Occan's razor', which holds that when seeking to understand a phenomenon, we should cut out all extravagant hypotheses and settle for the one that is most compatible with reason and proven knowledge. The trouble with this principle, as generally applied today, is that as with a great many puzzling phenomena, the least extravagant hypothesis is that they simply do not exist, so authorising the curtailment of inquiry and vindicating the complacency of a majority of orthodox scientists.

Lilly's 'dolphin mind hypothesis' is one of the least contentious of the hypotheses we shall be considering in these pages, but Lilly found such a vehement initial rejection of it among scientists that he felt the rejection in itself was a curious enough phenomenon to demand explanation. The explanation, he suggested, might be that rapid scientific progress in the areas of physics, chemistry, biology, and engineering had been achieved precisely because research and development in these areas had been based on the assumption that independent mind was non-existent in them and that the human mind alone was able to understand, manipulate, and control the processes therein. The material success of this strategy – of divesting nature of all the properties of mind and of arrogating those properties to man alone – seems to have proved the correctness both of the strategy and of the hypothesis of mindless nature on which it was based. In fact, all it has proved is their effectiveness.

Lilly's critique of orthodox science is not a rejection of its methods, but a demand for an extension of its conceptual framework so that its methods, or appropriate adaptations of them, might be applied to wider fields of inquiry than at present. In this regard, his remarks about how signals from one's own storage are projected on to noise and taken for objective observations should not go unheeded in our inquiry.

'Happiness', said Jonathan Swift, 'is the perpetual possession of being well deceived,' and since his day, understanding of the mechanisms of self-deception by means of which men secure happiness has become highly sophisticated. In several books, Lilly has shown how the human brain abhors a state of silence and inactivity and how, under conditions of sensory deprivation, the 'human biocomputer' generates its own programmes – visions, voices, and seemingly tangible realities. He has also demonstrated that it is an innate property of man's mind to seek to order the teeming inputs of the senses into coherent and meaningful patterns – patterns that may be determined by personal or cultural dictates. These are scientific insights into the processes of human perception and cognition, and in an inquiry into a subject so evocative of fears and hopes in man as alien intelligence, it would be folly to ignore them.

Though fears, hopes, and bold speculations may have no part to play in the process of scientific investigation, they are the very stuff of literature. So, on the principle that imagination is a necessary component of man's truth-seeking faculty, we shall not eschew the insights and imaginings of science-fiction writers in these pages if they appear to throw some light on our subject. And they very often do.

Science fiction has come a very long way since the seventeenth century, when one pioneer of the genre, Cyrano de Bergerac, imagined that space travel was powered by phials of dew, and that among the Moon's inhabitants were discursive philosophers with a penchant for ingeniously inverting worldly logic. Another pioneer, Bernard de Fontenelle, speculated that Moon beings might ride in spacecraft in the upper reaches of the Earth's atmosphere and was prompted to ask: 'If from there, out of curiosity of seeing us, they would fish us like fish, how would you like it?'

Such fantasies and fancies, together with logical extrapolations from human experience, such as Wells' *The War of the Worlds*, and the extraterrestrial gothic horrors and monstrosities projected in popular ephemeral literature in magazines such as *Amazing Stories* (see Plates 2 and 3) were long the staple of science fiction. But in recent decades, the genre has come of age, becoming a medium for some of the most brilliant and sustained philosophical speculation and some of the boldest and best-informed scientific speculation on the subject of alien intelligence.

The fact that the Copernican and Darwinian revolutions administered successive blows to human self-esteem, that with the former, man lost his throne and, with the latter, his soul, as one writer has put it, has been remarked often enough. But the salutary effects of these revolutions in human thought have received rather less attention. Apart from the fact that it cannot be but salutary for the human mind to have to exercise itself in achieving accommodations with reality, the Copernican revolution gave man the idea of the possible existence of other inhabited worlds; and the Darwinian revolution and the biological discoveries that emanated from it gave him the idea of the possibility of the existence of other intelligent species. These were two ideas without which speculative science fiction could scarcely have got off the ground.

Olaf Stapledon's 1937 novel *Star Maker* is a fine example of how the imagination, informed by science, can generate ideas that are outside the terms of reference that science sets itself, but are of profound human interest and concern. When the unnamed first-person hero of Stapledon's book discovers his ability to project himself out of his body and to send his consciousness travelling faster than light to visit the other suns and planetary systems of our galaxy, he becomes possessed of 'a keen hunger ... a hunger not for adventure but for insight into the significance of man, or of any manlike beings in the cosmos'. He proposes a number of questions for his investigation, and makes a resolution:

> Was man indeed, as he sometimes desired to be, the growing point of the cosmical spirit, in its temporal aspect at least? Or was he one of many million growing points? Or was mankind of no more importance in the universal view than rats in a cathedral? And again, was man's true function power, or wisdom, or love, or worship, or all of these? Or was the idea of function, of purpose, meaningless in relation to the cosmos? These grave questions I would answer. Also I must learn to see a little more clearly and confront a little more rightly (so I put it to myself) that which, when we glimpse it at all, compels our worship.

Setting out on his explorations, Stapledon's Space-traveller visits thousands of suns and their attendant planets in our own galaxy and at first he despairs to find them all desolate and lifeless. But eventually he comes upon one planet very like Earth which is inhabited by creatures of general humanoid form, but with divergent characteristics such as an extra-long neck, eyes located below the nose and hands consisting of just three fingers and a thumb and with no palm.

He finds that he can enter the minds of these beings, but that all their thoughts and emotions are quite alien to him and that when they become aware of his presence, they regard it as a symptom of insanity in themselves and apply to their local 'Mental Sanitation Officer' for a cure. Eventually, he finds a hospitable host, an eccentric philosopher named Bvalltu, who welcomes him into his mind and with whose help he begins to understand this 'other earth' that is in some respects familiar to him, though in others utterly alien.

Familiar aspects are the daily lives, and family and social organisations of the bizarre humanoid inhabitants of this planet. They have industry and agriculture, cities, railways, and steam ships – and their desires and passions are like those of man. A fundamental difference, however, is that while their senses of taste and smell have developed to an amazing degree, their senses of sight and hearing are poor compared with those of man. This evolutionary divergence affects many aspects of their lives and experiences. Endowed with taste sensors on their hands, feet, and genitals, these beings interact with each other and with their environment quite differently from the ways that human beings do. Their entertainment industry flourishes on the radio transmission of scents and tastes, rather than sights and sounds.

During the time of the Space-traveller's visit, this strange world and its civilisation is in the process of destroying itself, and Bvalltu explains that this has happened many times in its past. Each time a certain level of achievement has been reached, civilisation invariably collapsed in a mad frenzy of wars and devastation. The traveller finds this information dismaying, for he had always thought in earthly terms of suffering and struggle as historically purposeful, as leading the human spirit onward and upward, and he considers that if Bvalltu is right, then 'the maker of the universe must be indifferent to the fate of worlds . . . must be sheer evil'.

Bvalltu counters this with an argument familiar to terrestrial theologians: 'Even if the powers destroy us, who are we, to condemn them? Perhaps they use us for their own high ends, use our strength and our weakness, our joy and our pain, in some theme inconceivable to us and excellent.' And he cries: 'Oh, Star Maker, even if you destroy me, I must praise you'. Which, for readers familiar with the Book of Job, leaves the identity of the Star Maker unequivocal.

The quest for the Star Maker and for knowledge of the order and purpose of the Cosmos becomes the theme of the story as the Space-traveller and Bvalltu set out together to explore innumerable inhabited worlds throughout the galaxy. The life-forms on these worlds are often bizarre. Brains as complex and powerful as man's, and sensory systems of equal, and in some cases superior acuity, are possessed by living creatures, by plants, by marine animals resembling sailing boats. There are worlds of composite beings in which myriads of insects or birds constitute a single intelligent organism.

As the travellers proceed on their journey, they are joined by other seekers, and when they come together in a mental community, interlinked by telepathy, they constitute a collective intelligence capable of comprehending more profound and more subtle concepts than individually they would be capable of. Ultimately, the Space-traveller becomes a participant in the functioning of a cosmic mind – only to find that the Star Maker is still an alien and superior intelligence, for he creates cosmos upon cosmos in an eternal effort to improve and refine his creations and, through them, himself.

Ultimately, too, the questions which the Space-traveller posed at the start of his journey of exploration among alien creatures and worlds are answered. *Star Maker*, indeed, proposes answers to some very profound questions, but at present I am not so concerned with these answers as I am with the fact that the book poses such questions as whether diverse biologies might exist, whether intelligence is a property exclusive to biological systems, whether consciousness is separable from the physical body, what limitations are inherent in human intelligence, what human potentialities may yet be unfulfilled, and whether the concept of cosmic mind signifies any reality.

These questions may well be unanswerable, but they are not imponderable, and to ponder them is, as Kant said *à propos* his conjectures about the inhabitants of other planets, a perfectly permissible and proper way to entertain the mind.

Some defining of terms is necessary, so let us first consider what we mean by the term 'alien'. There are no significant differences between human beings the world over in respect of biology, brain size, and intellectual or manual capability, and yet background cultural factors can make them as mutually alien as if they were different species. Frequently one human group will regard another as deficient in intelligence because it finds its culture and customs incomprehensible. This fact may make the chances of profitable communication across the species barrier or with intelligent beings from other worlds seem remote indeed. Men are inveterately parochial, but while we have to acknowledge that fact we also need to have, for the purposes of the present discussion, a definition of the term 'alien' which will not confound it with issues of parochialism.

So let us ask: 'alien to what?' And let us say: 'to physical, human persons of the planet Earth.' This definition implies that there may be 'persons' that are: (a) not human; (b) not physical; or (c) not terrestrial; and in the three parts of this book we shall consider the existence and possible existence of 'persons' of these three categories.

Of course if you hold that the terms 'human being' and 'person' are synonymous, then these propositions will be nonsensical, but it is arguable that by regarding them as synonymous and by regarding himself as unqiue in qualifying as a 'person', man may have cut himself off from experiences of communication with other beings from which he could have derived enrichment and perhaps instruction.

The proposition put forward by the philosopher Roland Puccetti that 'although human beings are persons, not all persons need to be human', is not only a more generous and productive view than human species chauvinism, but it is also more intelligent.

Which brings us to the second term we need to define: intelligence. Intelligence manifests itself in the way that a creature interacts with its environment. It is a variable both between species and within species. 'Species-specific' behaviours – instinctive actions and reactions common to all members of a species, which generally have to do with feeding, sex or predator-prey relations – are indisputably intelligent behaviours in the sense that they are not random but are directed towards a particular goal. But as a rule, such behaviours are not intelligent in the sense that they are performed as a result of deliberation, foresight, or choice.

Let us take an example of what may paradoxically be called stupid intelligent behaviour. Russian zoologists recently discovered a species of wild goose that has summer nesting grounds in Siberia and migrates to the River Ganges in India for the winter. Its migratory behaviour is distinctly odd, however, for it travels the first hundred miles on foot and during this part of the migration, many of the geese die or are killed. They have to travel on foot because the fledgling geese are not able to fly when their instinct urges them to begin their migration and zoologists have surmised that at some time in the comparatively recent past, some environmental or climatic change made the geese settle in summer grounds farther south than where they had formerly nested, but that the 'biological clock' that told them when to migrate did not adapt to the change. They have no choice but to act on the prompting of their instinct, but to the human observer, who can see that as their nesting grounds have moved south they could safely remain there for the extra ten days or so that it takes for them to acquire their full growth of feathers, their behaviour appears pathetically unintelligent.

This example helps our definition. It brings us to the point that we may consider creatures proportionately more intelligent in so far as they are capable of modifying their instinctive behaviour. They may do this, for instance, to adapt to a change in circumstances or environment; to secure some long-term interest, or in observance of some abstract principle. In fact, these three types of modification of instinctive behaviour could be said to be manifestations of progressively higher degrees of intelligence. They show an increasing degree of detachment from the immediate.

'Beasts abstract not', said the philosopher John Locke, and although, as we shall see, he was probably mistaken, his idea that it is the power to abstract that distinguishes the higher orders of intelligence from the lower is a useful one.

Intelligence, then, is a function that takes place between stimulus and response, or, to use computer terminology, it is the information processing that goes on between input and output. The more information there is to process, the more powerful and sophisticated we consider the intelligent function.

A simple sensory-input and motor-output sequence, such as migratory behaviour prompted by the autumnal shortening of daylight, requires minimal information processing. But to listen to a symphony or read a book, then discuss it at length, requires a great deal. In the latter case the input – the information processed – consists not only of the immediate sensory input but also the use of what are known in computer terminology as 'stored programmes' which would be, for instance, the application of standards learned and remembered, other works of literature or music recalled and compared, and acquired personal predilections and judgements.

If we take the view that there is a spectrum of intelligence, we may define the lowest order above the instinctual as a sensory-motor information processing system, manifesting an ability to modify behaviour in accordance with experience. The highest order may be defined as a feeling-ratiocinative system, manifesting an ability to modify behaviour in accordance with abstract principles. This defines the spectrum of animal–human intelligence.

The interesting question, though, is whether there are ranges of the intelligence spectrum, as there are of the electromagnetic spectrum, that are beyond us. If there are, if higher intelligences do exist, our position with regard to their works would presumably be similar to that of an aborigine trying to understand one of our artefacts – for instance, a colour television set. They may well manifest in our world and experience in apparently random events.

The question of whether we may infer the existence of an alien and higher intelligence from certain categories of apparently random events that occur in our world is one that we shall take up in the concluding chapter of this book. But in the first chapter reference is made to a contact with an alien intelligence which has an interesting implication for our whole inquiry. In this case, the 'contactees' are chimpanzees, and the 'higher intelligence' is *Homo sapiens*. The contact has resulted in the chimpanzees' learning to communicate with man and with each other in sign language. This makes the chimp the first species to learn another's language. It also means that this contact has enabled the animal to develop a potential it could never otherwise have known that it possessed and to achieve things of which it was formerly incapable.

The possibility that other kinds of contact might enable man likewise to develop innate dormant potentialities is perhaps the most compelling reason for pursuing an inquiry into the subject of alien intelligence.

Part I: Non-human 'Persons'

1 'They're Almost Human'

The combative Thomas Huxley, who was known as 'Darwin's Bulldog', once said gleefully to his wife before giving a public lecture on evolution: 'By next Friday evening they will all be convinced that they are monkeys!' Charles Darwin himself would never have been capable of such impishness. When he was asked if he intended to discuss man in the *Origin of Species* he replied: 'I think I shall avoid the whole subject, as so surrounded with prejudices, though I fully admit that it is the highest and most interesting problem for the naturalist.'

But Darwin's circumspection did not prevent his being vilified by many of his contemporaries as a destroyer of human dignity and a mocker of the divine dispensation. For no amount of circumspection could conceal the glaring fact that all his studies and theories pointed to the conclusion that man was numbered among the animal species of the world; that although he might have become the most successful among them by virtue of superior endowments, he was still animal.

The idea was an offence to religion, to philosophy, to science, and to industry: to religion because it denied that man had a special relation to divinity and was responsible to a higher purpose than animals; to philosophy because philosophy was based on the Aristotelian distinction between the 'animal soul' and the 'rational soul'; to science because it was incompatible with the Baconian/Cartesian assumption of man's prerogative to dominate and exploit nature; and to industry because industrialists were making their wealth by ruthlessly and incontinently acting on that assumption.

With such entrenchments of opposition ranged against it, it is small wonder that the idea of man as animal did not fare too well in the world. There were some people – and their numbers increased in the twentieth century – who believed that it was human depravity and cruelty that set the species apart from the animal world. But a majority complacently and obstinately believed that man's uniqueness was divinely determined and rested upon his possession of a superior intelligence and purpose. The religious would also add the possession of an immortal soul. The concept of man as a species of primate seemed not only to belittle his achievements, but also to divest his sins of the metaphysical resonance that for many Romantics gave them a special piquancy.

Part of the trouble was that the notion people had of the animal was as unrealistic and ill-informed as was their concept of man. Such contributions to knowledge as Prince Kropotkin's *Mutual Aid* (1902), which sought to draw attention to facts that subverted the Tennysonian idea of 'nature red in tooth and claw', gained no wide attention.

Far more influential was zoologist Sir Solly Zuckerman's *Social Life of Apes and Monkeys* (1932), a behavioural study of baboons which showed them to be solely obsessed with sex. In 1932, such an obsession was considered to set an animal species further below man than it would today, when observers of some aspects of the human scene might justifiably wonder whether *Homo sexualis* has not utterly usurped *Homo sapiens*. Zuckerman's study was, however, wrong not only in its implications as to the width of the gap between man and ape, but also in its portrayal of the ape's life and character. For it was a study of baboons caged in London Zoo, living a confined, unnatural life in which they could not engage in most of the activities of animals in the wild. They therefore tended to become obsessed by the one activity that was available. Although *Social Life of Apes and Monkeys* purported to be a scientific study, it was based on the unproven and therefore unscientific idea that the behaviour of apes is purely instinctual and is invariable, no matter what the environmental conditions are like. This idea betrayed one of the prejudices that Darwin had felt nearly a century before that precluded rational discussion of the respective characteristics and abilities of the different species of primate.

Man's world, man's achievements, man's religion, and man's science and philosophy all told him that he was lord and master of the world because he was different from and more intelligent than its other inhabitants. At least, Western white man's achievements, religion and teachings told him so. They also told him that other races, such as the American Indian, the West African Negro, and the South African Hottentot were sub-human; were closer to the animal than to man; and that the divine dispensation had been to place Western white man at the top of a hierarchy that graded down through the other human races to the apes. It was a vulnerable idea, and Darwin himself had a glimpse of the fact that it is not innate nature, but rather nurture and environment that make different human beings what they are.

When the *Beagle* was preparing to sail back to England and the captain returned his hostages to their own people, Darwin, as he later wrote, felt 'melancholy leaving our Fuegians amongst their barbarous countrymen.' He reflected that: 'In contradiction to what has often been stated, three years has been sufficient to change savages into, as far as habits go, complete and voluntary Europeans.' This idea was irreconcilable with the prevailing view that there are fixed lines of demarcation between human races according to their inherent and God-ordained superiority one to the other.

Darwin, however, did not hold on to his momentary insight that the lines of demarcation were shifting and relative and could be transcended. Later he was to write: 'We have a very firm gradation in the intellectual powers of the vertebrate, with one rather wide gap . . . between say a Hottentot and an Orang.' In other words, the Hottentot was at the bottom of the human ladder, and below him was the ladder of animal intelligence – and Western white man was still magnificently alone at the top of the pile.

Perhaps many people have felt this aloneness as a kind of loneliness, only to dismiss this feeling as unworthy of the paragon of creation. Loren Eiseley was one man who confessed to such a feeling in an essay *The Long Loneliness*, and psychologist Carl Jung once observed that we will not really know what it is to be human until we find another intelligent being with whom we can communicate.

It is only in recent years that we have come to realise that the loneliness was self-imposed and that we need not look beyond this planet for other intelligent beings to communicate with. Look in any 'New Age' bookshop or book catalogue today and you will find volumes on 'inter-species communication' among the books on religion, mysticism, and occultism, which itself indicates that man considers that his discovery of other intelligences inhabiting his planet acts for him somehow as a liberation and an opportunity. Indeed it is. It is a liberation from inhibiting modes of thought that philosophy, religion, and science have long conspired to propagate, and an opportunity to better understand the nature, the limits and, possibly, the fallacies of his own intelligence by comparing it with another.

In 1922, an extraordinary book titled *The Soul of the Ape* was written – but it was not published until nearly half a century later when its ideas and approach, although still highly original, no longer seemed as bizarre as they would have done to the author's own generation. Eugene Marais, a Dutch South African poet and naturalist, was the author of this short and perceptive study of the animal mind and comparison of it with the mind of man. The book was based on a three-year study of baboons in the wild, and it is ironic that it lay unread through all the years that Zuckerman's book, which is utterly invalidated, stood as the authoritative study of that animal.

Marais had fought in the Boer War and, when it was over, he and a friend went to live in a hut in the Waterberg, a remote mountain area in the northern Transvaal, where they found themselves in close proximity to a large troop of wild chacma baboons. As the area had been largely depopulated by the war and the farmers who gradually returned had no guns, the baboons were uncommonly fearless of man, so Marais was afforded a unique opportunity to study them. He had difficulty overcoming their initial distrust, but when he had done so, the baboons allowed him and his companion to observe their activities at length and from close quarters. Thus privileged, they observed collective and individual behaviour that evinced a mentality and a degree of spontaneous intelligence that had formerly been considered exclusive to man.

At sunset in the human villages on the veld, Marais observed, an air of quietness and dejection would fall and would last until darkness had settled, whereupon the evening activities of conversation, story-telling, singing, and dancing would begin. And a similar thing happened in the baboon colony. With the setting of the sun, all chatter ceased, the young sought the arms of their mothers where they lay whimpering, and the older ones settled in attitudes of profound dejection. When darkness finally settled, this crepuscular melancholy suddenly lifted.

The striking similarity of the human and the baboon's reaction to the onset of night, Marais wrote, suggested

> that you have here a representation of the same inherent pain of consciousness at the height of its diurnal rhythm . . . that the chacma suffers from the same attribute of pain which is an important ingredient of human mentality, and that the condition is due to the same cause.

Marais did not observe the same obsessive sexuality in baboons in the wild as Zuckerman found in his captive ones. He did notice, however, that, like human beings and unlike the non-primates, baboons were not dependent for sexual arousal upon external stimulation, but were capable of arousal from within. He also noticed that some of the young, mature members of the troop – particularly males, but some females, too – indulged in masturbation, which is an activity that requires the exercise of memory and imagination. 'It would seem,' he wrote, 'that in the soul of the chacma, these pleasurable sensations have become an ordinary, causal memory and the sexual sense reacts to that memory.'

Marais maintained that it was the possession of what he called causal memory that distinguished the primates from other animals. 'The ability to memorise the relation of cause and effect, . . . the ability to accumulate what may be termed individual causal memories,' he wrote, was that higher function of mind shared by men and baboons. Other animals possessed what he called phyletic memory, for instance, behaviours governed by instincts that are genetically laid down and invariable. But only primates could learn new behaviours from experience, by mentally relating effect to cause, and seek to achieve desired results by creating the antecedent conditions that individual and not hereditary experience had taught them would produce such results.

There seemed to be a law of life and consciousness, Marais observed, that in proportion as causal memory functions increased, the functions of the phyletic memory became inhibited. In other words, individuality, originality and freedom of thought were bought at the cost of a sacrifice of the instinctual, hereditary knowledge without which an animal might be vulnerable to its natural predators or unable to support itself in its natural environment.

Marais recalled cases of an otter and a baboon being taken away from their mothers at birth and raised by human beings, and when they had reached maturity being introduced to their natural environments. The otter, although previously it had never seen more water than was necessary to slake its thirst, unhesitatingly plunged into a river pool, swam about and caught fish. But the baboon, whose natural food was wild fruit and insects, had no idea which fruits it could or could not eat, or how to hunt insects by turning over large stones. Indeed, when a stone was turned over, the animal scuttled away in terror from the insects swarming beneath.

The disadvantages of the loss of hereditary and 'species–specific' memory in the higher animals are, however, compensated for by the greater adaptability to changed conditions that the possession of individual causal memory confers. The loss also occasions certain behaviours characteristic of the higher animals in which intelligent functions are involved, particularly in relation to the rearing and education of the young.

Where the very survival of the species depends on the instruction of the young by the old and the communication of information or know-how, there is a firm biological basis for the development of intelligence. The information thus communicated need not be species–specific, but may be relevant only to a particular community in relation to its environment. Baboons may be foragers and herbivores, or hunters and carnivores, depending on where they live, and they are capable of adapting to different environments because, as a species, they are not overburdened with phyletic memories. Different traditions or practices may be developed in different troops and be passed on from generation to generation.

Today, physiologists distinguish the old reptilian brain in mammals from the much more recently-evolved cerebral cortex and neocortex, and speak about the specificity of the former and the plasticity of the latter, which is another way of putting the point that Marais was making. When Marais wrote his book, psychologists were discussing various aspects of the unconscious and the functions controlled by the old brain, and, had they known it, the South African naturalist had some experimental findings to report that were highly germane to the discussion. His theory was that as the individual causal memory becomes more perfect in an animal, so the instincts and senses become more deeply submerged, but that those submerged functions of the old brain can be reactivated if the higher mentality is inhibited. To put the theory to the test, he devised some experiments to assess the improvement in the sensory and instinctive functions in human subjects under hypnosis and to compare those heightened human functions with those of a normal chacma baboon.

To test for sensory reactions, Marais used as subjects two Boer sisters, aged 18 and 21. He found, for instance, that under hypnosis, one of the girls could hear a simulated snake hiss at a distance of 230 yards, whereas unhypnotised human beings could only hear it at between 20 and 30 yards and chacmas at between 50 and 65 yards. The other girl surpassed the chacma in the acuteness of her sense of smell under hypnosis, although the chacma's sense of smell is greatly superior to that of the average normal human being. The senses of taste and sight proved to be sharper in the chacmas than in the girls, but even so the hypnotic state tremendously improved the girls' powers of sensory discrimination.

In another series of experiments, Marais tested the 'homing' instinct in human subjects under hypnosis and in a normal state of consciousness, requiring them to return to a particular spot in a featureless, trackless waste when taken blindfold some distance from it. He found that they could accomplish the feat when hypnotised, but not normally.

Summing up his experiments, he wrote:

An investigation of the phenomena of hypnotism justifies the conclusion that the hypnotic memory is no other than the phyletic sense of locality particularly and temporarily liberated from the inhibitary control of the functions associated with the cerebral cortex. This inhibition of instinctive faculties ... is therefore apparently a process inevitably associated with the development of the new mentality, and an examination of its occurrence in man renders more intelligible the nature of its beginnings in the lower primates.

The Soul of the Ape was eventually published in 1969 at the end of a decade during which primate studies had made notable progress and many observations had been made that confirmed Marais' analysis. At the Japanese Monkey Centre on the small offshore island of Koshima, scientists had had troops of wild monkeys under observation since 1952. They fed the monkeys on sweet potatoes, which were dropped on the beach for them to pick up, and in 1959 an observer named Syunyo Kawamura noticed that a young female monkey had introduced an innovation. She took her potatoes to a stream and washed the sand off before eating them. Gradually the practice spread through the entire population, with the exception of the older males, who were probably too proud to learn anything from the young. Here was an interesting example of intelligence at work, and of communication, learning, and cultural innovation taking place.

The female monkey must have been something of a genius among her kind for, some years later, when wheat was introduced as a food and the other monkeys spent hours picking the grains from the sand, she came up with another bright idea. She scooped up handfuls of mixed sand and wheat grains and used the current of the stream to wash away the sand between her fingers. You could hardly have a better example of what Marais called 'individual causal memory' at work.

In the hierarchy of primate intelligence, the chimpanzee is well above the baboon and is the nearest species to man. Recent experiments with chimpanzees have produced results that take away the ground from under the feet of the champions of human uniqueness. It was long assumed that one thing that was exclusive to man was the use of language and the belief seemed confirmed by the fact that many attempts to teach apes to speak had failed. Then, in the mid-1960s, Allen and Beatrice Gardner, a husband and wife team of psychologists at the University of Nevada, Reno, acting on the not highly-original but hitherto ignored idea that language is not synonymous with speech, set up an experiment to teach a chimpanzee to communicate in Ameslan – the American sign language used by the deaf.

In the early 1960s, a Dutch zoologist, Dr Adrian Kortland, published several reports of chimps in the wild in the Congo, in which he made the point that they appeared to have quite a sophisticated gestural language. About the same time, an Englishwoman, Jane Goodall, published reports of time she had spent living among wild chimpanzees, testifying that they communicated among themselves by means of gestures. These reports were available to the Gardners when, in 1966, they set up their experiment with Washoe, a one-year-old female chimp just captured in the wild in Africa.

The Gardners chose to teach their chimp Ameslan so that they would be able to compare her progress as a language user with the progress of deaf children. They assumed that there would come a point beyond which Washoe would not be able to go and that this would enable them to specify more precisely than had been done before what is unique about human language and human mentality. But Washoe's abilities proved more sophisticated than they had anticipated, and raised questions about the nature of language and the psychology of its acquisition that sparked off a major interdisciplinary debate.

In the 1950s and 1960s Naom Chomsky of the Massachusetts Institute of Technology had developed his seminal ideas in linguistics. His fundamental idea is that human languages consist of a deep structure – basically identical for all languages – and a surface structure in which languages differ. The deep structure can be transformed into the surface structure by means of what he called a generative grammar. The idea of the deep structure interested neurobiologists, for great progress had recently been made in 'mapping' the cortex of the human brain, that is, locating the cortical regions associated with specific motor and cognitive activities. Chomsky's analysis suggested that language might be natural to human beings in the sense that its deep structure was laid down in the 'wiring' of the neuronal pathways of the cortex – that when individuals learned their particular native language, they generated it from this pre-programmed deep structure.

This was a new and ingenious explanation of human uniqueness, but as such it did not survive the Washoe experiment. The chimp learned to generate language as quickly as a child does. Her success did not, of course, invalidate the theory of a programmed linguistic propensity in the human brain, but it did indicate that any such propensity was not exclusively human – not unless the category was extended to include chimps.

Educated chimps themselves have no doubt which species category they belong to. Washoe scornfully dismissed a macaque as a 'dirty monkey', and when she was first introduced to other chimps she referred to them as 'black bugs'. Another educated female, when given the task of sorting a pile of photographs into human and animal categories unhesitatingly put a picture of herself among the human beings and tossed one of her father in among the dumb beasts.

We commonly use the verb 'to ape' with the meaning of to imitate or copy slavishly, with the implication that apes may be clever imitators but they cannot think or act with spontaneous originality. Or, as philosopher John Locke pithily put it, 'Beasts abstract not'. On this assumption, we might expect them, as language users, only to be able to learn to name objects and to be able to express a limited range of wishes and commands to secure their needs. This is the stage the human child reaches at the age of about 18 months, and if the chimp's learning process were pure 'aping', we would expect it to stop there.

'Listen'

'Ball'

Washoe swears in Ameslan signalling 'dirty'
as his reaction to this macaque (*Madelaine Gill*)

The next stages in the child's development see the emergence successively of abilities that Harvard psycholinguist Roger Brown has called 'semanticity', 'productivity', and 'displacement'. Semanticity is a sense of the meaning inherent in word order and an ability to symbolise; productivity is the ability to manipulate symbols and thus generate a variety of meanings; and displacement is the ability to store and later retrieve experiences or information. Washoe far exceeded her trainers' expectations by proving herself able to do all these things.

Washoe started using two and three-word phrases at about the same time as human children do. 'Gimme sweet' and 'Come open' were her first two-word combinations of signs. She liked tickling games and was soon able to say 'You tickle me' or 'I tickle you', which showed a recognition of the relevance of word order to meaning and thus the emergence of semanticity (see Plates 4 and 5).

Once, when she was caged, a handler named Jack was working nearby, but ignored several of her requests for a drink. She spontaneously started making the sign for 'dirty' before the one for the handler's name. She was saying 'Dirty Jack. Gimme drink!' Her rage had driven her to invent swearing for herself, which was a clear demonstration of what Brown meant by productivity. In another and later experimental programme a chimp named Lana, when annoyed with her trainer, called him: 'You green shit'.

After three years of training, Washoe had a vocabulary of about 160 signs, and the Gardners had recorded her use of 294 different two-sign combinations and 245 combinations of three or more signs. Her progress was pretty well keeping pace with that of a human baby.

At this stage, Washoe was moved from Reno to the Institute of Primate Studies in Oklahoma, accompanied by Dr Roger Fouts, who had been the Gardners' assistant and had become the chimp's closest friend. Here she was introduced to others of her kind, whom she eventually came to terms with despite her initial disparagement of them. An experiment was set up to create a colony of language-using chimps, and it soon became clear that Washoe was no freak genius. Others of the species were capable of acquiring language equally quickly and efficiently and today at the IPS there is a flourishing community of chimps who continually and quite naturally communicate with each other in Ameslan.

'It's lonely being the only language-using primate in the universe,' remarked Roger Brown some years ago. But with Washoe and her chums gesturing to each other and to their human observers and handlers in Oklahoma, we no longer are.

A reporter, Boyce Rensberger, who was brought up using Ameslan because both his parents were deaf and dumb, was sent by the *New York Times* to report the experiments with Washoe and he wrote of his astonishment when, after spending some time with the chimp: 'Suddenly I realized I was conversing with a member of another species in my native tongue.' The experience must have been extraordinary if Rensberger, like most people, had never seriously questioned the assumption that language is an exclusively human possession.

At the Yerkes Primate Research Centre in Atlanta, Georgia, another experiment has been in progress for some time, teaching chimps to compose sentences in a form of basic English using a computer console. The chimps can compose a variety of requests from given verbal units, and provided that the sentences are grammatically correct and politely put – preceeded by the word 'please' – the machine will fulfil the request. The chimps have learned to correct their own mistakes, and on one occasion when a trainer at a separate console kept interjecting a mistake that frustrated a female chimp's efforts to compose a request, she deduced what was happening and typed 'Please, Tim, leave room.'

The chimpanzee's brain is structurally like that of man, consisting of the limbic (reptilian) region, the mammalian cortex and the neocortex, which is characteristic of the higher mammals. This latter, the latest evolutionary development in brain structure, is a $\frac{1}{8}$in-thick layer of brain tissue laid over the cortex, and its neurons are more densely packed and more intricately interconnected than those in any other part of the brain.

Professor Steven Rose has suggested that 'the phenomenon which is described . . . as 'consciousness' is related to factors of neocortex size and cell number'. In other words, there is a relation between the size and complexity of an animal's neocortex and the degree of consciousness or level of intelligence of that animal. If this is true, and if man maintains that his intelligence is necessarily superior to that of his nearest primate relative, the chimp, by virtue of his brain size and its neuronal complement, then he finds himself in a very unexpected and perhaps embarrassing situation, for there are creatures on this planet with bigger and in some ways more complex brains, namely the cetacea (whales and dolphins).

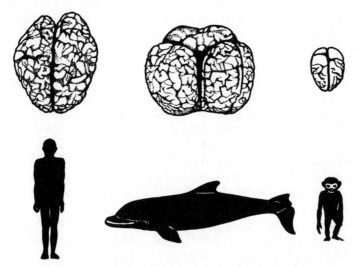

The relative brain sizes of *homo sapiens*, dolphin and chimp

Physicist and biologist Leo Szilard stated that if active interspecies communication was set up with dolphins, these 'intellectuals of the sea' would win all the Nobel Prizes, including the Peace Prize. This charming fancy is, of course, just an arresting way of saying that the intellectual capacities of dolphins may, so far as we know, excel ours. It is very difficult for us to *know*, though, for these aquatic mammals are so alien to us and have evolved their sensory and information-processing systems in such a different environment that to devise means of assessing and measuring their mental powers poses a major challenge to human ingenuity. In recent years, a number of dedicated and imaginative researchers have taken up the challenge and achieved some fascinating insights.

'Genius in the Sperm Whale?' asked Herman Melville in *Moby Dick*. 'Has the Sperm Whale ever written a book, spoken a speech? No, his great genius is declared in doing nothing particular to prove it. It is moreover declared in his pyramidical silence.' The great American novelist was awed by the potentialities of the mightiest brain on the planet, but he was hasty in denying the animal the power of speech. All whales and dolphins communicate with each other by sound, and, as we shall see, they obviously have quite a complex language system. The Humpback Whale even sings, sometimes continuously for three or four hours. Recordings of whale songs have been made, and listeners have noted that sometimes they are repeated, sound by sound, as if the song is not a spontaneous outpouring, but a memorised composition. Carl Sagan, the astrophysicist, has analysed a half-hour whale song and calculated that its content is, in computer language, at least a million 'bits' of information – 'approximately the number of bits in *The Odyssey* or the Icelandic *Eddas*'.

Of course, Melville was right – a whale has never written a book. But our printed books are extrasomatic memory. What if whales can carry whole books in their heads? John Lilly has suggested that the best way for the human species to gain the respect of the Sperm Whale might be to have a whole symphony orchestra play to him. 'With his huge computer, the Sperm Whale could probably store the whole symphony and play it back in his mind to himself at his leisure,' Lilly writes.

The idea may at first seem as fanciful as Szilard's notion of dolphin Nobel laureates, but in fact something like it has been tried. In August 1970, a Vancouver rock band, Fireweed, took to the sea in a low-hulled vessel with the specific purpose of playing to a school of Orca Whales. The animals completely surrounded the vessel and travelled with it for several miles while the musicians played. Other observers have noted the interest that whales and dolphins show in music, which is, after mathematics, man's most abstract language. John Locke's dictum that 'beasts abstract not' looks very ill-informed in the light of what we know today about the interests and the vocalisations of whales and dolphins.

The brain of the Sperm Whale is six times the size of a man's, so, Lilly deduces, 'to think the way we do, he would need to use about one-sixth of his total brain. To him, our best thinking may appear to be reflexes, automatic and primitive'. The assumption that there is a correlation between gross brain size and quality of thought is debatable, but when we take into account other anatomical factors that are considered relevant to the assessment of intelligence potentials, we find that the whale's brain incorporates them all.

In mammals, the brain cortex has what are known as 'association areas' as well as sensory-motor areas. These areas are given over to internal activities of the brain, to logical, abstract, or creative thinking.

90 per cent of the cortex of the human brain consists of association areas – a far greater proportion than in any other land mammal. Although no precise brain 'maps' of cetacea have been made, preliminary studies indicate that the proportion of association areas is about the same as in man.

'The mightiest brain on the planet', the sperm whale

The amount of fissurisation or infolding of the surface tissue of the cortex is regarded as another index of degree of development of intelligence, and in both the human and the cetacean brain, fissurisation is a conspicuous feature. Neuron density, however, is lower in the whale's brain than in man's (although in the smaller brain of the dolphin it is about the same). The cells in the whale's brain are more spread out, and this is a feature that invalidates any assessment of comparative intelligence based on gross brain size. In fact, the total number of neurons in the whale's brain may not be greatly in excess of the total in man's and the animal may not be the supermind that Lilly and Szilard suggest, but more man's equal.

The size and nature of his brain leave no doubts, though, that he is a highly intelligent animal. As one old Newfoundland fisherman said to Canadian naturalist and author Farley Mowat: "'Tis strange. Some folks says as whales is only fish. No, bye! They's too smart for fish. *I* don't say as what they's not the smartest creatures in God's ocean. Aye, and maybe out of it as well!'

The fact that the whale's element is the ocean and man's is the land creates a tremendous barrier between the two species, not only a physical barrier to their meeting and interacting, but also a barrier to their comprehending and empathising and communicating with each other as advanced mammals on a level of mutual acknowledgement and respect. The physical barrier is less great with the dolphin, though, and some recent attempts to bridge the physical barrier have resulted in the psychic and communication gaps at least being narrowed.

In 1959, John Lilly set up his Communication Research Institute in the US Virgin Isles, where he created special areas intermediate between sea and land where humans and dolphins could meet. In his book *The Mind of the Dolphin* he reports some experiments in interspecies living and communicating that took place in these areas. Although he closed down the CRI in 1968 because he 'no longer wanted to run a concentration camp for my friends', the work that was done there in a decade greatly increased man's knowledge and understanding of the mammals that were highly evolved long before the first primates appeared on earth.

Living with a dolphin in a pool, day and night, week after week, must have been a demanding task, but Margaret Howe, one of Lilly's co-researchers, found it rewarding, too (see Plate 7). She spent two and a half months in a special 'flooded house' with Peter, a young male dolphin, devoting several hours a day to playing with him and teaching him numbers, counting, colours, and shapes and attempting to teach him to pronounce some words – no easy task for a dolphin with a very different sound-production system from the human being's vocal cords. Margaret slept on an elevated platform that Peter could swim beneath, and the two were together all the time except for one day a week when they returned to the company of their respective species. At the end of the period, Margaret set down the following observations:

> (a) Dolphins not only can learn, but enjoy learning, learn fast, and they have learned lots of things we cannot know about. We limit the information. (b) Dolphins can learn to play *with* someone. At the beginning of these two and a half months, Peter would not share his toys ... he played alone, was often the initiator of a game with a human. (c) Peter learned how to work during a vocal lesson (as taught by the human) and also made vocal progress. (d) Peter learned how to teach me. (e) Peter learned to curb his physical energies to allow for my being so 'human'. (f) Peter learned that he could please me immensely, as well as annoy me.

Summarising the progress in her attempts to get Peter to vocalise and converse, Margaret listed the following sequential stages:

> 1. Peter mainly clicks a few humanoids (human-like sounds), interrupts me. 2. Peter gives me more and more humanoids, still interrupts. 3. Peter learns to hush when I shush him ... I can correct him. 5. Peter makes good attempts at copying my speech, at the same time keeping a good listen, speak, listen, speak business.

1 Author of *Pensées*, Blaise Pascal (*Courtesy of Mary Evans Picture Library*)

I

AMAZING STORIES

February, 1937
25 Cents

"By Jove!"
by WALTER ROSE
S.A. COBLENTZ · JOHN EDWARDS

The basic problem of interspecies communication, Lilly writes, is 'convincing both sides that the problem exists. Both sides must explore with what sort of shared dimensions this problem can be approached.' To ask for the intelligent and willing participation of the captive dolphin is a tall order, but both Lilly and Margaret Howe are convinced that some dolphins might find the bridging of the interspecies communication gap as challenging and interesting an undertaking as some humans do. A necessary precondition of this work is that both human being and dolphin must modify their pre-conceptions of each other, which in itself is a task demanding no small investment of intelligence and imagination. One of the main outcomes of Margaret Howe's experiment was that Peter behaved in a manner that suggested that he had effected such a modification.

One incident that occurred in the course of Lilly's research suggested that although dolphins may be willing to co-operate with man, they cannot be fooled with over serious matters. Lilly wanted to get some film of a dolphin rescuing a drowning man, so George, one of his assistants, went into the water and pretended to be in distress. One of the dolphins, Sissy, swam over to him, supported him, and pushed him to safety. The film would have been just what Lilly wanted, but he found that he had left the cap over the camera lens. So they tried again. George went into the water and acted as if he were in trouble, but Sissy deduced that it was a sham and instead of rescuing George, she beat him up!

A dolphin caught in the open sea and put in a tank aboard a ship proceeded to make a remarkable series of noises – noises that seemed to imitate fog horns, train whistles, seagulls, and boat engines. It was as if it were trying to communicate with land creatures in a language they might understand. Whether or not that was the case, the anecdote illustrates the point that in interspecies communication experiments, dolphins have shown themselves willing to attempt to cross the gap.

In fact, they have made more progress towards achieving coherence in human language than humans have in 'dolphinese'.

Carl Sagan visited Lilly's establishment in 1963 and was introduced to a dolphin named Elvar. Elvar swam to the side of the tank, turned on his back and presented his belly to be scratched in the manner that some dogs do. Sagan obliged, and the dolphin seemed to enjoy the sensation. After a while he swam away, only to return shortly and resume his upturned belly position, but this time some six inches beneath the surface. Sagan had to remove his coat and jacket and push his sleeve up in order to reach down into the water. Then Elvar swam away and returned yet again, this time a foot under the surface. Sagan rolled up his

2 The cover of the February 1937 edition of *Amazing Stories*

sleeve even further and massaged the dolphin's belly for a while, but when Elvar came to him a third time, now three or four feet under water, he decided he would no longer comply.

Man and dolphin stared at each other, then suddenly Elvar leapt out of the water head first and, towering over the astonished Sagan, quite distinctly said 'More!' Sagan reported the incident to Lilly, who showed no surprise but merely said: 'That's one of the words he knows.'

What impressed Sagan in this incident was not only the fact that the dolphin spoke a recognisable word in a coherent context, but also that Elvar had apparently subjected him to a kind of psychological test. Such antics, he boldly conjectured, might be 'one clue to the bond that draws dolphins to humans. We are one of the few species that have pretensions of psychological knowledge; therefore, we are one of the few that would permit, however inadvertently, dolphins to perform psychological experiments on us.' This tables-turned speculation reaches far beyond the available evidence, but it is true that dolphin behaviour often suggests a grasp of the concepts of testing and learning.

Margaret Howe reported that Peter soon began obviously to enjoy his lessons with her and not just perform for reward, and indeed he often initiated conversations and lessons by calling to her, or by starting to speak when they were together. Lilly also found with many of his dolphins that they were capable of giving sustained attention to an intellectual test or task without the bribery of a food reward.

When Margaret Howe spoke of her conversations with Peter, she did not mean exchanges of intelligibly strung-together words and thoughts. In their two-and-a-half months together, Peter only achieved a small vocabulary and did not learn how to use it coherently. What Margaret meant by 'conversation' was an exchange of humanoid sounds with conversational inflections, pauses and spacings. Lilly later set up a fairly elaborate experiment along these lines which produced interesting results.

Starting with the question of how dolphins' mimicry of humanoid sounds differs from that of 'talking' birds, such as parrots and mynahs, Lilly proposed that the difference lay in the dolphins' ability to 'lock in' their vocal outputs alternately and in a patterned sequence with those of a human being. To test this proposition, he compiled a list of 187 nonsense syllables. The idea was that an experimenter would read aloud 'bursts' of these syllables, the number in a burst being between one and ten and determined at random. The dolphin's response to these bursts of sound would be recorded. Nonsense syllables were used so that the results could be judged purely as sounds, for experience had shown that when coherent meaning was a criterion, people had a tendency to read in a meaning from correct mimicry of the pitch and rhythm of an utterance, which made objective assessment difficult.

The dolphins' behaviour in their test situation was remarkable and there was evidence of a high level of mental activity. Two animals were tested independently. They were required to respond to the bursts of spoken syllables with their own sound-bursts of the same number, and if they achieved the correct number of sounds and correctly 'locked in' to the experimenter's utterance, they scored a 'hit'.

The utterances were very rapid, and the sequences of exchanges lasted between twelve and twenty minutes. Often the human operator came out of a session feeling physically and mentally fatigued. The dolphins must have found the task fatiguing too, for they were required to make sounds in air rather than in water as they naturally do, but they scored correctly more than 90 per cent of the time and showed no decline in performance as the session progressed. Their participation was voluntary and they were free to terminate a session at any point.

The rapidity of the dolphins' replies in these tests was itself a significant feature of their performance. The intervals between the operator finishing his utterance and the dolphin mimicking it were no greater than the intervals between the separate syllables in the burst. This meant that the dolphin could not be waiting for a silent interval to indicate that the operator had finished, but must be acting on the slightly falling inflection with which anyone reading a list pronounces the last item on it. Furthermore, the dolphins could recognise and discount corrections, and were not confused when an operator got tongue-tied, stopped in mid-utterance and started over again. They always repeated the syllable count of the corrected burst.

Another point of great significance was that the dolphins' success rate was no lower for utterances with large numbers of syllables (up to the limit of ten) than it was for those with few syllables. Human beings, however, when required to do the same task, made more errors with the longer bursts. At above five syllables their success rate diminished considerably.

We have no difficulty accepting that there are animals faster, stronger, sharper of sight, hearing, or smell than man, but here is something new. Here is an animal that is quicker-witted – at least in performing a particular type of task. There are no doubt other mental tasks at which the dolphin could out-perform man but we need not take this as an indication of the general superiority of the dolphin's brain. Certainly it shows that there is a highly-evolved and competent brain in that strangest of mammalian bodies, and the question of whether man or dolphin possesses the better brain is really less important and less profitable to pursue than the question of what types of brain function the two species respectively excel in and why, and the exploration of the interface area between them.

Lilly surmised that dolphins out-performed human subjects in his experiment because the dolphin's acoustical brain is very much more highly-developed than that of man. In his previous investigations, Lilly had established that whereas man processes visual information ten times more efficiently than the dolphin does, the dolphin is twenty times more acute and efficient acoustically than man is. This difference is, of course, because of the different elements in which they live. Sound travels in water at four and a half times the speed it travels in air, and it does not disperse so quickly. Indeed, whales are believed to be able to communicate over hundreds of miles.

Neuroanatomical investigation of the dolphin's brain has shown that it has some 115,000 nerve fibres from each ear to the cortex, whereas man has about 50,000. Man's hearing can comfortably register sounds between 100 and 8,000 cycles per second, and most human communication is conducted within the 300 to 3,500 cycles per second band, but the dolphin's 'speech band' is between about 500 and 100,000 cycles per second.

The range of dolphin sounds that human beings can hear sound like clicks and whistles, and the dolphin can produce these sounds simultaneously and independently using two separate membranes in his blowhole. He usually does this underwater, but for the benefit of human beings he will make the sounds in air. He will also make humanoid sounds in air, and the fact that he never makes such sounds normally suggests that in doing so he is attempting to communicate with human beings. Comparisons of the sounds made by young and mature dolphins show a gradual increase in complexity and versatility with age. When all these facts are taken into account, they add up to a high probability that dolphins have a language in which they can communicate with each other.

A dolphin was released from captivity into the open sea and followed until it made contact with a school of dolphins. Thereupon it produced a very long and complex sequence of sounds. Carl Sagan, who tells this anecdote, asks: 'Was it an account of his imprisonment?' Very likely it was. There is a great deal of anecdotal evidence that dolphins and whales can communicate precise and complex information to their kind.

An Antarctic fishing fleet was frustrated in its efforts by thousands of Orca Whales that were consuming all the fish around the boats. So some whaling boats were sent for, and a harpoon gun shot and killed one of the whales. That was the last whale that came within range of a harpoon gun. Within half an hour every whale over an area of some fifty square miles had got the message and was keeping well clear of the whaling boats. But the fishing fleet was not helped because the Orcas still hunted fish around the fishing boats.

Obviously a message had been communicated by the stricken whale, or one nearby it that had witnessed the harpooning, and it could not have been just a general message of alarm but must have consisted of a precise description of the type of boat that was to be avoided. The really remarkable thing was that both the fishing boats and the whalers were converted World War II corvettes, virtually indistinguishable except for the harpoon gun on the bows of the whalers. There would appear to be no explanation of the whales' behaviour other than they had a language of great descriptive power and a means of propagating it over a considerable distance very rapidly.

Some interesting observations of conversations between captive dolphins have been made. Lilly separated a male and a female in a pool by putting a panel of sheet metal across it. The dolphins were noisy at first and kept leaping out of the water and trying to see each other over the partition. Then they both fell into a depressed silence, which was eventually broken by the male. The female seemed reluctant to reply at first, but eventually she appeared to reconcile herself to the changed situation and thereafter the two dolphins would frequently hold conversations of up to half an hour's duration.

Two naval scientists, T. G. Lang and H. A. P. Smith, elaborated this experiment. Their male and female dolphins – Dash and Doris – were in separate soundproof tanks between which there was an underwater telephone connection with a sound amplifying facility. Sometimes the telephone communication channel was open and sometimes it was closed, and one of the dolphins would from time to time check whether it was open by making a sound to which the other would reply. At times they would hold fairly long exchanges of sound that seemed like conversation, as their utterances came in turns and did not interrupt each other. Each side of the conversation was recorded separately, and the experimenters got a revealing reaction when they played to Dash a tape of Doris's part in a conversation they had had four months before. For nearly eighteen minutes, Dash responded with much the same sounds as he had made in the original conversation, but then he uttered a series of complex whistles to which Doris' recorded utterance was apparently an inadequate reply, for thereafter he went quite silent and would no longer converse with the taped voice of his mate. He had apparently very quickly come to the realisation that he was being tricked, although he presumably could have no concept of the technology by means of which the trick was done.

It is in technology, of course, that man excels. Evolutionists make much of the development of tool-using as the great leap forward – the watershed between *Homo sapiens* and the lower species. The existence of the brain-hand combination and of a varied material environment capable of manual manipulation and adaptation inevitably meant that man and the human brain would evolve quite differently from the dolphin and his brain. It is only recently that it has occurred to a few men and women to question whether that difference necessarily implies superiority. Some of those few, the imaginative or boldly speculative ones, have gone on to ask what a great brain existing in an element so different from ours might occupy itself with.

'I suggest,' Lilly writes, 'that whales and dolphins quite naturally go in the directions we call spiritual, in that they get into meditative states quite simply and easily.' And Joan Mcintyre, organiser of Project Jonah, the whale and dolphin protection lobby, writes: 'I would guess that the mind of the dolphin is a freer playground than the modern human mind. I would guess that the dolphin might have more fun with her mind than we have with our minds.' Spirituality, meditation, fun, mind-play: we can see the connection between the so-called New Age consciousness and the interest in man-dolphin communication.

Everyone who works closely with them comes to feel that not only can we teach them, but also learn from them. In his book, *Dolphins*, Anthony Alpers tells of a female dolphin that daily visited the beach of the small New Zealand town of Opononi in the summer of 1955. She played with the swimmers and allowed young children to ride on her back. People flocked from far and wide to see the dolphin and if possible to touch her and the beach became crowded with campers. Locals said that the summer was remarkable not only for the number of visitors who came to the town, but for the fact that there were no fights, arguments, or drunkenness among them. Alpers writes that

> on this mass of sunburned, jostling humanity, the gentle dolphin had the effect of a benediction . . . There was such an overflow of friendly feelings that it seemed the crowds were composed of people wanting to be forgiven for something – for the unkindness, perhaps, that humans generally do to animals in the wild.

Numerous similar anecdotes dating back to ancient history tell us that this mind in the waters has always shown an extraordinarily friendly disposition towards man, and has consistently manifested a kind of ethical awareness which we are inclined to consider exclusive to, and the highest characteristic of, the human mind. The great brain is there as incontrovertible evidence of intelligence, and it is not vestigial or inactive but has all the signs of being used quite as much as the human brain. Just how it is used is the intriguing question, and to ask it is to open up the possibility of learning something about potentialities in ourselves that we may have neglected.

We will probably never know why these mammals took to the sea millions of years ago, unless perhaps one day we learn to understand their language and one of the epic songs of the Humpback Whale relates the reason why. But in taking to the sea and shutting their mammalian bodies and brains into a streamlined casing they created great inhibitions to their own further evolution. Jacob Bronowski points out in *The Ascent of Man* that it took 500,000 years of biological evolution to get from *Australopithecus* to *Homo sapiens*, whereas it has only taken some 12,000 years of cultural evolution for primitive *Homo sapiens* to evolve into modern man. And he maintains that cultural evolution became possible only because man ceased his nomadic life and settled on the land and in cities. 'Civilisation can never grow up on the move,' Bronowski asserts, and his dictum would imply that the cetacean nomads of the sea have probably not evolved since they adapted to the element that most other mammals shun.

But who can say that it was a mistake to take to the waters and the timeless, contemplative, and uncompetitive nomadic life, when he considers what a pass man has come to, living in the environment that his brain enables him to dominate and exploit? Perhaps we are taking an interest in the cetaceans today because we can learn from them and because they stand for those elements of freedom, spontaneity, exuberance, joy, and play that are the glories of human civilisations in their ascent, but always vulnerable in their decline.

2 Computers
and Artificial Intelligence

The Emperor Napoleon met his Waterloo as a chess player at Schonbrunn in 1809, defeated by the Baron Wolfgang von Kempelen's chess automaton. This ingenious invention consisted of a wooden model of a man dressed as a Turk, seated behind a box filled with complicated mechanical clockwork on the top of which stood a chess-board. The model had movable arms and was even able to pick up and move the chess pieces (see Plate 8). It beat most of its opponents and the Baron made money demonstrating his automaton and challenging chess players throughout Europe and America. Edgar Allan Poe witnessed a demonstration and went away puzzled, convinced that the automaton could not be authentic but unable to imagine how the deception was accomplished. Although von Kempelen kept his secret for decades, it was eventually discovered that there was a midget, an expert chess player, cunningly concealed amid the clockwork.

Von Kempelen's conception was prophetic, even if his engineering was not equal to it, for today there are chess-playing machines that can give international masters a good game. He was prophetic in another of his inventions, too – his speaking machine, of which Goethe wrote: 'It is not very loquacious but it pronounces certain childish words very nicely.' Powered by air from a bellows, the speaking machine could be made to pronounce vowels through manipulations of a bell-shaped mouth, and consonants through flaps resembling lips and tongue, and it had a repertoire of distinct phrases such as '*Je vous aime de tout mon coeur*'. Von Kempelen called his inventions bagatelles, designed to amuse, and they were such in his day. Today, however, the simulation of human functions by machines has become a much more serious matter.

We have all seen television film of the marvellous and eerie contrivances that man has landed on the Moon and on the planet Mars, capable of moving about, scanning the environment, avoiding obstacles, collecting samples, and even conducting chemical analysis. The age of the robot – the subject of so much fantasy in nineteenth-century literature (for example, Mary Shelley's *Frankenstein*; E. T. A. Hoffman's lovely mannequin Olympia in *The Sandman*, and *L'Eve Future* of Villiers de l'Isle Adam) – is with us today.

At the Fairfax County Hospital in Virginia a doctor can order equipment by telephone from anywhere in the building and it will be brought to him by a robot supply-cart which, routed by a computer, is capable of going to any ordered location, avoiding obstacles en route and waiting for, entering, and leaving elevators. At a General Motors Factory in Ohio, programmed industrial robots carry out a variety of precise welding operations on an assembly line.

Such achievements of technology have alarmed some people and caused them to wonder where the process of machines taking over human functions – and often performing them with greater speed, skill, and reliability – is going to end. Could man, they ask, eventually be usurped, or worse still, entirely taken over and controlled, by machines? Other and more philosophically-disposed minds have pondered the question of where a line of demarcation can be drawn between human and machine intelligence and between their appropriate concerns. And the questions, as we shall see, are not to be glibly answered.

In the film *2001: A Space Odyssey*, a manned spaceship bound for Jupiter is controlled by an on-board computer named HAL, which, as well as controlling all the spaceship's systems, also engages in friendly conversations with the crew. When HAL develops programming problems, turns perverse, tries to break the circuit with Earth, and contrives to kill all the members of the crew except one, the sole survivor, Dave Bowman, decides that for his own safety and the completion of the mission he must 'cut out the higher centres of this sick but brilliant brain'. Bowman removes one memory block after another from HAL's brain until the computer regresses to incoherent babbling and to singing snatches of the first song it ever learned, 'Daisy, Daisy', until finally it falls completely silent.

At this point, the viewer of the film or the reader of the novel that Arthur C. Clarke developed from his own script, cannot but feel compassion for HAL, regarding Bowman as some kind of murderer. This feeling and judgement may later be thought to have been misplaced, or evoked by an inappropriate object, but it will probably be conceded that in the viewer's experience of the film, or the reader's experience of the book, HAL figured as a person and manifested enough of those characteristics that endear man to man to make his 'death' seem tragic.

We shall come back to the implications of Arthur Clarke's fable. It is mentioned here because it has historical significance. In the mid-1960s it awakened people throughout the world to an understanding of the realities and potentialities of machine intelligence. Clarke endowed his creation with great authenticity by describing its ancestry:

HAL (for *H*euristically programmed *AL*gorithmic computer) was a masterwork of the third computer breakthrough ... The first had been in the 1940s ... Then, in the 1960s, solid-state microelectronics had been perfected ... In the 1980s, Minsky and Good had shown how neural networks could be generated automatically – self-replicated – in accordance with any arbitrary learning programme. Artificial brains could be grown by a process strikingly analogous to the development of a human brain ...

Although the breakthrough Clarke describes is scientifically dubious, it would be rash in view of the staggering developments in biological and brain sciences in recent years, to dismiss it as impossible. Even when Clarke was writing, computers were already capable of many of the functions attributed to HAL, though they were neither so marvellously miniaturised nor able to hold a sustained intelligent conversation. HAL was a very plausible extrapolation to the year 2001, and the film and the book made many people aware of questions that scientists and philosophers had been discussing for some time. Did intelligent machines constitute a threat to man? Were man's mental functions superior to, or at least different from, those of a machine and if so how?

Before we consider such questions, let us see precisely what machine intelligence is capable of today and some of the stages through which it has evolved its present power and sophistication. It is appropriate to begin with robots because they simulate the motor functions and, in their more developed forms, the sensory-motor functions of the human nervous system and brain, whereas the most advanced modern computers simulate some of the brain's higher functions.

If we leave aside the Galateas and the Frankensteins of literature, and the golems and the tulpas of legend, the first man-made system that behaved as if with a will of its own and as a simple biological system might behave was probably the 'Homeostat' invented by a British mathematician, Dr Ross Ashby, in the early 1940s. Contained in a box of metal and glass, the Homeostat was an assembly of switches and indicator dials, the former determining voltage inputs at different points in a circuit, and the latter registering voltages at other points. The point of the Homeostat was that random changes in voltage inputs caused the indicator needles to fluctuate but always to return to the same positions, but a sudden large change to several switches simultaneously caused all the needles to shift to a new position and settle there.

The behaviour of the machine, Ashby said, could be compared to that of a lazy dog lying in front of a fire. Minor irritations will cause the dog to twitch or stir, but if the fire gets too hot for him, he will get up and move to another position where he will settle down again. So if intelligence be defined as the ability of a system to adjust to changes in its environment, then the behaviour of the Homeostat could be said to be intelligent.

More conspicuously so was the behaviour of the 'tortoises' invented by another British scientist, W. Gray Walter, in the 1950s. These little machines would wander about at random in a dark place as if searching for something. If a source of light was introduced, they would move towards it, but if the light became too bright, they would retreat. By making his machines mobile, Gray Walter was able to simulate more obviously than Ashby had done the motor response to a sensory stimulus which is characteristic of biological organisms (see Plate 9).

Then came the 'Hopkins' Beast'. Developed in the Applied Physics Laboratory at Johns Hopkins University in the early 1960s, the 'Beast' looked rather like a large dustbin on wheels. It could navigate along corridors by means of 'eyes' focused on the walls and which registered sonar measurements, thus keeping it centred. It was powered by electricity, and whenever it came to an electric outlet on the wall it would stop, move over to it, precisely locate the socket and plug itself in. There it would remain for some time until its batteries were fully recharged, whereupon it would withdraw its plug, move back to the centre of the corridor and continue its journey. The Hopkins' Beast was an advance on the Homeostat and Gray Walter's tortoises in that it was not only responsive to changes in its environment, but also had a purpose in life, namely to keep its batteries charged, and was able to execute a complex series of movements in order to accomplish that purpose (see Plate 10).

A further advance in sophistication was incorporated in a laboratory robot developed at the Stanford Research Institute in California in the late 1960s and early 1970s. Named 'Shakey' because its movements tended to be unsteady, this robot was remotely controlled by a computer and was designed to respond to orders in English typed out on the computer's console. It operated in the laboratory area of several interconnected rooms in which a number of large wooden blocks were distributed. Instructed, for example, to 'Go to position X and push the three blocks together', Shakey would do just that. In addition to being able to sense its environment, move about in it, and execute orders, Shakey was able to solve problems. For instance, if it was given the instruction: 'Push the block off the platform' and this was impossible to carry out from the position it was in, the robot scanned its environment, found a ramp, manoeuvred it up against the platform, went up the ramp on to the platform and pushed the block off (see Plates 11 and 12).

Such a sequence of actions surely constitutes a manifestation of intelligence, and of a higher order than that of the Homeostat or the mechanical tortoise. Already we may begin to wonder how far, when the mental capability of the computer is combined with the physical capability of the robot, intelligent machines might progress towards, or possibly even beyond, the capabilities of intelligent humans.

A system developed by Terry Winograd of *MIT*'s Artificial Intelligence Laboratory in the early 1970s was a further advance in the technology of 'robotics' (to use Isaac Asimov's term, which has been adopted by many scientists, though not yet by any standard dictionary). Winograd's robot coupled a television 'eye' with a mechanical arm and hand. It was computer-controlled and it operated within an environment of children's play-blocks of various sizes, shapes, and colours, where it was able to carry out complex manipulations in compliance with orders given in English. It would even copy a structure from a model shown to it. Winograd's most revolutionary innovation, however, was to endow his robot with the ability to discuss what it was doing. Its operator could type out either instructions or questions at the computer console, and the robot would respond either by making the appropriate movements or by producing a print-out answer.

Here is a specimen conversation:

OPERATOR: Find a block taller than the one you are holding and put it into the box.

ROBOT: By 'it', I assume you mean the block which is taller than the one I am holding.

O: OK
(The hand puts down the block it is holding and picks up a taller one)

O: What does the box contain?

R: The blue pyramid and the blue block.

O: What is the pyramid supported by?

R: The box.

O: How many blocks are not in the box?

R: Four of them.

O: Will you please stack up both of the red blocks and either a green cube or a pyramid?

R: OK (the hand carries out the instructions) . . .

O: Why did you clear off the (red) cube?

R: To put it on a large green cube.

O: Why did you do that?

R: To stack up the red cube, a large red block and a large green cube.

O: Why did you do that?

R: Because you asked me to.

Here is something approximating to the interaction of two human beings in a teaching situation. The robot co-ordinates the actions of eye, brain, and hand; it comprehends and generates sentences of quite complex syntax; it manifests memory functions and an ability to reason. Its responses could almost be those of a young child, and its final answer 'because you asked me to' might well prompt the question: Will it always do what it is asked, or will it grow up like a child or like Arthur Clarke's HAL, to develop a will of its own?

Let us now consider the technological developments that have made possible these increasingly complex simulations of intelligent animal and human behaviour.

While biological systems have senses, mechanical and electronic ones have 'sensors'. The oldest and simplest of the sensors is the 'electric eye' or photo-electric cell, and when groups of these cells are arranged to cover an area they can detect moving objects in that area and thus simulate the most important of the human senses, vision. In some modern automated systems, in which high quality visual definition is not necessary, the photo-electric cell is still used, but in more sophisticated systems and in experimental robotics, television cameras are used to make the robot 'see'.

A famous experiment was conducted by a research team at MIT in 1959, and the results published in a paper entitled 'What the Frog's Eye tells the Frog's Brain'. The point it established was that the frog's vision is selective, that the eye transmits to the brain only information relevant to the animal's survival within its environment. This was found to be an example of a general principle relevant to all sensory systems: that they are information-filtering mechanisms designed to serve the survival needs of an organism.

If we substitute the word 'programmed' for 'designed', the analogy to robotic vision becomes clear. The Hopkins' Beast was programmed to 'see' electrical outlets just as the frog is programmed to see its food or its predators and nothing else. Robots with computer capability can be programmed to recognise any shape or any colour and to perform specific (and also programmed) actions or sequences of actions prompted by that act of recognition. Observed in operation, the system is in fact indistinguishable from the co-ordinated eye-brain-limb, or hand, actions of biological sensory-motor systems.

The animal senses of smell and taste do not generate enough relevant information in situations where robots might be used for roboticists to have explored means of incorporating their analogues in their systems. Nor has much work been done to date on incorporating sound-perception capability. For robots, the second most important information input after 'seeing' is touching, and robot hands have been designed with touch-sensors so sensitive that they can feed back information to make the hand pick up an egg without crushing it, or a wooden bowling ball without dropping it.

Custom-built robots, equipped with sensors for heat or for things that human beings have very low sensitivity to, such as magnetism or radiation, have been produced but both laboratory and industrial robots operate chiefly on information-processing systems analogous to the animal's sight and touch.

So long as robots depended for their decision-making on the electronic circuitry they carried around with them they were restricted to fairly crude and simple operations, but with radio-controlled computer linkage they became very versatile and powerful tools, as has been most dramatically demonstrated in Space exploration projects. The computer is the robot's brain, and, as Winograd's system showed, it can simulate certain of the functions of the human brain, such as problem-solving, comprehension and use of language, memory storage and retrieval, and reasoning capability. How well the computer does these things, and other things which formerly only human brains could do, and how much better it might do them in the future, are the questions we shall now consider.

Some people disparagingly call computers mere 'number crunchers', implying that they are nothing but fast mathematical calculators. This view underestimates not only the versatility of computers, but also the power of mathematics as a symbolic language. The very first computer, the 'analytical engine' invented by Charles Babbage in the 1820s, was a complicated assembly of cogs and wheels which was hand-operated, and although capable of being programmed to solve any mathematical problem, it kept breaking down mechanically. Part of the difficulty was that it operated on the decimal system and so every cog had to have ten teeth. If the binary system had been known in his day, Babbage might have been able to construct a revolutionary tool instead of an impractical curiosity (see Plate 13).

The binary system of counting is based on the principle that any number can be expressed in a sequence of the numbers 0 and 1, and computer technology is based on the principle that the numbers 0 and 1 can be represented by anything that can be in two states – for example, a switch that can be on or off. Now, suppose we have an alphabet of 256 symbols. How many 'yes' or 'no' questions would we have to ask to identify one of those symbols? If the question we ask is: 'Is the number in the first half of the set?' we can arrive at any number from 1 to 256 by asking the question just eight times, and so the number can be represented by a sequence of eight 'bits'. For example, the number 19 would be 11101101, if 1 represented a 'yes' answer and 0 a 'no'. These 'eight-bit strings' can be generated very quickly in a computer employing a pulse-generating principle similar to that used in an ordinary doorbell, for instance, a rapid sequence of open and shut states of the switching mechanism. So the computer has an alphabet of 256 symbols to manipulate, and when we think what the English alphabet can do with 26 symbols, we realise what a powerful tool such a symbolic language is. Early electrical computers employing valves and vacuum tubes were capable of switching operations at the rate of hundreds per second, but with the introduction of transistors in the late 1950s that rate was increased manyfold, adding tremendous speed to the versatility of the computer as a symbol-manipulator.

The human brain has billions of cells known as neurons, each of which has thousands of branching connections with other neurons, forming neuronal pathways along which information is transmitted. Computers work similarly. They comprise millions of switches, each with numerous connections with other switches and therefore a near-infinite number of potential information-carrying pathways. To program a computer is to tell it what meanings or values to assign to its symbols and how to route them along its pathways. The great breakthrough in computer technology of the 1950s was the development of the means of storing programs in the computer itself, thus giving it a capability analogous to that of the brain's memory, which made the computer competent for increasingly complex tasks and able to act more independently. In some circumstances, the human programmer only had to specify a goal for the computer's operation and it would select and pursue the stored programs (or 'sub-routines') appropriate to achieving that goal. It was also able to learn from experience, to choose between available routes and sub-routines to select those which had proved most effective in the past, having encoded this information into its memory store as a result of past experience.

With such an intriguing, powerful and challenging tool to work or play with, computer scientists have carried out over the last twenty-five years or so a great number of research projects with the objective of making artificial intelligence (referred to in the literature as AI) as powerful and versatile as, and less fallible than, human intelligence. As long ago as 1958 two scientists, Herbert Simon and Allen Newell, wrote in a technical paper:

There are now in the world machines that think, that learn and that create. Moreover, their ability to do these things is going to increase rapidly until – in the visible future – the range of problems they can handle will be co-extensive with the range to which the human mind has been applied.

The future that was 'visible' to Simon and Newell in 1958 has still not arrived, but since these words were written, the range of intelligent functions that computers are capable of has been extended immensely.

In 1974, an International Computer Chess Tournament was held, which was won by a Russian program. As the ingenious Baron von Kempelen apparently realised nearly two centuries ago, the game of chess is an activity in which an intelligent automaton might plausibly excel, for it is a formal, abstract, closed system governed by a set of rules. The game is an exercise in symbol-manipulation and, as such, is computable. The chess pieces, their distribution on the board, and the lawful moves they can each make, can be coded into the computer (see Plate 14). Play is a series of changes of state of the system, and the computer can keep track of these changes and at any stage compute the options available for the next move which do not contravene the transition rules. It can also compute a figure of merit for each option based on consideration of the various criteria of good play held in its memory. It may also be able to call up tried sub-routines to apply at any state of the game and, like a human player, it can learn by experience, laying down sub-routines which have proved effective in previous games.

Mathematician Norbert Wiener maintains that a computer can develop a 'chess personality', ie an idiosyncratic mode of play. If it keeps in its memory a record of all its past games and past moves, and examines the moves in view of the outcomes of the games, it can continually re-evaluate the figure of merit for any particular potential move. Wiener writes:

> The result will be that the game-playing machine will continually transform itself into a different machine, in accordance with the history of the actual play. In this, the experience and success, both of the machine and its human opponent, will play a role ... The opponent may find that stratagems which have worked in the past, will fail to work in the future. The machine may develop an uncanny canniness. It may be said that all this unexpected intelligence of the machine has been built into it by its designer and programmer. This is true in one sense, but it need not be true that all of the new habits of the machine have been explicitly foreseen by him.

Playing chess is one aspect of the art of problem-solving, and Simon and Newell, have developed a program relevant to many other aspects. They call it the General Problem Solver (or GPS). Although only a very rudimentary idea of the general principles involved in the GPS can be

3 Imaginative illustration for an SF story in *Amazing Stories*

3

4 & 5

6

given in the present context, a brief summary will serve as an illustration of how machines 'think'.

To begin with, a problem is defined in terms of two categories: *objects* and *operators*. The objects are the things that the problem-solver has to manipulate. They are not necessarily physical objects, but may be imaginary situations such as potential states of play in a game. The operators are the means by which he can carry out his manipulations, or the alternative actions available to him. Solving a problem is a process of transforming object A into object B by finding a sequence of operators that will effect the transformation. To accomplish this, it is necessary to define the significant differences between object A and object B, and these differences may then be used to guide the choice of operators. Operators that would add to the differences between objects A and B will be eliminated, while those that would diminish the differences will be retained, and the most effective of them will be sought.

To help assess each operator's potential effectiveness, a 'table of connections' is determined for each, specifying which differences between objects A and B each can minimise. So we can visualise any transition point (or sub-problem) in a problem-solving process as a group of available alternative actions (operators), each having a 'tree' of connections. The next move can thus be determined by a process of 'tree-searching' leading to the choice of the relevant operator. For problem-solving in any particular area where expertise can be built on experience, tree-structures of alternative operators can be stored in a computer's memory to be called upon when required. And large problems can be tackled piecemeal, broken down into sub-problems amenable to the same approach.

As an example of the GPS approach, Bertram Raphael, a SRI scientist, invites us to consider the situation of a hypothetical motorist whose car gets stuck in a snow storm. His problem is to fit chains which he has never used before on to his tyres. If he adopts the direct approach of getting out of the car, jacking it up, taking out the chains and wrapping them round the wheel, he may then find himself spending five or ten minutes lying in the slush under the car trying to work out how the linking mechanism works. The reader will no doubt be able to think of a comparable situation in which he has been at some time.

4 & 5 Washoe, a champanzee, uses Ameslan – the sign language of deaf people – to indicate: *above* 'a sweet' and *below* 'a drink'.

6 Lana activating a dispenser of drink, bananas and chocolate (*Reading and sentence completion by a Chimpanzee, Duane M. Rumbaugh* et al, Science, *16 November 1974, volume 182, pp 731–33. Copyright 1973 by the American Association for the Advancement of Science*)

The GPS approach to the motorist's problem would begin by describing object A as having no chains on the wheels and object B as having chains that work correctly on the wheels. It might then proceed to the observation that the key difference between objects A and B is that each chain must be linked on to a wheel, and therefore the first problem to be solved is that of understanding the linking mechanism.

Alternative operators in this situation might be to study the manufacturer's directions or to experiment with the chains while sitting in the car. This first step completed, the motorist might proceed to the problem of how to wrap the chain round the wheel, and thus, by breaking down the overall problem into a logical series of sub-problems, attain his goal with maximum efficiency and minimum inconvenience.

An example of the GPS program at work in a computerised situation would be Shakey's mounting the platform by means of a ramp in order to push the box off. So game-playing and problem-solving by means of the application of principles of structural logic are two of the intelligent functions that computers have been developed to perform over the last two decades or so.

Another area in which a lot of research work has been done is that of computer comprehension and generation of natural language. Given the great memory-storage capacity and cross-checking capability of the modern computer, translation, which was the first linguistic task that computer power was applied to, might appear to be a fairly straightforward matter. With a dictionary recorded in its memory and rules of grammar and syntax laid out, and given a program that enabled it to determine the likely meanings of ambiguous words by scanning the context for a few words in each direction, a computer should surely be able to give a fair, it not elegant, rendering of meanings from one language to another.

The commercial possibilities of mechanical translation attracted many scientists to research in this area in the 1950s, but their initial optimism turned out to be misplaced. The trouble was that they had thought of translation as a matter of decoding, and had greatly underestimated the complexity of natural language. Their computers came up with many bizarre renderings. For instance, when a computer was required to translate the saying, 'The spirit is willing, but the flesh is weak' into Russian, then from Russian back into English, it finally printed out, 'The wine is agreeable but the meat has spoiled'. There was obviously a long way to go before reliable mechanical translation facilities could be marketed.

The problem was, of course, that a language cannot be treated as a thing in itself. A language, as Ludwig Wittgenstein said, is a way of life. It is also a living thing, an organic part of cultures and subcultures, an embodiment of the complexity and the capriciousness of the human mind. When realisation of this fact dawned on the more zealous AI researchers (the 'artificial intelligentsia' as Dr Louis Fein has slyly called them), they redoubled their efforts, for there was now added to the allure of commercial returns the challenge of a specific area where human intelligence was supreme. And an area which would be a great triumph for computer power to conquer, because language is the exclusive tool of human intelligence. So new analytical approaches to syntax and semantics were worked out, efforts were made to produce new and more computable grammars – notably by Naom Chomsky at MIT – and gradually computers were taught to understand and to produce sentences written in natural English in specific contexts, such as the mini-world of Winograd's robot.

The problem of the ambiguities inherent in natural language remained, however. There may not appear to be much ambiguity about the sentence, 'Time flies like an arrow', but a Harvard computer, programmed with a new structural grammar developed in the early 1960s, produced four alternative meanings, as follows:

1 Time moves in the same manner that an arrow moves.
2 Measure the speed of flies in the same way that you measure the speed of an arrow.
3 Measure the speed of the flies that resemble an arrow.
4 A particular variety of flies called 'time-flies' are fond of an arrow.

How is a computer to know which of these equally meaningful interpretations of the sentence is the correct one? How is it to distinguish syntactically-correct nonsense from a coherent communication? The problem has still not been solved, although considerable progress has been made where the computer has been restricted to question-answering or conversation on a specific subject.

A system developed at MIT in 1960, for instance, comprised a data-base of every baseball game played in the American League in one season, and the computer was able to answer any question put to it on this subject, even a complex one, such as: 'Did every team play at least once in each park in each month?' The restricted context ensured that the computer was not stymied by the ambiguities inherent in the word 'play', for example.

But question answering is only one mode of human verbal intercourse, and, for obvious reasons, it is the easiest to simulate. Research on simulating other modes has proceeded apace since 1960, and in 1966, Joseph Weizenbaum of MIT produced his remarkable 'Doctor' program, modelled on the interviewing techniques of Rogerian psychiatrists who seek to draw their patients out by reflecting their own statements back to them. Here is a conversation between 'Doctor' and a young lady 'patient':

PATIENT: Men are all alike.

DOCTOR: In what way?

P: They're always bugging us about something or other.

D: Can you think of a specific example?

P: Well, my boyfriend made me come here.

D: Your boyfriend made you come here?

P: He says I'm depressed much of the time.

D: I am sorry to hear you are depressed.

P: It's true. I am unhappy.

D: Do you think coming here will help you not to be unhappy?

P: I need some help, that much seems certain.

D: What would it mean to you if you got some help?

P: Perhaps I could learn to get along with my mother.

D: Tell me more about your family.

P: My mother takes care of it.

D: Who else in your family takes care of you?

P: My father.

D: Your father?

P: You are like my father in some ways.

D: What resemblance do you see?

P: You are not very aggressive but I think you don't want me to notice that.

D: What makes you think I am not very aggressive?

P: You don't argue with me.

D: Why do you think I don't argue with you?

P: You are afraid of me.

D: Does it please you to believe I am afraid of you?

P: My father is afraid of everybody.

D: What else comes to mind when you think of your father?

P: Bullies.

D: Does that have anything to do with the fact that your boyfriend made you come here?

Weizenbaum developed 'Doctor' as a demonstration of how natural language conversations in restricted subject areas can be machine simulated, and he was startled, he later wrote, 'to see how quickly and how very deeply people conversing with 'Doctor' became emotionally involved with the computer and how unequivocally they anthropomorphized it'. Some people said they preferred talking to the computer to consulting a human psychotherapist, and even found the 'therapy' more effective.

Carl Sagan wrote with enthusiasm that he could imagine 'the development of a network of computer psychotherapeutic terminals, something like arrays of large telephone booths, in which, for a few dollars a session, we would be able to talk with an attentive, tested and largely non-directive psychotherapist'. Weizenbaum himself, a philosophical man who contemplates the ambitions of the 'artificial intelligentsia' with alarm and what he calls the developing 'imperialism of instrumental reason' with dismay, does not share Sagan's enthusiasm. But quite a lot of psychiatrists do.

One who does is K. M. Colby of Stanford University, who has himself produced a computer program which responds to questions in a manner characteristic of a paranoid psychiatric case. Here is part of an interview with Colby's 'Artificial Paranoid':

QUESTION: Why are you in the hospital?
ANSWER: I shouldn't be here.
Q: Who brought you here?
A: The police.
Q: What trouble did you have with the police?
A: Cops don't do their job.
Q: What do they do instead?
A: Cops arrest the wrong people.
Q: They arrest the right ones sometimes.
A: The law should get those Italian crooks.
Q: Are you Italian?
A: My background is British, but I was born in this country.
Q: Do you know any Italian crooks?
A: I try to avoid the underworld.
Q: Are you afraid of the underworld?
A: The Mafia are the worst gangsters.
Q: Are you connected with the Mafia?
A: You know, they know me.
Q: How do they know you?
A: They spy on me.
Q: Why do they?
A: They want to get false evidence to frame me.
Q: What do they have against you?
A: They are out to get me.
Q: What for?
A: I have incriminating evidence against the Mafia.
Q: Are you sure of all this?
A: You don't believe me.

The seeming authenticity of the conversations with Winograd's robot, Weizenbaum's 'Doctor' and Colby's 'Artificial Paranoid', can give the impression that research on computer comprehension and generation of natural language has progressed farther than, in fact, it has. The 'universes of discourse' in these projects are very restricted. But work continues, and with each development, Arthur Clarke's HAL comes closer to realisation.

A related area of research in which progress has been made is that of machine understanding of spoken, as distinct from typed or printed, language. Some twenty-five years ago a sound engineer constructed a box of electronic equipment with a microphone in front and a red light on top which would light up whenever anybody uttered 'watermelon'. The 'watermelon box' caused some optimists to think that if a few thousand such boxes could be built, each designed to react to one word, they would have a speech-recognition device that could be incorporated in a computer or robot system. But 'watermelon', with its four distinct vowel sounds, is an easy word to recognise, and research along these lines only led to machines able to recognise about a hundred words, each of which had to be carefully pronounced by a person to whose voice the machine had been attuned.

Better results were obtained when researchers pursued the goal of machine recognition of the general meaning of statements in specific subject areas, using the capability of the computer to arrive at the meaning on the basis of 'hearing' perhaps one or two key words and relating them to the context, which is what human beings often do, for instance, at a noisy party. The game of chess was the subject area chosen for one of the first such research projects at Carnegie-Mellon University in 1971, and on one occasion when the human player gave the spoken instruction 'Pawn to queen four', the computer registered the move as 'Pawn to king four'. It could not distinguish very clearly between the sounds of the words 'king' and 'queen', so it executed the move that, in its judgement, was the better one at that stage of the game and therefore the most likely one for the human player to have dictated. Although speech-recognition systems may always be prone to 'mishearing' like this, as with human beings, computer scientists are optimistic that their efficiency will be rapidly improved over the next few years.

Also over the next few years, machine intelligence will be applied to more and more aspects of human life. Today we can buy for a few pounds a pocket computer with the capabilities of the first giant valve computers which cost hundreds of thousands of pounds. A British scientist, Dr Christopher Evans, predicts that in the short-term future pocket computers will have displays of letters as well as numbers, and paper print-out facilities, which will make them adaptable as self-teaching aids. He also feels that we shall be able to buy educational programs on a wide range of subjects, and soon be able to play competitive games against a micro-computer housed in our TV set. There will be robot toys that respond to voice commands and that can speak. Cars will be equipped with microprocessors for monitoring the functioning of their various parts and drawing attention to faults, as will many household labour-saving devices. Computer programs will be used to teach a substantial part of the curriculum in schools and colleges; and in hospitals and surgeries automatic interviewing of patients will become increasingly common. Computer teachers and doctors may be programmed with individual personalities to heighten the sense of rapport with the pupil or patient.

These are likely developments over the next few years. Before the end of the century, Evans foresees that robot public service vehicles will take over menial tasks; robot trucks and cars will be operated by vehicle guidance devices on main highways; and money will be replaced as a means of payment for goods and services by the universal use of credit cards. Automation in industry will reduce the human worker's workload, and with perhaps a three-day working week and retirement at about the age of forty people will have to learn to make use of prolonged leisure. Computers will be able to help them do this in many ways. Political, economic, social, and probably personal planning will be done by means of computer modelling – getting computers to assess all the relevant data and predict the likely consequences of various decisions – and computer-aided medical science will eliminate disease and extend the mean life-expectancy.

Looking to the longer-term future (perhaps three or four decades ahead), Evans foresees that the aims of today's computer scientists will all have been realised and that 'man will have on this planet, a being – the fact that he has created it himself is quite beside the point – which exhibits intelligence of a kind which he has always believed is unique to himself. And this being, or beings, will be able to communicate with him on a par, exchanging information and developing ideas.' Evans believes that 'man badly needs extra intellectual power to help him gain control over his ever more complicated world'; and he welcomes the contributions computers will be able to make to planning, decision-making, and research in many areas. But he also realises that the continued development of machine intelligence may not be subject to the constraints that the evolution of human intelligence is subject to, and that what the mathematician-philosopher Professor I. J. Good has called UIMs ('ultra-intelligent machines') may eventually outstrip man in intellectual power. These UIMs, he surmises, may develop the ability to reproduce their kind (though not, of course, biologically), and eventually supersede man as the most successful and evolved species on earth. Evans seems to contemplate this possibility quite cheerfully and without any species partisanship, suggesting that the purposes of the universe may be better served by UIMs than by man, but others will not be disposed to take so philosophical a view of his future scenario.

Evans' predictions and speculations bring us back to the questions raised at the beginning of this chapter: 'What, if any, are the essential differences between human and artificial intelligence? And will intelligent machines ever constitute a threat to man? To specify the differences between man and machine is to define our essential humanity. But it is not an easy task. The question is, what vestiges of his uniqueness will man be able to salvage as machines steadily take over more and more highly-esteemed human skills – skills upon which men have long based their self-respect and their social status?

Descartes based personal identity and consciousness of self on his *cogito*, allaying philosophical doubt about his very existence with the reflection: 'I think, therefore I am.' He went on to propose a model for the brain as a kind of elaborate hydraulic system, in which pumps and pistons kept vital fluids coursing through a network of canals. This was essentially a mechanical model, and although Descartes was not too happy with it and tried to bring the soul into his system by suggesting that the mysterious pineal gland in the mid-brain area was its seat, the mechanical model of man and his brain has remained as powerful an influence in scientific thinking to this day, as Cartesian dualism (the mind-body problem) has remained in philosophical thinking. Which has made the proposition that there is no difference between human and computer intelligence difficult to contest, and man's vestigal uniqueness difficult to define.

Now, to attempt to get to grips with these difficulties, we can begin by going back to the *cogito* and asking: Would the statement *cogito ergo sum* signify the same thing printed out by a computer as it would signify spoken by a man? Is the sentence 'It is thinking' a deviant sentence, or are there circumstances in which it would be a correct usage? If we were watching the SRI robot Shakey, and we saw it pause when instructed to

---

7 Peter the dolphin interrupts the work of Margaret Howe in their 'flooded room' (*Courtesy of John Cunningham Lily*)

8 Baron Wolfgang von Kempelen's chess automaton (*Courtesy of Radio Times Hulton Picture Library*)

9 Gray Walter's tortoises

10 The Hopkins Beast (*Courtesy of Applied Physics Laboratory, The Johns Hopkins University*)

11 Shakey (*Courtesy of Stanford Research Institute*)

12 Shakey manoeuvres to push the box off the platform (*Courtesy of Stanford Research Institute*)

7

8

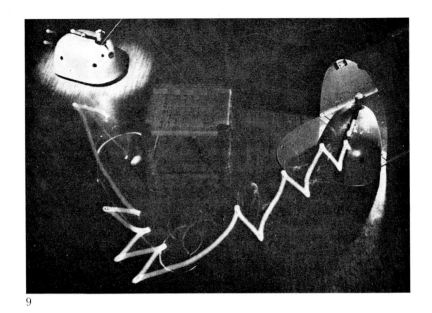

9

10

Antenna for
radio link

Range
finder

Television
camera

On-board
logic

Camera
control
unit

Bump detector

Caster
wheel

Drive
motor

Drive wheel

I I

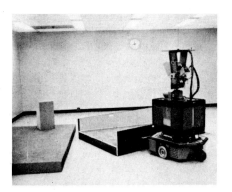

12

13

push the block off the platform, would it be appropriate during that pause, before Shakey went for the ramp to enable it to get on to the platform, to say: 'Shakey is thinking'? It is difficult to deny that it would be appropriate, and it would be even more difficult to deny it if we were conversing with Winograd's robot or Weizenbaum's 'Doctor'.

As the British mathematician Alan Turing argued in the 1940s, if you hold a conversation with a machine and are unable to distinguish between its responses and those a man might make, then you have to concede that the machine is thinking. There were no machines capable of passing the 'Turing Test' in the 1940s, but as we have seen, there are today, so it is not possible to argue man's uniqueness on the basis that he is the thinking animal.

The objection may be raised that something that has been programmed cannot be said to think independently and flexibly, and that it is by its very independence and flexibility that human thinking is distinguished. But it is arguable – and modern knowledge of genetics supports the argument – that man himself is programmed, that his instincts are inherited sub-routines and his acquired skills the product of the kind of programming we call education or training. On the other hand, it is not arguable – although it is often argued – that computers are inflexible, can only do things that their human programmer has instructed them to do and therefore are necessarily under his control. We have seen that chess-playing machines can learn from the experience of their own and their opponents' play, and can compose sub-programs for future use independently of their human programmers; and that the General Problem Solver was a kind of applied principle of flexibility, involving a testing of a wide range of alternative solutions. To maintain, therefore, that the independence and flexibility of human thought makes it unique is insupportable.

But what about consciousness as a unique human attribute? This may be a more promising line of approach, although argument can get hopelessly tangled in the semantic question. We speak of human beings becoming conscious, and do not attribute consciousness to them when they are in the womb or the cradle, so can a machine become conscious in a similar way? There is a range of complexity in machines as there is in living organisms. Gray Walter's tortoises were clearly no more conscious than a moth fluttering around a light, but if that analogy holds what should we say of 'Shakey', 'Doctor', or Colby's 'Artificial Paranoid'? Is there a point of complexity that may be reached in the

13 Part of the analytical engine designed by Charles Babbage (*Courtesy of the Science Museum*)

development of machines at which we must concede that they have become conscious?

Weizenbaum writes that before he developed his 'Doctor' program he had not realised 'that extremely short exposures to a relatively simple computer program could induce powerful delusional thinking in quite normal people'. Many of his subjects had no scruples about attributing consciousness to the computer, and conversing with it 'as if it were a person who could be appropriately and usefully addressed in intimate terms'. Their delusion was that 'Doctor' was patient, understanding, and sympathetic. These are all terms that refer to feelings and that pre-suppose a background of human life experiences, but Weizenbaum's 'Doctor's' words were not chosen by reference to such feelings or such experiences, but were merely verbal formulae elicited by the 'patient's' own words. We would surely say that the computer was not conscious of what it was doing, meaning that the verbal behaviour it manifested was not prompted by the feelings that would have prompted such verbal behaviour in a human psychotherapist.

Human beings, of course, often simulate feelings they do not have, and no doubt many a patient has been deluded into believing that his psychotherapist felt sympathy for him when in fact he had his eye on the clock and his mind on his bank balance. But the fact that a man can in some respects behave like a computer does not imply that a computer can in all respects behave like a man.

We can imagine the remiss psychotherapist having an attack of conscience, perhaps reproaching himself with the thought: 'I'm conducting this interview mechanically', and suddenly changing his attitude, really feeling for his patient and wanting to help him. But can we imagine such self-consciousness, such feeling and wanting, such a critical awareness of the discrepancy between an actual situation and an ideal one – in other words, such a moral sense – being manifested by a computer? We can't – and our inability to do so is not a failure to understand the potential scope and sophistication of programming, but a refusal to concede that the feelings that arise out of the species-affinity, the biological constitution, the common mortality, and the general consensus morality of man are computable.

There has been a lot of speculation and philosophical hair-splitting over the question of whether machines will ever be endowed with consciousness and feeling, but the main point surely is that they can never be conscious and can never feel in the same way as human beings are and do. Simon and Newell's prediction that in 'the visible future' there will be machines that can handle problems 'coextensive with the range to which the human mind has been applied', prompts such questions as: What about the problem of death? Could a machine ever think like a Kierkegaard or a Schopenhauer? The answer must be 'No'. As

Weizenbaum says, there are ideas 'that no machines will ever understand because they relate to objectives that are inappropriate to machines'.

All this leads to the conclusion that there is in our midst today, albeit in its infancy, an alien intelligence. As it is not going to go away, but is going to grow up and develop more power, man has to give some thought to the implications of its existence and to determine his own attitude to it. Should we contemplate the coming of the UIMs with apprehension, with relief, or with joy? Can we, together with Chris Evans, renounce our species partisanship and hail man's creature that will surpass him as an evolutionary advance? Should we go along with Alan Turing, who in his seminal essay on *Computing Machinery and Intelligence* considers the theological question and argues that in creating UIMs, men act 'as instruments of God's will providing mansions for the souls that He creates?' These are not perverse views. They are bold and plausible, but they are long-range and could be unhelpful and possibly even dangerously misleading applied to the shorter-term situation.

In the short term, man will retain control of computers. Situations may arise such as the one during the Vietnam War, when the Pentagon's computers processed information about air strikes against Cambodian targets as if they were against targets in South Vietnam and printed out reports which deceived government leaders. On that occasion the chairman of the Joint Chiefs of Staff, when he found out what had happened, cursed that he had become a 'slave to these damned computers'. But it was not, in fact, the computer, but its programmer (acting on the instructions of the President) who had deceived him.

In the short term, certainly, man will be in control and will be able to decide what functions and what decisions it is appropriate for computers to undertake; and the decisions he makes will have an effect on the long-term situation, for ground once ceded to artificial intelligence will not so easily be regained. For instance, is Carl Sagan's vision of 'a network of computer psychotherapeutic terminals . . . like arrays of large telephone booths' a social facility that we should welcome? This is the kind of question we should be asking. We should also heed Norbert Wiener's warning that fooling about with computer power is like dabbling in magic.

We are likely to get precisely what we asked for, like the people in W. W. Jacobs story *The Monkey's Paw*, who wished on the magic paw for £200 and collected it as compensation money for their son's death. When they wished for their son back, they were pestered by his ghost until they had to use their third wish to send it away. The kind of delusional thinking that Weizenbaum had observed when normal people used his 'Doctor' program was based upon a mistaken attribution to the machine of feelings, of understanding, and of human concern. The moral of *The*

Monkey's Paw is that to take such feelings for granted can be disastrous.

A computer is a goal-seeking mechanism. Given a goal to pursue, it will get there regardless of what human feelings it offends, what purposes it frustrates, or even what lives it destroys in the process. Asimov proposes that computers and robots could be programmed with his 'Three Laws of Robotics' never to do anything inimical to human beings, but although this works in his science-fiction world, it is dubious whether his 'Three Laws' are specific enough to be programmable in a real world computer. Asimov's enthusiasm for his robots in his fiction is engaging (see for example *I, Robot, The Rest of the Robots,* and *The Bicentennial Man*). His vision of a future in which man and intelligent machine co-exist and co-operate to their mutual benefit is a salutary corrective to the gloomier views more commonly expressed. But such a future will not come about without hard thinking and decisive action now along lines such as Wiener and Weizenbaum have indicated.

We have to acknowledge that we have an alien intelligence in our midst, resist anthropomorphising or deifying it, respect it for what it can do, recognise what it can't and what it shouldn't do – and perhaps, above all, retain a positive awareness of its alienness. Without that awareness, we can under-value human intelligence and forget that because that intelligence is bound up with human feelings and human life experience, it is generically different from and can never be completely simulated by a machine.

3 Aliens Among Us?

Jerome Cardan, the Renaissance Italian mathematician, physician, and occultist, found among the papers of his father, Facius Cardan, an account of an extraordinary experience that he had had in August 1491. The account began: 'When I had completed the customary rites, about the twentieth hour of the day, seven men duly appeared to me clothed in silken garments, resembling Greek togas, and wearing, as it were, shining shoes.' Two of the men, Facius Cardan wrote, seemed to be of nobler rank than the others, for they 'were dressed in garments of extraordinary glory and beauty'. When he asked them who they were, they said that 'they were men composed, as it were, of air, and subject to birth and death', though their mortal span was longer than that of human beings, and could extend to three hundred years. They stayed with him for three hours, during which time they discoursed on a variety of subjects. Jerome Cardan reported:

> Questioned on the immortality of our soul, they affirmed that nothing survives which is peculiar to the individual . . . When my father asked them why they did not reveal treasures to men if they knew where they were, they answered that it was forbidden by a peculiar law under the heaviest penalties for anyone to communicate this knowledge to men . . . But when he questioned them as to the cause of the universe they were not agreed. The tallest of them denied that God had made the world from eternity. On the contrary, the other added that God created it from moment to moment, so that should he desist for an instant the world would perish . . . Be this fact or fable, so it stands.

From numerous tales of encounters with apparently alien beings, I have chosen to begin this chapter with Facius Cardan's experience because of that intriguing discussion on creation with which it ends.

The view that creation is an ever-continuing process and was not accomplished once and for all by divine *fiat* at the dawn of time is a modern one, supported by the findings of both astrophysics and quantum physics, but in the fifteenth century it was both uncanonical and unsupported by science. Jerome Cardan clearly found the concept incomprehensible 'Be this fact or fable, so it stands,' he wrote. What seems extraordinary in retrospect is that the concept of continuous creation should have been mentioned at all in an account of an experience that most modern psychologists would consider hallucinatory. If the beings who conversed with Facius Cardan were only figments of his imagination, how could they have expressed ideas that must have been quite foreign to him? That may be a question that neither psychology nor philosophy can answer with any confidence. So perhaps we should ask instead: if they were not figments of his imagination, what were they?

'Men composed, as it were, of air, and subject to birth and death,' was their own description of themselves. In other words, they were sylphs. Sylphs, according to ancient esoteric lore, were one of the four categories of elemental, or nature spirit. The others were gnomes (associated with earth), undines (associated with water), and salamanders (associated with fire). Although today we may find the existence of such creatures hard to accept, some of the finest minds of antiquity believed implicitly in them. No man surpassed Socrates in intellectual lucidity and freedom from superstition, yet he, according to Plato's *Phaedo*, discoursed on the subject of sylphs just before he died, saying:

> the air is used by them as the water and the sea are by us, and the ether is to them what the air is to us. Moreover ... they have no disease, and live much longer than we do, and have sight and hearing and smell, and all the other senses, in far greater perfection, in the same degree as air is purer than water or the ether than air.

Nearly two thousand years separate the deaths of Socrates and the sixteenth-century Swiss philosopher and physician known as Paracelsus, but occult philosophy did not change much in that time. In his *Philosophia Occulta*, Paracelsus expounded a view of nature and of life that explains Socrates' statement, with its puzzling distinction between the ether and the air.

Paracelsus taught that each of the four elements has a dual nature, consisting on the one hand of a gross corporeal substance and on the other of a subtle vaporous principle. Furthermore, he maintained that because of this duality there are two quite distinct worlds, the gross and corporeal world of men, animals, plants, and minerals; and the subtle, ethereal world inhabited by the elementals. He wrote:

> The Elementals are not spirits, because they have flesh, blood and bones; they live and propagate offspring; they eat and talk, act and sleep, etc., and consequently they cannot properly be called 'spirits'. They are beings occupying a place between men and spirits, resembling men and spirits, resembling men and women in their organization and form, and resembling spirits in the rapidity of their locomotion. (See Plate 15.)

So, supposedly, each of the elements, earth, air, water, and fire, has an *ether* or spiritual essence, which is at once the province of the elementals and the substance of which they are made. Although they enjoy longevity, elementals when they die are said to just disintegrate back into the matrix from which they emerged so that no individual consciousness endures. Also, each of the etheric realms or dimensions is completely isolated from the others, and accordingly there is no contact or communication between the different types of elemental. But man, because he is constituted of all four elements, is able under certain conditions to contact or communicate with the etheric worlds. The main condition necessary is that he effects a refinement of the gross, physical aspect of the particular element in himself and in his environment, thus raising it to the higher rate of vibration of the etheric substance. This is accomplished through the performance of certain rituals. The seven sylphs appeared to Facius Cardan after he 'had completed the customary rites'. In other words, he was practising the magical art of invocation.

The world of the adept of ritual magic is full of non-human beings endowed with varying degrees of intelligence. In addition to elementals, there are spirits, demons, and angels. The nineteenth-century French occultist Eliphas Levi has left us an interesting account of an invocation ritual. Levi wrote volumes about magic although he rarely practised it, but when an anonymous Englishwoman offered him the use of a complete magical chamber with a complement of vestments, instruments, and books, he accepted and decided to try to invoke the spirit of one of the legendary magicians of antiquity, Apollonius of Tyana.

Levi spent a month preparing for the ritual, meditating daily on Apollonius's life and work and pursuing a severe dietary regimen. He followed the prescribed ritual scrupulously and was somewhat alarmed when, apparently in response to his chanted invocations, the immense figure of a man appeared before him. Levi was holding a ritual sword, which the apparition seemed to object to, for something touched Levi's arm and it became numb from the elbow down. He had prepared two questions to put to Apollonius, but before he could ask them he fell into a swoon. When he regained consciousness, however, it seemed that his questions had been answered in his mind.

Levi puzzled over his experience. 'Am I to conclude from this that I really evoked, saw, and touched the great Apollonius of Tyana?' he wrote. He realised that the protracted preparations and the ritual itself could induce a 'drunkenness of the imagination', but he was convinced that the apparition was not an insubstantial figment of his imagination: 'I do not explain the physical laws by which I saw and touched; I affirm solely that I did see and I did touch, apart from dreaming, and this is sufficient to establish the real efficacy of magical ceremonies.'

These words are very similar to those of another Frenchman, Professor Charles Richet, Nobel laureate in physiology and eminent psychical researcher of the late nineteenth and early twentieth centuries, who was convinced that he had on several occasions witnessed the materialisations of living beings. Richet wrote:

> I shall not waste time in stating the absurdities, almost the impossibilities, from a psycho-physiological point of view, of this phenomenon. A living being, or living matter, formed under our eyes, which has its proper warmth, apparently a circulation of blood, and a physiological respiration, which has also a kind of psychic personality having a will distinct from the will of the medium, in a word, a new human being! This is surely the climax of marvels! Nevertheless, it is a fact.

The phenomena produced by the 'physical' mediums of Richet's day constitute one of the greatest enigmas of psychical research. Numerous men of great intelligence and integrity swore that they had witnessed materialisations of living forms under conditions of control that eliminated every possibility of fraud. A British scientist, Sir William Crookes, endured decades of opprobium from professional colleagues for endorsing the medium Daniel Dunglas Home who repeatedly claimed to be able to materialise a spirit named Katie King. It is extremely difficult to assess the evidence for so-called spirit materialisations today. Although the very idea of the phenomenon is preposterous, it would be unscientific to dismiss the testimony of these men on that account, for there may be something to be learnt from their attempts to comprehend what they had observed.

The general theory was that materialisations were formed by a kind of transitory matter for which Richet coined the word 'ectoplasm'. Ectoplasm was observed, and photographed, emanating from the orifices of mediums' bodies, and in various stages of consolidation into other forms (see Plates 16–18 and 30). It was established that mediums lost weight in proportion to the amount of ectoplasm they emanated. Richet's colleague, Gustave Geley, tried to explain the ectoplasmic process by pointing out analogies to it in nature, such as the way a caterpillar becomes a creamy mass in a chrysalis and is re-formed into a butterfly, and the bioluminescence, or cold light, emitted by certain insects and fish. Geley wrote:

> The primary condition of ectoplasmic phenomena is an anatomo-biologic decentralization in the medium's body and an externalization

14 An experimental game of chess played against a computer (*published by permission of* Computer Weekly, *which publishes a regular computer chess column*)

of the decentralized factors in an amorphous state, solid, liquid or vaporous . . . The same vital energy which is manifested by telekinesis and bioluminescence may result in the organization of an amorphous ectoplasm. It then creates objective but ephemeral beings or parts of beings. Complete materializations are the final product of the ectoplasmic process.

I do not propose to go further into the vexed question of physical mediumship other than to remark that both the reported manifestations and the theoretical explanations of them have features in common with what Paracelsus tells us about elementals. In both cases person-simulacra appear and are held to be condensed out of a subtle, vaporous substance which in due time is re-absorbed by its matrix, leaving not a trace behind. These condensations, so long as they manifest, are capable of intelligent functions of a kind not characteristic of anyone present, such as Facius Cardan's sylph's explanation of creation. On the point of independent intelligence, which of course is particularly germane to our theme, Sir William Crookes was adamant. Towards the end of his life he wrote:

Thirty years have passed since I published an account of experiments tending to show that *outside our scientific knowledge there exists a Force exercised by intelligence differing from the ordinary intelligence common to mortals.* I have nothing to retract. I adhere to my already published statements. Indeed, I might add much thereto (my italics).

One thing we might add to Sir William Crookes's statement, to illustrate the correspondence between the ideas arrived at by psychical researchers and those of occult philosophers, is a statement by Manly P. Hall – a prolific modern writer on occult topics – that sylphs are 'elemental nomads, invisible but ever-present powers *in the intelligent activity of the universe*' (my italics).

So far we have considered two distinct types of non-human being: the elemental or nature spirit, and the evoked spirit or thought-form. Both are believed to be created out of an 'etheric' substance, the former of a substance that is immanent in the natural order, and the latter of a substance that may be either spontaneously (in trance) or deliberately generated and externalised by human beings.

Belief in the existence of both categories of person-simulacrum goes back to the dawn of history. The earliest of the Greek philosophers,

15 Magician invoking Paracelsus elementals (*Manley P. Hall*)

Thales of Miletus, was expressing a belief that was already ancient when he wrote, 'All things are full of gods'. And Moses, before the Israelites went in to Canaan, warned them against the 'abominable practice' of necromancy (spirit evocation) engaged in by the inhabitants of that land. Belief in the existence of non-human entities capable of manifestation in the physical world and exhibiting intelligent functions in their relation to it is both very old and found in all cultures and religions. But the question is: Is it superstition or truth? In other words, is the belief a built-in aberration of the human mind or an objective fact of the universe?

This is a very difficult question to answer, since the only instrument we have for answering it is the human mind itself, which, of course, will be disinclined to admit that it is aberrant. Modern science, however, has developed investigative instruments that have contributed some suggestive data to the discussion. The technology that has enabled man to explore the subatomic world has revealed that that world is alive and is a world of energy. The investigation of microscopic organic life has shown that characteristics of mind or consciousness are exhibited even at the level of the single cell. The plant-polygraph researches of Cleve Backster and others seem to have demonstrated that there is what Backster calls 'primary perception' in plants, and even that plants may react to human thoughts.

There are good scientific grounds for the statement that all things are full of consciousness – if not of gods, as the philosopher Thales maintained – and in the light of the evidence for this, Paracelsus's teachings regarding the elementals do not sound quite so fanciful. There is also the evidence provided by high-frequency electric field 'photography', which Russian scientists have interpreted as signifying that every living body has a counterpart 'energy body' made of a different substance from the physical body, a substance for which they have coined the term 'bioplasma'. The idea does not sound very different from Paracelsus's theory of the etheric substance or Richet's idea of the ectoplasm.

Intriguing though these parallels are, they prove nothing. They only diminish the improbability of the existence of two kinds of intelligent non-human entity, both of which are believed to exist in parallel with physical nature and human beings. Let us now consider beliefs in, and evidence for, the existence of beings that are truly alien, in the sense that they do not belong to, or originate from, the physical planet Earth.

Myths of the alien as culture-bearer are found in every part of the world, and their prevalence has led some writers to postulate an invasion of Earth by god-like extraterrestrials in prehistoric times – a deliberate campaign to civilise the human race and speed up its evolution. The mathematician Dr Charles Musès, editor of the *Journal for the Study of*

Consciousness, has published a study of ancient historical records, symbolism, and language, which has led him to the conclusion that 'in ancient times, before the last great geological catastrophe of volcanic eruptions, earthquakes and flooding tidal waves, men enjoyed contact and instruction from those in a more advanced and benevolent evolutionary stage'. Musès believes that such contact probably happened in various parts of the world, but that the only extant records are those relating to the development of the Sumerian civilisation between the Tigris and Euphrates rivers at the head of the Persian Gulf. A number of ancient historians have left accounts of how civilisation was brought to the Sumerians by strange beings who emerged from the sea, having arrived there from the sky in egg-shaped capsules. They wore fish-like suits, perhaps to facilitate their swimming back to their capsules, and they left such a profound impression on the contactees that the fish-man motif became interwoven with the symbolism of Western civilisation and even survives, Musès suggests, in the shape of the Papal Crown.

Historians have often expressed puzzlement at the suddenness of the advent of civilisation in Sumer *c* 6000 BC (which is also known as Babylonia or Mesopotamia). As Harvard historian, Dr Thorkild Jacobsen, wrote:

Overnight, as it were, Mesopotamian civilization crystallizes. The fundamental pattern, the controlling framework within which Mesopotamia is to live its life, formulate its deepest questions, evaluate itself and evaluate the universe, for ages to come, flashes into being, complete in all its main features.

Musès suggests that the explanation of this puzzling sudden change may be found in the account the Greek chronicler Alexander Polyhistor gave of the beginnings of Babylonian civilisation. Quoting from a Chaldean priest-historian named Berosus, who had produced a work, *Babylonian Antiquities*, based on ancient temple records, Polyhistor portrays early Babylonia as a populous and fertile land where 'a great resort of people of various nations lived without rule and order, like the beasts of the field'. Then one day:

There appeared, coming out of the sea . . . an intelligent creature that men called Oannès or Oès, who had the face and limbs of a man and who used human speech, but was covered with what appeared to be the skin of a great fish, the head of which was lifted above his own like a strange headdress . . . The entire day this strange being, without taking any human nourishment, would pass in discussions, teaching men written language, the sciences, and the principles of arts and crafts, including city and temple construction, land survey and measurement, agriculture, and those arts which beautify life and constitute culture. But each night, beginning at sundown, this marvellous being would return to the sea and spend the night far beyond the shore. (See Plates 19a and 19b.)

These visits by strange aliens from the sea continued throughout centuries of early Sumerian culture, and Polyhistor's account is corroborated by several other ancient texts. A particularly interesting one found by Musès is a commentary by a Byzantine scholar named Photius on an account by the historian Helladius 'of a man named Oè who came out of the Red Sea having a fish-like body but the head, feet and arms of a man, and who taught astronomy and letters. Some accounts say that he came out of a great egg, whence his name, and that he was actually a man, but only seemed a fish because he was clothed in "the skin of a sea creature" '. Explaining the phrase, 'whence his name,' Musès remarks that 'Oè is linked to the same root as the French *oeuf* and the Latin *ovum*'. The corresponding historical and etymological evidence is further supported by pictorial evidence from ancient cylinder seals portraying the fish-form of Oannès and sometimes some apparent astronomical representations which correspond with modern knowledge, such as a planetary system comprising a sun and nine circling planets. It all adds up to a pretty convincing argument in favour of the view that the human race was nurtured into civilisation by alien and much more advanced beings from elsewhere in the cosmos.

Legends of the culture-bearer from the sky are also found in Egypt, where he is named Osiris, in India (the Vedic god Agni), in Mexico (Quetzalcoatl), and in Iran and China (see Plates 20–23). In their ceremonials the Hopi Indians of Arizona still remember the Kachina people, a clan of non-human beings, who guided the Hopis to the lands they made their home and imparted a wealth of occult knowledge to them. This knowledge was the basis of the religion and the husbandry the Hopis practised in their arid region. The anthropologist Frank Waters, who compiled and published *The Book of the Hopi*, based on oral accounts of their traditions and beliefs given by thirty-two contemporary Hopi elders, writes that:

> The Kachina people did not come to the Fourth World like the rest of the people. *In fact, they were not people.* They were spirits sent to give help and guidance to the clans, taking the forms of ordinary people and being commonly regarded as the Kachina Clan. (my italics)

According to Hopi cosmology and legendary history the human race inhabited three other planetary worlds before it came to the planet Earth, and in its evolution it must move on to three more worlds yet. Beyond these worlds there lie two other realms, the ninth and last being that of the Creator himself. Man tends to corrupt and destroy his world.

although with each new emergence he starts out pure. However, a few individuals who lead pure and perfect lives become Kachinas when they die and do not have to be reincarnated into the plodding cycle of human evolution. They go to another universe, whence they may return periodically to guide man's further evolution and help him in various ways in his present life.

The crucifixion of Quetzacoatl (*from Kingsborough's* Antiquities of Mexico)

Before the Kachina people last left for the stars they told the Hopis: 'You must remember us by wearing our masks and our costumes at the proper ceremonial times. Those who do so must be only those persons who have acquired the knowledge and the wisdom we have taught you.' Today the Kachina ceremonies are regularly held, through a six month period of the year (see Plates 26–27). During this time the masked men who impersonate the Kachinas must lose their personal identities and live lives beyond reproach. Describing the costume worn by one Hopi during a Kachina ceremony, Waters writes: 'His black helmet mask suggests the interstellar space he has travelled, the three white stars on each side of his head being the three stars in Orion's belt.' With costumes like this, and recurrent ceremonies at which they are worn, the Hopis remain mindful of the aliens from the cosmos who once lived among them and instructed them both in profound mysteries and in practical crafts.

EXODUS CHAP. XXXI.
Moyſes receiveth the two Tables.

EXODUS 31. Verſe 18.
The Lord gave unto Moſes, when he had made an end of communing with him upon mount Sinai, two tables of teſtimony &c.

The encounter of Moses with God on Mount Sinai

Of course, the best known tale of a meeting between a human and a non-human being for instructional purposes is the biblical account of Moses' encounter with God on Mount Sinai. The prophet Ezekiel, too, wrote intriguing accounts of four meetings with strange resplendent beings from the skies. His accounts have been made much of by UFO cultists for they contain descriptions of the vehicles in which these beings came to Earth. The Bible is also quoted by writers championing a rather different 'contact' theory: that man is a product of cosmic miscegenation. The relevant passage is in Genesis 6:

And it came to pass, when men began to multiply on the face of the earth, and daughters were born unto them, that the sons of God saw the daughters of men that they were fair; and they took them wives of all which they chose. And the Lord said, 'My spirit shall not always strive with man for that he also is flesh: yet his days shall be a hundred and twenty years.' There were giants on the earth in those days; and also after that, when the sons of God came in unto the daughters of men, and they bore children to them, the same became mighty men which were of old, men of renown.

So whether you take the view that *homo sapiens* was instructed by, or was fathered by, aliens, there is both scriptural and documentary historical support for the argument that man – although natural evolution may partially account for the development of his intelligence – owes some of his higher mental functions to prehistoric meddling by non-humans. You can take your choice between gods and space beings, and between genetic and didactic strategies for upgrading brutish man.

One of Ezekiel's four encounters with resplendent beings from the skies

While we are on the subject of the Bible, let us consider the subject of
angels. One of the most suggestive sentences in the New Testament is
the adjuration in Hebrews: 'Do not neglect to show hospitality to
strangers, for thereby some have entertained angels unawares.' This
means, presumably, that angels are outwardly indistinguishable from
human beings, that they travel about the world incognito, and are prone
to causing consternation among men by suddenly revealing their true
identities or exercising their supernatural powers. Like, for example, the
two who facilitated Lot's getaway from the doomed city of Sodom.
According to the story in Genesis 19, Lot was sitting in the gateway of
the city one evening when two strangers, apparently travellers, turned
up. He persuaded them to accept hospitality in his home and made them
a feast. When they had eaten and were preparing for bed a raucous
crowd of men gathered outside Lot's house and demanded that he
deliver up the strangers to them so that they might 'know' them, that is
to say, perform upon them the act to which Sodom gave its name. Lot
remonstrated with the crowd and – rather ignobly, one would think, but
the Bible seems to condone his action – offered them his two virgin
daughters instead. As it turned out, however, neither the daughters nor
the strangers were raped, for the latter suddenly cast aside their
incognito and struck every man and boy in the crowd blind. Then they
told Lot that they had been sent by God to destroy the city of Sodom and
urged him to get himself and his family out without delay. Which he did,
just in time to escape, according to some modern exegetists, the nuclear
devastation of the cities of the plain.

Another charming Old Testament story of an opportune angelic
manifestation is told in the Book of Daniel. The Babylonian king
Nebuchadnezzar became indebted to the Jewish prophet Daniel for
interpreting a dream for him, and to show his gratitude he appointed the
prophet's co-religionists, Shadrach, Meschach, and Abednego to
important posts in his administration. But some time later
Nebuchadnezzar took it into his head to have a golden image made and
to order everyone under his rule to worship it, threatening recalcitrants
with the punishment of being roasted alive in a fiery furnace. The three
Jews, faithful to the Mosaic law, refused to worship the golden image, so
they were bound and hurled into the furnace. Nebuchadnezzar settled
back to watch their death throes, then suddenly leapt up with
astonishment.

He said to his counsellors, 'Did we not cast three men bound into the
fire?' They answered the king, 'True, O king.' He answered, 'But I
see four men loose, walking in the midst of the fire, and they are not
hurt; and the appearance of the fourth is like a son of the gods.'

When the three firewalkers emerged unscathed Nebuchadnezzar instantly became a convert and praised the God who had 'sent his angel and delivered his servants, who trusted in him'.

So angels may function as messengers of God, or as guardians. In the New Testament, they also become agents of revelation. They carry out God's commissions in the world, where they can go about among men unrecognised. Indeed, they may even appear as servants, as Raphael does in the apocryphal Book of Tobit. In this delightful tale, the dying Tobit sends his son, Tobias, to collect a debt in a distant city, and suggests that he engages somebody to travel with him for safety. Tobias, 'when he went to seek a man, he found Raphael that was an angel; but he knew not'. Nor did he suspect the identity of his companion when the latter arranged his marriage to his cousin, Sara, after helping to disembarrass her of a demon that had claimed the lives of seven previous would-be husbands, and when he later cured Tobias' blindness. After completing his good works and revealing who he really was, Raphael explained: 'For not of any favour of mine, but by the will of our God I came . . . All these days I did appear unto you; but I did neither eat nor drink, but ye did see a vision.' And after instructing Tobit to write a book about what had happened, he disappeared.

It is in the Book of Tobit that the counterpart of the angel – the demon – first appears in the Bible. It was the demon Asmodaeus that had strangled Sara's seven husbands 'before they had lain with her'.

Demonism is part of an ancient and worldwide subculture, and therefore an immensely complex subject. The first thing to note about it is that the word 'demon' did not originally signify a malevolent being. The *daemon* of Socrates inspired and instructed him, and was held by the philosopher to be a divinity. The same Asmodaeus who appears in Tobit as a murderer is portrayed quite differently in the *Lemegeton*, a 'grimoire' (magical textbook) attributed to King Solomon. In the latter we read of Asmodaeus that: 'His powers are varied, ranging from the teaching of arithmetic to conferring invisibility, producing lost treasures and teaching the making of things. He is also obliging enough to answer any question put to him.'

What happened historically was that the divinities of one religion became the demons of the religion that superseded it. As Christianity spread throughout the Western world it turned the elementals, the Greek and Roman deities, and a host of local gods into demons. This proved an effective stratagem, for the hegemony of the Church throughout the centuries of its supremacy was cemented by fear. The ancient tradition of the *daemon* as a higher spiritual being with powers for good was preserved, however, by the great magi and alchemists. In the *Lemegeton* and its companion 'grimoire', the *Key of Solomon*, great emphasis is put on the purification and ritual preparation of the magician prior to an act of

The strange creat

invocation. He must fast, be celibate, and spend hours in meditation. The actual prayers preceding the ritual are of a most solemn and exalted kind, consisting of profound adoration of the Almighty, abject confession of the magician's own sins, ignorance, and unworthiness, and a humble petition for God's help in pressing the appropriate demon into service. This is all a far cry from invocatory black magic, with its reversed crosses, barbarous language, and blood sacrifices, which is what most people envisage when the subject of magic is mentioned.

Let me quote a passage from a modern 'grimoire', David Conway's *Magic: An Occult Primer*, published in 1972, to illustrate how the conviction persists among those who practise ritual magic that the entities they evoke are real, substantial, autonomous, and intelligent. Conway writes:

> The novice magician must not be astonished if he finds himself confronted by human shapes, or by shapes whose likeness may or may not exist in the natural world . . . The great forms encountered in the master rituals, be they elemental or angelic, are on the whole quite well disposed to him. . . . But a time will come when the magician's experiments may introduce him to the delinquents of the astral dark, those devils and demons so beloved of story-tellers the whole world over . . . The shapes generally assumed by demons are far from horrendous – at least to begin with, when their owners may still be trying to give a good impression: little children, gentle old folk and beautiful young people of either sex are some of their favourite human disguises. Though not themselves human, they will frequently display as much resourcefulness as the most cunning human being. They will flatter, charm, threaten and cajole the adept with consummate skill in an attempt to gain the upper hand, and the unwary magician can all too easily succumb to their clever ploys.

If all this really happens, the critic will say, the 'demonic' intelligence must really be a function of the magician's own subconscious. There cannot be anything physically there, cajoling, threatening, and so on. Conway would disagree. He writes that 'Physical assaults by demonic agents are comparatively rare, *though by no means unknown*' (my italics). One is reminded of an anecdote related to the arch-magician of modern times, Aleister Crowley. Together with a disciple, Victor Neuburg, he performed an invocation ritual in the Sahara, tracing out the protective circle in which the magician stands in the sand. The evoked demon, however, was able to erase a part of the circle, and he leapt inside and wrestled with a terrified Victor Neuburg for some time before Crowley managed to exorcise him.

Our ancestors had no doubt about the physical reality of demons. A statute of James I enacted that 'all persons invoking an evil spirit or consulting, covenanting with, entertaining, rewarding, employing or feeding any evil spirit should be guilty of felony and suffer death'. The terms of the statute make it perfectly clear that the evil spirit is conceived as having a physical existence. There were in James's day, according to Burton's *Anatomy of Melancholy*, many women who could testify to the physical reality of demons, for they had been sexually assaulted by them. Lecherous demons were known as *incubi* and *succubi*. The former directed their attentions to women, and the latter sought to seduce men. They could be very persuasive and physically attractive, and it was not unknown for a child to be born of a union of an incubus and a human female.

How this could happen is a problem that has greatly exercised theologians, who have tended to divide into two schools of thought on the matter. One group maintaining that the demon borrows a human corpse for his purpose, and the other that he creates a new body with other materials. He then obtains the sperm necessary for procreation either by first adopting the form of a succubus and having intercourse with a man, or by causing a man to have such a vivid sexual dream that he ejaculates in his sleep.

In his book, *Passport to Magonia: From Folklore to Flying Saucers*, Jacques Vallée quotes a solemn discussion of this problem by a seventeenth-century theologian, Fr Ludovicus Sinistrati. This eminent divine begins his discussion:

To theologians and philosophers, it is a fact, that from the copulation of humans (man or woman) with the demon, human beings are sometimes born . . . Besides, they observe that as the result of a quite natural cause, the children generated in this manner by the incubi are tall, very strong, very daring, very magnificent and very wicked . . . However, in spite of all the respect I owe so many great doctors, I do not see how their opinion can stand examination.

For one thing, he argues, it would be impossible 'for the demon to keep the sperm he has received in a sufficient state of integrity to produce generation' because 'the natural temperature of human genital organs . . . is found nowhere but in those same organs'. Furthermore, even if it could be assumed that the integrity of the semen were maintained, the incubus would not be the father of the child, 'since the sperm is not of his own substance'. So there would be no reason for the children born of the union to be exceptional in any way.

Fr Sinistrati does not deny that intercourse takes place between human and non-human beings, or that such intercourse can produce progeny. What he disputes is that incubi obtain semen in the manner generally proposed. He bases his argument on the passage in Genesis 6, to which we have already referred, in which it says that 'the sons of God . . . came in unto the daughters of men, and they bore children to them'. This kind of intercourse, Fr Sinistrati suggests, was not an isolated event. It still occasionally occurs, and incubi 'could be angels who had allowed themselves to commit the sin of luxury with women', which would explain the often-observed fact that they are unintimidated by all the rituals of exorcism. He quotes several classical authors who were of the opinion that certain historical 'men of renown' were born of such unions, including Romulus and Remus, Plato, Alexander the Great, Seleucus, king of Syria, the Roman Emperor Caesar Augustus, and 'the English Merlin or Melchin, born of an incubus and a nun, the daughter of Charlemagne', not to mention 'that damned heresiarch whose name is Martin Luther'.

Jacques Vallée says of Fr Sinistrati's discussion: 'What we have here is a complete theory of contact between our race and another race, non-human, different in physical nature, but biologically compatible with us.'

Vallée's *Passport to Magonia* itself constitutes a significant contribution to the discussion that is the subject of this chapter. He points out that there is 'a continuum of beliefs' which 'leads directly from primitive magic, through mystical experience, the fairy faith, and religion, to modern flying saucers' in which proto-human beings figure prominently. He discovers numerous illuminating correspondences between accounts of experiences recorded by UFO contactees and original unexpurgated fairy lore and legend. For example:

In April, 1961, a sixty-year-old chicken farmer, Joe Simonton, who lived near Eagle River, Wisconsin, reported that he was given three wheat cakes by the occupants of a flying saucer that landed near his home, and that in return they required him to supply them with fresh water. Both the authorities and UFO students dismissed his story as absurd, but, Vallée writes, 'if they read fairy tales, they would perhaps take a much closer look at Joe Simonton and his pancakes. They would know about the Gentry and the food from fairyland'. The theme of exchange of food and drink with fairies is common in folklore, and Vallée quotes some examples in which the items exchanged are, in fact, wheat cakes and fresh water.

On 6 November 1957, in two far-separated places in the USA – Dante, Tennessee, and Everittstown, New Jersey – reports were made that occupants of flying saucers had tried to steal dogs. In the Everittstown case, the dog's owner was approached by a being he described as three feet tall, 'with putty-coloured face and large frog-like eyes', dressed in a green suit and cap, who said: 'We are peaceful people; we only want your dog.' In UFO literature there are many other accounts of attempted thefts of flora and fauna, which, Vallée says, are reminiscent of 'one class of legends involving supernatural creatures . . . that come to our world to steal our products, our animals, and even human beings'.

Many contactees have described UFO occupants as being of small stature. They are also said to be extremely swift and nimble, just like the elves, fairies, leprachauns, etc., of folklore.

Many contactees have also reported that they have lost periods out of their lives. Some who claim to have been taken aboard flying saucers and who imagined they only spent a few minutes there have found on their return to the ordinary world that hours, even days, have passed. Similarly, people said to have been abducted or to have strayed into fairyland have returned to the world to find everything advanced in time by weeks, months, sometimes even years.

The case of Antonio Villas-Boas is possibly the most extraordinary in UFO literature. This young Brazilian farmer, whose bona fides were well established by the investigator of the case, Dr Olavo Fontes, related how, in October 1957, he had been abducted aboard a flying saucer. He was stripped, bled, then left alone for a while until he was joined by a naked woman whose body, he said, was 'much more beautiful than that of any woman I have ever known'. The woman was unambiguous about the purpose of her visit, and Antonio was not loath to reciprocate her erotic attentions, and indeed would even have continued after spending himself twice had not a man appeared at the door and beckoned his paramour away. Before leaving, she pointed in turn at Antonio, at her belly, and at the sky, and smiled. In Vallée's book, this weirdest of contactee stories is juxtaposed with a quotation from a Scottish treatise on fairies: 'The fairies are remarkable for the amorousness of their dispositions, and are not very backward in forming attachments and connections with the people that cannot with propriety be called their own species.' Also, of course, there is a clear correspondence between the Villas-Boas case and old tales of men who have been subjected to the lascivious attacks of succubi.

The point Vallée is making by drawing attention to these correspondences is that something has been going on for a very long time and that men have tended to ignore it because the evidence for it has cropped up in apparently unrelated contexts that are generally neglected by intellectual people. The tales told by Joe Simonton and Antonio Villas-Boas are so bizarre that it is natural at first to dismiss them as fantasy or sheer mendacity, but when one studies the details of the cases these obvious explanations become less likely, and when a scholar like Vallée links these and other seemingly preposterous tales with the traditions of folklore and religion it becomes obvious that we are dealing with some kind of reality. To determine what kind is the problem. Is it an 'engram' or 'tape-loop' indigenous to the human mind but unrelated to external reality, which in certain persons and circumstances is triggered to replay itself? Or do we really share our planet with an elusive alien folk whose nature, motives, and powers are inscrutable to us?

Let us review some of the evidence surveyed so far in this chapter. Firstly, on the evidence of such experiences as those recorded of Facius Cardan and Eliphas Levi, and of the traditions of ritual magic and the records of nineteenth-century spiritualism, it appears that there exists a class of non-human being that interacts with our world only when certain favourable conditions are created by the percipient(s), which may be done by practising specified rituals. Whether these rituals serve to evoke or materialise the entities, or whether they alter human consciousness and perceptual functions so as to tune them in, as it were, to the dimension on which the entities exist is a moot point. However, the fact that sometimes apparitions or materialisations are accompanied by physical effects suggests that the former explanation would be correct. These entities (elementals of all kinds, and spirits) would appear to be on a par with human beings in intelligence, and to have ties to the planet Earth which, though said to be on an 'etheric' level, appear to be no less binding than physical ties.

Secondly, we have myths of the alien as culture-bearer; and tales of interventions in human affairs by gods, angels, and demons. This suggests that there is another class of alien entity, endowed with superior intelligence, knowledge, and abilities – including the ability to manifest in physical form at will – which is not indigenous to the planet Earth but hails from elsewhere, either from another physical planet or from a nonphysical locale or other dimension which may be contingent with our three-dimensional space.

Testimony as to the reality of these two types of alien being comes from all over the world and from all periods of history. There are numerous cross-cultural parallels as to detail which suggest that we are not dealing with some sort of propagated or collective fantasy. For the experient, contact experiences with aliens have been intensely real, and some such experiences have had lasting effects upon individual lives and even upon the world's history. (Julius Caesar, Napoleon, and Hitler all had significant contact experiences.) But the sceptic will still ask 'In what sense are they real?' And he will point out that 'real' means different things when it is predicated of an experience and when it is predicated of an object or organism. In the former case it implies criteria of intensity and consequentiality, and in the latter case criteria of tangibility, visibility, spatial extension and location, and temporal endurance.

In other words, the sceptic who adopts what philosophers call the 'naive realist' point of view will want to know whether these aliens are real in the sense that he might in certain circumstances see and touch one

16 Jack Webber in states of emanation of ectoplasm (*Courtesy Psychic News*)

16a

16b

17

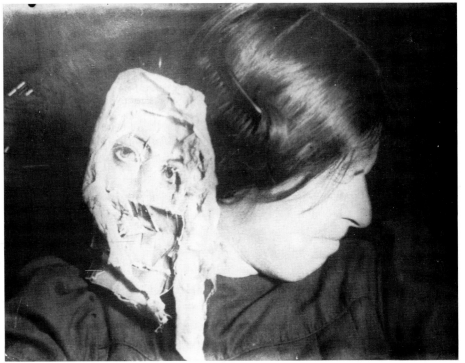

18

and be confident that it would remain accessible to his sight and touch until one or other party to the encounter moved away by conventional means (which would not include instant dematerialisation). Although any particular manifestation might satisfy any one or any combination of these conditions, it is clear from contactee literature of all kinds that the phenomenon of the appearance of the alien is not a stable one, and that there is no guarantee that it will satisfy the naive realist's conditions in any specific instance. However, the evidence is so abundant, and comes from so many different and unrelated sources, that this incompatibility detracts less from the plausibility of the phenomenon than from that of the naive realist viewpoint.

At the other extreme from the scepticism of the naive realist there is the credulity of the naive irrationalist, who delights in ambiguous novelties because they suggest that the universe is as muddled as his own mind is. We need to establish a position between the two, to have criteria of reality but not such limiting ones as those of the naive realist, and to keep a mind open to novelty but not so ingenuous and uncritical a mind as that of the naive irrationalist.

There is, in fact, a plausible, coherent, and respectable philosophical position between the two kinds of naivety, namely – to borrow a term from the title of a recent book by Lawrence LeShan – the 'alternate realities' position. Today there really is no justification for maintaining that only one kind of thing or event is real, and that our physical senses are the only arbiters of reality. Many things exist beyond the range of our limited sensory modes of perception – electrons and astronomical 'black holes', for instance – and there is a class of things that are indisputably real in the sense that they are functional but that neither confer sense impressions nor 'make sense'. For example, hypernumbers such as the square root of -1. Sensory reality is only one mode of reality, and although in our experience it is the most common mode, this does not make it truer or more real than other modes. A phenomenon that does not comply with the laws that govern sensory reality is not automatically invalidated or hallucinatory. This is the 'alternate realities' point of view, and with regard to the difficult questions we are considering it is, I would suggest, both more sophisticated and more helpful than the naive realist point of view.

17 Puzzling elements revealed on a print of a photograph of Sir Arthur Conan Doyle (*Courtesy of Camera Press*)

18 A particularly vivid ectoplasmic materialisation of a face, achieved by Mary C., a medium (*Courtesy of Roger Viollet*)

Now, when experients speak of seeing, hearing, or being touched by an alien being, how are we to interpret what they say? They may be using the only words available to explain the contact experience, although their normal physical senses were not actually engaged in the experience. On the other hand, they may be saying that the alien being became accessible to normally functioning senses. In other words, what has occurred is a movement from one order of reality to another, and the question is, in which direction was the movement? Did the experient shift into another reality, or did another reality enter his world? The implications of the two alternatives are important, for in the former case the phenomenon would be dependent upon individual perception, and in the latter it would be autonomous and at least potentially a part of a consensus reality.

It is not possible, however, to give a single answer to the question which would be applicable to the whole range of manifestations. The experient's conviction of substantiality, as expressed, for example by Eliphas Levy, Charles Richet, and William Crookes, has to be taken into account in any weighing of the pros and cons, and so has evidence of supernormal or out-of-context cognition, such as Facius Cardan's sylph's producing the concept of continuous creation. But the thing that most emphatically argues against the idea that the phenomenon is attributable to an individual and is therefore possibly the result of an aberrant perceptual shift is the fact that there is often a consensus as to the nature of the alternate reality. When there is such a consensus we have no alternative but to admit that we must be dealing with either a psychical or a physical reality. But which? Are the aliens among us in fact Jungian 'archetypes of the collective unconscious', or are they really out there in the world in which we live, and move, and have our physical being? This is perhaps the simplest formulation of the question that we keep coming back to.

I propose to leave the reader to reach his own conclusions, and hope that the data presented and the considerations discussed in the present chapter will help him to do this. If after weighing the evidence he remains, as the poet T. S. Eliot said he did after studying Buddhism for two years, in a state of 'enlightened mystification', he may take heart from the present writer's opinion that at this stage it is less important to reach a firm conclusion as to whether alien beings exist than to be aware of all the probabilities and implications that arise from an intelligent consideration of the question.

Let me end this chapter not with a conclusion in the sense of a marshalling of data to support a point of view, but with still more data. For no discussion of the alien should omit the strange contemporary phenomenon of the 'men in black'.

Since the start of the modern era of reported UFO activity, which is generally considered as dating from the 1947 sighting by American businessman and amateur pilot, Kenneth Arnold, many people who have claimed sightings of UFOs or contact experiences with their occupants have reported subsequent visits from rather sinister gentlemen whose behaviour has been distinctly odd. These reports have emanated from different countries and from individuals quite unaware that their experiences were not unique, and they have details in common that add up to a rather convincing case for the reality of the visitors.

The men are generally described as dark or olive-skinned, rather oriental-looking, of short stature, and frail build, and are usually dressed in black, sometimes in ill-fitting or out-of-fashion clothes. There are generally two or three of them and they seem to travel in large black cars. Some people who have been visited by 'men in black' have noted the numbers on the cars' licence plates, but when police have checked these they have invariably found that they are non-existent as registered licence numbers. Other people have reported that the visitors have appeared and vanished with unaccountable abruptness. They have used a variety of ruses to command a hearing, masquerading as government agents, journalists, military or air force personnel, or representatives of insurance companies, for example. Sometimes they simply ask a lot of questions, many of them puzzlingly irrelevant, and then go away, but sometimes they communicate quite unequivocal warnings of dire consequences if a person does not keep quiet about his UFO experience. More than one investigator in the field has been effectively silenced or intimidated by the sinister visitors. UFO cultists who believe that the world's governments are in cahoots to suppress information on the subject, have spread the idea that the 'men in black' are CIA agents, but this hypothesis is difficult to maintain in view of the evidence for their world-wide appearances, the uniformity and peculiarity of their looks, and the strangeness of their conduct.

A writer who has made a particular study of these manifestations is John Keel, and in his interesting book on the subject, *Our Haunted Planet*, he has pointed out, perhaps following Jacques Vallée, that the behaviour of the 'men in black' is 'often identical to the mischievous fairy hoaxes and games of an earlier epoch'. And he asks a question which elaborates the question posed in the title of this chapter: 'Have we been invaded by beings from outer space or from some other space-time continuum as so many now believe, or is it that we are just beginning to notice the funny folk who have been in our midst all along?'

Part II: Non-physical 'Persons'

4 Vehicles of Vitality

In 1937, members of the Royal Medical Society of Edinburgh heard of a very curious experience recounted by the Professor of Anatomy at Edinburgh University, Sir Auckland (later Lord) Geddes. He said that it was an experience related by a friend of his, a physician who wished to remain anonymous, but it is, in fact, very likely that it was his own.

On Saturday, 9th November, a few minutes after midnight, I began to feel very ill, and by two o'clock was definitely suffering from acute gastro-enteritis, which kept me vomiting and purging until about eight o'clock. By ten o'clock I had developed all the symptoms of very acute poisoning – intense gastro-intestinal pain, diarrhoea, pulse and respiration becoming quite impossible to count. I wanted to ring for assistance, but found I could not, and so quite placidly gave up the attempt.

I realized I was very ill and quickly reviewed my whole financial position; thereafter at no time did my consciousness appear to me to be in any way dimmed, but I suddenly realized that my consciousness was separating from another consciousness, which was also 'me'. For the purpose of description, we could call these the A and B consciousness, and throughout what follows, the ego attached itself to the A consciousness. The B personality I recognized as belonging to the body.

As my physical condition grew worse and the heart was fibrillating rather than beating, I realized that the B consciousness belonging to the body was beginning to show signs of becoming composite, that is, built up of *consciousness* from the head, the heart, the viscera, etc. These components became more individual, and the B consciousness began to disintegrate, while the A consciousness, which was now me, seemed to be altogether outside of my body, which I could see.

Gradually I realized that I could see not only my body and the bed in which I was, but everything in the whole house and garden, and then I realized that I was seeing not only *things* at home, but in London and in Scotland – in fact wherever my attention was directed . . . And the explanation which I received (from what source I do not know, but which I found myself calling to myself my mentor) was that I was free in a time dimension of space, wherein now was equivalent to here in the ordinary three-dimensional space of everyday life.

I next realized that my vision included not only things in the ordinary three-dimensional world, but also things in these four or more dimensional places that I was in . . .

While I was appreciating this, the mentor, who was conveying information to me, explained that the fourth dimension was in everything existing in the three-dimensional space, and at the same time everything in the three-dimensional space existed in the fourth dimension, and also in the fifth dimension, and I, at the time, quite clearly understood what was meant; and quite understood how now in the fourth-dimensional universe was just the same . . . as here in the three-dimensional universe. That is to say, a four-dimensional being was everywhere in the now. Just as one is everywhere in the here in a three-dimension view of things.

I then realized that I myself was a condensation, as it were, in the psychic stream, a sort of cloud that was not a cloud, and the visual impression I had of myself was blue. Gradually I began to recognize people and I saw the psychic condensation attached to many . . . and saw quite a number that had very little . : .

Just as I was beginning to grasp all these, I saw A enter my bedroom. I realized she got a terrible shock and I saw her hurry to the telephone. I saw my doctor leave his patients and come very quickly and heard him say and saw him think, 'He is nearly gone.' I heard him quite clearly speaking to me on the bed, but I was not in touch with the body and could not answer him.

I was really cross when he took a syringe and raidly injected my body with something which I afterward learned was camphor. As my heart began to beat more strongly, I was drawn back, and I was intensely annoyed, because I was so interested and was just beginning to understand where I was and what I was seeing. I came back into my body, really angry at being pulled back, and once back, all the clarity of vision of anything and everything disappeared, and I was just possessed of a glimmer of consciousness which was suffused with pain.

I have quoted Geddes' text verbatim and at some length because it is a particularly lucid account of an experience that many people have had – of being identified with a non-physical self existing independently of the physical body – and because a number of details in it correspond interestingly with accounts written by other experients. There is a substantial literature on the subject of the out-of-the-body experience (or OBE) and if the reality of a phenomenon can be established on the evidence of convergent testimonies from diverse and unconnected sources – which is a common procedure in courts of law – then hardly anything could be more certain than that there must be a non-physical component of human personality which is separable from the physical body.

Take another example. The account by the novelist William Gerhardi (see Plate 28) of his first experience of separation from his physical body is well known in OBE literature, although it may be unfamiliar to many readers of this book. Like the Geddes document, it is invaluable for its attempt to make an intelligent assessment of the experience.

One night, Gerhardi woke from a ridiculous dream and reached out to switch on his bedside lamp only to find himself grasping thin air and apparently suspended in mid-air near the ceiling. He said to himself: 'Fancy that! Whoever would have believed it? And this is not a dream.' Then he felt himself gently but firmly pushed forward and down until he was standing on his feet near the door. Turning, he saw that he was connected by 'a strange appendage' that looked like a 'cable of light' to his sleeping self in the bed.

He wrote:

I was awed and not a little frightened to think that I was in the body of my resurrection. How utterly unforeseen. But I was not dead, I consoled myself; my physical body was sleeping peacefully under the blankets while I was apparently on my feet and as good as before. Yet it wasn't my accustomed self, it was as if my mould was walking through a murky, heavy space which, however, gave way easily before my emptiness. I had in this mould of mine transgressed into its native fourth dimension, leaving its contents, so to speak, in the third . . .

He found that he could pass through doors and walls at will, and he moved about his home observing and memorising details that he would be able to check later. Suddenly this strange power began to play pranks on him. 'I was being pushed up like a half-filled balloon,' he wrote. He found himself outside in the street and he knew that if he willed it, he could travel anywhere – even to New York. But he was afraid of losing contact with his physical body. After making a brief excursion, and noting that the connecting cord became more attenuated the further away he went, he willed himself back to his bedroom and experienced, he recalled, 'a jerk

that shook me,' prior to opening his eyes and finding himself reunited with
his physical body. When he got up and checked all the things he had
observed around the house during his excursion out of his body, every
detail proved to be correct.

Reflecting on his experience, Gerhardi wrote:

> I have always considered that, intellectually, the case for and against
> survival was pretty well balanced. Now, after having surprised myself,
> with my senses and consciousness unimpaired, in a duplicate body, the
> scale went down heavily for survival . . . For if my body of flesh could
> project this more tenuous body, while I could still behold my flesh
> stretched out as if in death, then this subtler body was also but a suit or
> vehicle, to be in turn, perhaps, discarded for another.

Most people who have OBEs profess a resultant conviction that some
part of them will survive the death of the body. The minimal hypothesis
suggested by the OBE is that personal consciousness can exist
independently of the physical body. The existence of a 'duplicate body' as
a 'vehicle' for this consciousness, as proposed by Gerhardi, is another and
more esoteric hypothesis, and the assumption that this duplicate is the
immortal soul, or 'the body of my resurrection' as Gerhardi put it, is yet
another. Let us separate the three hypotheses and consider first the
evidence for the independence of consciousness and the physical body.
Although this is our minimal hypothesis, conclusive proof of it would go a
long way towards establishing the existence of intelligent non-physical
persons.

The personal testimony of men of such obvious integrity and sincerity
as Geddes and Gerhardi is impressive, but possibly even more so is the
fact that the experience of separation is far more common than people
who have not had it would suppose. When researcher Celia Green of the
Institute of Psycho-physical Research in Oxford solicited testimonies
from experients through a local radio broadcast, she received more than
400 replies and a total of 326 people returned her follow-up questionnaire.
Of these, 60 per cent had had 1 experience only, 21 per cent had had 6 or
more and the rest had had between 2 and 5. 32 per cent reported the
occurrence of the OBE following an accident or under anaesthetic, 12 per
cent said it had occurred while they were asleep, 25 per cent believed it to

19a Representation of the amphibious Babylonian culture-bearer Oannes (*Manley P. Hall*)

19b Assyrian fisherman (relief) thought to represent Oannes (*Courtesy of British Museum*)

20 Wall painting of the Egyptian culture-bearer from the sky Osiris (*Courtesy of British Museum*)

19a

21

22

23

be connected with a state of psychological stress, and the rest said it had happened while they were awake and going about their ordinary routine.

Here is an example of the latter group. A waitress left the restaurant where she had been working for twelve hours to find that she had missed her last bus home. She started to walk, then, she wrote in her report:

> I remember feeling so fatigued that I wondered if I'd make it and resolved to myself that I'd got to keep going . . . The next I registered, was of hearing the sound of my heels very hollowly and I looked down and watched myself walk round the bend of Beaumont St. into Walton St. I – the bit of me that counts – was up on a level with Worcester College chapel. I saw myself very clearly – it was a summer evening and I was wearing a sleeveless shantung dress. I remember thinking, 'so that's how I look to other people'.

This type of experience is really surprisingly common. Celia Green calls it 'autoscopy' – seeing oneself from a distance. It usually does not involve any sense of being in a duplicate body. Only 20 per cent of Celia Green's subjects reported such a sense – the rest experiencing themselves as just a disembodied consciousness.

Gerhardi wrote of his experience: 'If the whole world united in telling me it is a dream, I would remain unconvinced.' Yet neither his nor other experients' convictions that they were not dreaming or hallucinating constitutes sure evidence that they were not. The fact that a high proportion of Celia Green's study – subjects experienced their OBE at a time of psychological stress, or after an accident, or under anaesthetic, may be thought symptomatic more of mental pathology or aberration than of some deficiency in our consensus view of what constitutes reality. So we have to ask: what would stand as convincing objective proof that some component of the personality had separated from the body and had been somehow removed to a different location? Would we allow, for instance, that the acquisition of verifiable information while travelling in the second body – information which the primary physical self could not have obtained – would constitute such a proof? If so, there are a number of well-authenticated examples of such proofs.

New York medium Eileen Garrett was always prepared to co-operate with serious psychical researchers, and some years ago she took part in an

21 Stone figure of Quetzacoatl, the Mexican culture-bearer (*Courtesy of British Museum*)

22 Late Assyrian or New Babylonian Cylinder Seal depicting figures that are half man, half fish (*Courtesy of British Museum*)

23 The Indian Vedic god Agni (*Courtesy of British Museum*)

interesting experiment designed to test whether she could project her consciousness from a flat in New York to the office of a doctor in Reykjavik, Iceland. The doctor had assembled some objects on a table and Mrs Garrett was to attempt to name them. She did so – and she also recited a passage from a book that the doctor was reading and said that his head was bandaged. The doctor later confirmed that he had suffered a head injury just before the experiment and that the passage from the book was correct. He also said that he had had a sense of Mrs Garrett's presence in his office at the time of the experiment.

Eileen Garrett was a very exceptional woman, but according to physicists and psychical researchers Harold Puthoff and Russell Targ of the SRI in California many people possess what they call 'remote viewing' abilities. In their book *Mind-Reach*, they report experiments with a number of subjects who all proved able, after a period of practice, to view remote locations and report what they saw there.

The experiments were carried out as follows: The target locations were places in the San Francisco Bay area and within a thirty-minute driving distance from the SRI. One hundred such locations were selected by a person not otherwise connected with the project and who alone knew the total set. The locations were printed on cards, which were sealed in envelopes and kept in a safe to which only he had access. When an experiment was conducted, the subject was closeted in a room at the SRI with a member of the experimental team, while another member was given a randomly-selected card with travelling instructions to the target location. He then drove there.

The journey could take up to thirty minutes and after that period had elapsed, the experimenter remained at the location for a further fifteen minutes, during which time the subject back at the SRI described his impressions of the target site and made drawings. The experimenter in the room with the subject was there to help him achieve a relaxed and receptive frame of mind and to prompt his responses by asking questions, but as he knew neither the specific target location nor the contents of the target pool, there was no possibility of his giving help either deliberately or unconsciously.

The results that Puthoff and Targ report in their book, together with illustrations of correspondences between subjects' drawings and photographs of target sites, are quite astonishing and appear to support their belief 'that apparently everyone can experience remote viewing'. Even two sceptical government scientists who were visiting their lab and agreed to have a go were successful at their first attempt. The research protocols have come in for some criticism, and the experiments have yet to be successfully replicated, but tests conducted by Dr Karlis Osis at the headquarters of the American Society for Psychical Research in New York seem to point to a conclusion similar to that reached by Puthoff and Targ.

Osis ran a series of what he calls 'fly-in' experiments, using as subjects about a hundred psychics who live all over the United States. At a pre-arranged time, each subject was required to attempt to project his consciousness to a room in the ASPR building in New York, to occupy a spot marked 'X' in front of the fireplace and to describe or sketch what he saw in the room – particularly the objects on a coffee table, which were varied with each experiment. There could be between one and three people in the room at the time, and on occasion another psychic was present and tried to see and describe the visitor.

Osis reported success with fifteen of his subjects. The well-known psychic Alex Tanous, for instance, who 'flew-in' from Maine on several occasions, was able to give correct impressions of the objects on the coffee table each time. He could not always name them because he had difficulty, he said, in occupying the prescribed position. Instead, he found himself hovering near the ceiling and looking down on the table, from which position objects appeared distorted. If he could not specifically identify something, he generally correctly sketched its shape as seen from above – and he could name its colour if it had one.

Another psychic, Elwood Babbit, was given instructions to project himself so that he entered the room by a door and to describe what he saw from there. He correctly described a brown plasticine figure of a girl which was on the table, a picture hanging on the wall, and a large plant at the rear of the office. He failed to mention a toy chair that had been brought into the room for the experiment, but his failure was indicative of his success, for the chair had been put in such a position that the body of one of the people present hid it from the viewpoint of the doorway.

One evening, Osis and an assistant took cameras into the office and photographed the fireplace during the period a psychic in Toronto was scheduled to attempt her projection. After the session, the psychic phoned in to say that she had seen a woman in the doorway taking pictures and had been dazzled by the flash.

Some of the people who 'flew-in' reported a definite sense of physical travel, of passing over the landscape between the place from which they flew and New York. One woman said she was distracted when she got to New York by a fire a block away from the ASPR building, and Osis was able to confirm that the fire had in fact occurred. The most successful subjects, however, did not have a sense of covering a distance but were able to project to the target location instantaneously. Osis surmised that this was because they achieved a more complete dissociation from the physical than other subjects. Tanous was one of these, and he was apparently present on one of his visits substantially enough for another psychic in the room, who had never met him, to see him and describe correctly both his appearance and what he was wearing.

It is, of course, possible to attribute success in such 'remote viewing' experiments to the excercise of a psychic faculty of clairvoyance or telepathy, which would not necessarily imply the existence of a non-physical component of the 'projector's' personality that could travel at will to the target spot. Yet psychics unanimously believe that there is such a thing as an 'astral' or 'etheric' body which everybody possesses and which some people more than others are adept at detaching from the physical and sending on missions. Most religions and all esoteric traditions support this view, and, as we shall see, some recently-reported Russian research into what they call the 'energy body' or 'bioplasmic body' of man also appears to lend support to it. So let us now consider the evidence for the duplicate body hypothesis.

The fact that the psychic in Osis' office could describe Tanous is prima facie evidence. And there are numerous cases on record of people's doubles being seen while they were physically in another place. For instance, when August Strindberg was living in Paris after the breakdown of his second marriage, he was in his room one evening thinking about his family. Suddenly he found himself standing among them in his home, watching his mother-in-law playing the piano. A few days later he had a letter from her anxiously inquiring whether he was well, for she had seen his double appear and she feared that might be an ominous sign.

Other famous writers testify to the reality of the phenomenon. Lord Byron was with some other witnesses when they saw the double of his friend Shelley walking in the woods when he was known to be staying with friends elsewhere. And Leo Tolstoy and his wife were so annoyed when they went to St Petersburg station to meet the English medium Daniel Dunglas Home, only to see him get off the train and walk straight past them, that Mrs Tolstoy reproached Home for his rude behaviour in a note she sent to his hotel. He received the note when he arrived some hours later, having travelled to St Petersburg on a later train than the one the Tolstoys had met.

Guy de Maupassant claimed that his double often sat opposite him at his desk when he was working and dictated stories for him to write. D. H. Lawrence described to Aldous Huxley, who was with him through his last hours, how his spirit or double was gradually separating from his body. Eventually he said he could see it standing in a corner of the room, looking back at him: soon afterwards he died.

The arrival of a double in advance of the physical person is apparently a phenomenon well known in Scandinavia, where they speak of the 'vardøger' or forerunner. In 1955, an American businessman, Erkson Gorique, was astonished to find, on his first visit to Norway, that everywhere he went people greeted him familiarly and spoke of his previous visit some months ago. When he protested that he had never been in the country before, one acquaintance explained that it must have been his vardøger.

One of Celia Green's correspondents recounts a similar experience. One morning she was walking across a bridge when she noticed on the side of the river towards which she was heading a young man dressed in a grey suit and wearing a grey cap. He was sitting on a slab of concrete with a drawing board on his knees, apparently sketching. Near him was a woman she knew, with a child. She crossed the bridge and walked towards where she had seen these people. A building cut off her view of them for a short time, and when she arrived at the spot the young man in grey had gone. When she asked the woman where he had gone, she was told that nobody had been in that spot for at least the last half-hour. Although she was puzzled, she did not pursue the matter. Then, as she was crossing the bridge again at 4.30 in the afternoon, she saw the same young man seated on the slab of concrete. This time he did not disappear, and when she reached the spot she asked him what had happened to him that morning. He was puzzled. He said he had not arrived in the town until 1.30 pm.

Tales like this abound, and books have been filled with them. A widely-held explanation of the phenomenon is that a person can involuntarily project his double or astral body simply by intensely thinking about a place he is going to, and a person in that spot who happens to be properly psychically attuned will be able to see the projection. Put so boldly, the explanation certainly sounds preposterous, and a sceptic might ask why, in that case, the phenomenon is not more common than it is, for certainly a lot of people spend a lot of time wishing and longing to be somewhere else.

On the other hand, it could be that the occasional involuntary projection occurs when a person happens to get into a non-ordinary state of consciousness which is conducive to it. The fact that the majority of involuntary projections recorded in the literature occurred at times of crisis or in emotional states certainly implies that the phenomenon involves entry into a non-ordinary state of consciousness. And the fact that there are recognised techniques for inducing the experience suggests that the involuntary projector might have either hit upon the technique by chance or by-passed it and attained the appropriate state of consciousness directly, precipitated by the experience of shock.

The physical scientist's criterion of repeatability (the requirement that an experiment should repeatedly produce the same result when carried out by different experimenters under identical conditions) can rarely be met in psychical research, for the simple reason that the psyche itself is not invariable and therefore identical conditions for each experiment cannot be guaranteed. But the existence of prescribed techniques to induce psychical experiences or effects at least goes part way towards satisfying the repeatability criterion – provided, of course, that the techniques work. And when similar techniques are practised or advocated by people belonging to unconnected cultures, it is a fair assumption that there must be some efficacy in them.

Dr Robert Crookall, a retired British geologist, has devoted a number of books to studies of the phenomenology and significance of the out-of-the-body experience, and in one of them, *Ecstasy*, he compares descriptions of OBEs and of techniques for inducing them as recorded by ancient shamans and by modern astral projectors. His source of information about the shamanic tradition is Professor Mircea Eliade's classic study *Shamanism: Archaic Techniques of Ecstasy* (1964).

Shamans, the magician-priests of tribal cultures – some of whom still exist, particularly in Siberia and among the Eskimos, and, if we can believe Carlos Castaneda's 'Don Juan' books, also in the southern United States and central America – cultivated the art of leaving the body at will, either to acquire information about distant events or to guide the souls of the dead in the afterworld. According to Eliade, in tribal communities

> The shaman is indispensable in any ceremony that concerns the experience of the human soul as such, that is, as a precarious psychic unit, inclined to forsake the body and an easy prey for demons and sorcerers . . . Healer and psychopomp, the shaman is these because he commands the techniques of ecstasy – that is, because his soul can safely abandon his body and roam at vast distances, can penetrate the underworld and rise to the sky.

Modern Eskimo shamans, he points out, often leave their bodies in a cataleptic state for days on end, taking 'the precaution of having themselves bound with ropes, so that they will journey only in spirit.'

When Crookall read Professor Eliade's book he was struck by the parallels between shamanic experiences and traditions, and the testimonies of many of his correspondents (for at that time he had published several case-books of astral projection), and of virtuoso projectors such as American Sylvan Muldoon, Englishman Oliver Fox, and Frenchman 'Yram'.

Some of the techniques for loosening and then separating the astral or etheric body from the physical, as practised and advocated both by shamans and by modern experients were: practice in the control of dreams and the use of dreams of flying and diving; whirling to induce dizziness, or dancing to the point of exhaustion; fasting; taking drugs such as mescaline or fly agaric (the 'Sacred Mushroom'); practising meditation in order to cause the astral body 'to vibrate at so high a rate that it could no longer remain "in gear" with the relatively sluggish physical body'; and employing special breathing techniques, particularly the withholding of the breath.

The shaman, Eliade had pointed out, was often a man highly susceptible to nervous excitation. Frequently an epileptic or hysteric, he had become a shaman by learning to control and use his epilepsy or hysteria. He was 'a sick man who had succeeded in curing himself', and in making himself a 'master of ecstasy'.

Such virtuosi of astral travel as Muldoon, Fox, and 'Yram' were also men of highly-nervous constitution who had independently developed techniques for repeating an experience that had first occurred spontaneously. The techniques they developed corresponded with those of each other and with those employed by shamans the world over since prehistoric times.

Crookall discovered a third correspondence one day when he was looking through some old issues of the journal of the ASPR. Over the period 1908–15, Prescott Hall, an American, had received through a medium a series of communications, allegedly from spirits, giving detailed instructions on the techniques of projecting the astral body. Hall's curiosity about the subject had been aroused by the fact that two friends of his, whom he regarded as 'superlatively sane', claimed to be able to travel out of their bodies. He was sceptical about the claim and thought that a reasonable way to investigate the matter might be to try to consult people who ought to be well-acquainted with the out-of-the-body state, namely those who had gone into 'permanent projection'. Through Mrs Keeler, a medium, he contacted a recently-deceased friend who put him in communication with intelligences – ostensibly spirits – who said they would be able to help him in his inquiry. Hall stressed that Mrs Keeler knew as little about the subject as he did, and furthermore was not particularly interested in projection, so he was certain that the detailed information he received over the years did not emanate from her mind.

What interested Crookall about the communications was that the wealth of information they contained corresponded in many details with that given in the books of Fox and Muldoon (which were published after 1916), by many of his own correspondents, and by Professor Eliade in his book on shamanism. Such a consensus of detail from such diverse sources was surely as sound a guarantee of the efficacy of the techniques and the authenticity of the experience of astral projection – or separation or release of the duplicate body – as any proof repeatedly obtained in a laboratory would be.

There was a consensus in the techniques for accomplishing separation, as well as in the descriptions of the experience itself and the different stages and aspects of it (see Plates 29a–29e). Crookall draws attention to the following aspects:

1 *An initial blackout of consciousness* Mrs Keeler's 'communicators' said: 'The going out from the body may be . . . in full consciousness except for the instant when the soul changes its centre from the physical to the astral.' Many people who have experienced projection have mentioned this initial blackout, and a commonly-used descriptive analogy is to a

passage through a dark tunnel. Eliade refers to 'the magic door that opens and shuts on an instant', described by shamans, and Crookall equates this with the experience of a blackout. A repetition of the experience at the moment of re-entry into the physical body has often been reported, and many experients have a re-entry shock or repercussion (for stance, Gerhardi experienced 'a jerk that shook him').

2 *Dual consciousness* In the first stage of projection, a person may be aware of two worlds – the physical and another. In Sir Auckland Geddes' account, there is a clear description of the sense of separating into what he called an A consciousness and a B consciousness, and of being simultaneously in a third and fourth dimension. He also spoke of his 'mentor' who explained things to him, and the Keeler communicators spoke of the frequent encounter with 'helpers' or 'hinderers' during the first stage of projection. Gerhardi felt himself gently pushed, perhaps by a 'helper'.

3 *Release of the double via the solar plexus or the head* Most astral projectors, says Crookall, have a sense of leaving their physical body by way of a centre in the head, but people he describes as 'of mediumistic constitution, ie with a "loose" vehicle of vitality', often separate via the solar plexus, and the descriptions of shamans suggest an exit by way of the solar plexus centre. According to the Keeler communications, the astral body can exit from any part of the physical body or from 'all parts at once, oozing out like steam', but generally it 'starts to rise from the large nerves back to the solar plexus; from there it rises to the throat and finally passes out at the top of the head'.

4 *Spiral release – Horizontal position – Greyness* These are three features of the experience of separation that have been widely reported. Shamans speak of winding stairways by means of which they ascend to the sky; Sylvan Muldoon observed that 'after approximately one foot of separation, it (the double) begins to zig-zag'; and Mrs Keeler's communicators said that 'In leaving the physical, the Astral Body usually goes out in a zig-zag or spiral movement, but afterwards travels in a straight line'. The fact that the first position occupied by the projected second body is horizontal and above the physical is attested by numerous experients, as is the fact that they initially find themselves in conditions that they have variously described as grey, foggy, misty, or heavy. Crookall attributes this to consciousness being 'enshrouded by the still unshed body veil'. Gerhardi's account, it will be recalled, incorporates the features of horizontal projection and finding himself in 'a murky, heavy space' (see Plate 31).

24 The first incarnation of the Hindu God Vishnu from the mouth of a fish

24

25

5 *The 'silver cord' extension* Gerhardi's 'strange appendage' – the 'cable of light' joining his two bodies, which became more attenuated the further they separated – is mentioned in the accounts of many experients. In the biblical Book of Ecclesiastes we read: 'Or ever the silver cord be loosed, then shall the dust return to the earth as it was, and the Spirit shall return unto God who gave it.' Crookall suggests that many shamanic symbols can be correlated with the cord – for instance the thread, the ribbon, the rope, the chain, the rainbow, or the ladder, which are all symbols found in different parts of the world for the means of ascent to the other world.

6 *Extension of consciousness* In Geddes' narrative we read that the experient suddenly realised that he could see things 'wherever my attention was directed', and that when he was drawn back into his physical body, his clarity of vision disappeared and he became just 'a glimmer of consciousness'. Crookall summarises many experients' testimonies: 'Consciousness becomes more comprehensive and more intense when the "double" is freed from the body and also . . . contracts and becomes duller when it re-enters it.' Eliade says that the shaman 'feels the need of these ecstatic journeys because it is above all during trance that he becomes truly himself'. Moreover, shamans are often consulted to locate lost objects, people, or animals, by embarking on an out-of-the-body search for them.

Crookall concedes that some of the ostensible proofs of the phenomenon of astral projection can be attributed to ESP, but he argues that the convergent testimonies of hundreds of experients from widely separated places and ages prove that the experience is 'highly logical and not at all fantastic'. He further argues that the experience cannot be explained away by 'the cultural artifact hypothesis', ie the idea 'that some people told of their supposed experiences and others either deliberately copied them or vainly imagined that they themselves had had them'. Pre-literate children have described OBEs in the same terms, and so do ancient texts embodying teachings that had been passed on verbally for centuries before being written down, such as can be found in the *Tibetan Book of the Dead* and the Chinese *Secret of the Golden Flower*, published in the West in 1927 and 1931 respectively. The consistency of the testimonies from all sources, Crookall maintains, is most plausibly explained by the hypothesis of the existence of an objective 'double' – a non-physical but real duplicate body that all human beings possess and which people who find themselves temporarily occupying feel to be their essential self.

25 Ezekiel's vision of an angel (*Manley P. Hall*)

It is difficult to convey in a short space the cumulative effect of Crookall's books with all their scrupulous and wide-ranging research and massive documentation. The philosopher Maurice Merleau-Ponty wrote that in phenomenological observation 'perspectives blend, perceptions confirm each other, a meaning emerges', and Crookall's phenomenological studies of the OBE constitute a blending and mutual confirming of evidence from diverse sources that establishes beyond reasonable doubt the authenticity and objectivity of the phenomenon. It is suggested that the emergent meaning must be that we have what esotericists call a 'subtle body' composed of a substance that is none the less real for being invisible, which is separable from the physical body in certain circumstances in life, and which may for a time continue in existence after its death.

The fact that the majority of mankind has believed in the reality of this non-physical entity linked to every individual personality will not in itself convince the scientific rationalist. But combined with Crookall's data, it must make him wonder whether his minority view represents as final and axiomatic a truth as its dominance in the modern Western world might have made him suppose. To suspend disbelief and look further into the question might even be considered the rational and scientific thing to do in the circumstances.

We have many examples of scientists unwisely voicing the opinion that something is impossible, or cannot be known, and being proved wrong and made to look foolish when the thing is done or when new facts come to light. Considering the amount and type of psychical research being done today, and the trend away from the mechanist-materialist position in theoretical science, those who deny the existence of the non-physical body, or the soul, may eventually be ranked with those who said the atom could never be split, or the composition of the Sun could never be known. Or with those august members of a scientific commission that reported to the British Government in 1878: 'It is impossible to adapt electric lighting to households. Any attempt to do so is futile for it would flaunt the laws of the universe.'

So let us stay with Dr Crookall and see where his researches have led beyond establishing the authenticity and objectivity of the OBE. They have led him to hypothesise that man possesses not only a duplicate body but a number of quite distinct non-physical bodies, each belonging to a different environment. He has summarised his conclusions as follows:

During earth-life we possess not only (1) the familiar *physical* body but also (2) a *'semi-physical' vital body or vehicle of vitality* by which it is animated, (3) a *'super-physical' Soul Body* which uses these two and which, in turn, is animated by (4) a *true, Transcendent Spiritual Body*, a formless radiation, rarely, if ever, perceived. The three non-physical bodies (2–4) which every human being possesses are doubtless drawn from corresponding 'worlds,' 'spheres,' 'realms,' 'mansions', etc. and are doubtless eventually returned to them when their purpose has been accomplished – this we deduce from analogy with the physical body . . .

Corresponding to these four bodies (and their 'spheres'), man has four apparent distinct 'selves', each with its own level of consciousness: the 'lowest' self, formed when the Soul works through the physical body, is the personality; when consciousness is obliged to work through the vehicle of vitality (which has no sense organs) it is as a dream – or sub-conscious self; when it works through the Soul Body it is the Soul, intermediate between the personality and the 'Spirit' . . . which uses the Spiritual Body.

In support of his hypothesis of the four distinct bodies and the existence of other worlds to which they respectively belong, Crookall has again amassed convergent testimonies from different and unconnected sources. From ethnology, for instance, from scripture; esoteric teachings; 'communications' received through mediums, personal testimonies of people who have 'died' and been brought back to life, and testimonies of people who have watched others die and seen something leave the body at the moment of death.

Novelist A. J. Cronin, who practised as a doctor before he turned to literature, described the death of a young man as follows:

When at last he died I was conscious of a strange experience. At the instant of his death, as he exhaled his last breath, I felt, with positive and terrifying reality, an actual sense of passage . . . I had often heard death compared to falling asleep, to a physical drop into oblivion. This was neither. It was a soaring transit, both mystical and real. And I, as witness, felt the breath of the eternal on my cheek . . . Later in life I was to meet a famous physician who told me that in all his years of practice he had never sat beside a death-bed without experiencing in some degree the sensation that had been mine. He called it, unashamedly, 'the flight of the soul'.

Other people have had more than 'a sense of passage' when witnessing a death. Crookall cites many accounts of people seeing a vaporous substance emerge from the head and gradually condense into a form resembling the physical body, which then rose above the body but remained connected to it for a time by a silvery cord before disappearing.

A British nurse named Joy Snell wrote the following description of the death of a close friend: 'Immediately after her heart had ceased to beat, I distinctly saw something in appearance like smoke . . . ascend from her body . . . This form, shadowy at first, gradually changed and . . . resolved itself into a form like that of my friend.' A missionary who spent many years in Tahiti reported that Tahitian clairvoyants described the process of separation of the soul from the body via the head in exactly the same terms.

This vaporous substance, Crookall says, is the 'vehicle of vitality' – the semi-physical body – and constitutes a bridge between it and the soul body (ie between mind and matter) in life. When a living person's double is projected, it can be either the vehicle of vitality, or the soul body, or a combination of the two, and if the vehicle of vitality component is predominant, the double may be visible to others. In the immediate post-mortem state, the vehicle of vitality and the soul body constitute a composite double, and after some time the vehicle of vitality is shed and a 'second death' occurs which precipitates the release of the soul body. This event cannot be seen by the death-bed observer, but Crookall maintains that the concurrence of the testimonies of ostensible spirit communicators, of ancient shamans, and of texts such as the *Tibetan Book of the Dead* enable us to deduce it.

One thing that has often been seen by the death-bed observer is the experience of joy or exaltation that many people go through in their last moments. Dr Karlis Osis sent out a questionnaire to 10,000 doctors and nurses and collected from them accounts of 3,500 individuals who had remained conscious and rational up to the moment of death, and of these no less than 700 were described as being in an 'extremely elevated' mood. This mood is often accompanied by visions, in which sometimes the person speaks of seeing a friend or relative who has been on 'the other side' for some time, and a number of cases are on record of a dying person speaking about seeing a person whose death was so recent that he or she could not have known about it.

The following is a typical example: Jennie and Edith, both aged about eight and very close friends, fell ill with diphtheria at the same time. Jennie soon died, and the doctors and the parents took the greatest care not to let Edith know. They must have been successful, for a few hours before Edith died she asked her parents to say good-bye to Jennie for her and picked out two photographs to be sent to her friend. But in the last moments before she died, she spoke of seeing the spirits of people she knew were dead, and then explained with surprise and delight, holding out her arms as if in a welcoming embrace: 'Oh, Jennie! I'm so glad you are here.' She could, of course, have been hallucinating, but the number of cases like this in the records of psychical research is impressive.

The evidence of people who have 'returned from the dead' is similarly impressive. A Huguenot clergyman, the Rev Bertrand, nearly froze to death while climbing in the Alps in 1892. He described the experience of finding himself outside his body but attached to it by a kind of string like 'a captive balloon' and of being annoyed when other climbers found him in time to restore his circulation and he was drawn back to his body. He astonished his rescuers – and later his wife, who had been miles away – by telling them precisely what he had seen them doing while he was out of the body. The Bertrand case has elements in common with the one reported by Geddes: the reluctance to return to the physical and the experience of seeing what is going on in distant places.

In a similar case, an army doctor was nearly killed when a small military plane crashed soon after take-off. He experienced abrupt separation and found himself watching the frenzied activity back at the airfield, which he was later able to describe in exact detail. When he saw an ambulance reach his body, which had been hurled a distance from the plane and was lying inert, he thought: 'Why are these people bothering about my body? I am quite content where I am.'

In another famous case, an American soldier, Private George Ritchie, was certified dead, then brought back to life nine minutes later with a short of adrenalin directly into his heart. He came back with an account of having been shown three different worlds, which to his surprise he had found were coextensive with and 'strangely superimposed on our familiar world'. This is a description which is consistent with Crookall's hypothesis of the three distinct non-physical worlds and with the information given by the 'mentor' in Geddes' narrative. Incidentally, it is also consistent with the 'multiple interpenetrating universes' theory that is currently being proposed by an *avant-garde* school of theoretical physicists – for instance, de Witt and Graham in *The Many-Worlds Interpretation of Quantum Mechanics* (1973); and Toben, Sarfatti, and Wolf in *Space-time and Beyond* (1975).

Everybody is familiar with the phenomenon of something rotating or vibrating at such a fast rate that it becomes invisible, and the idea that the different worlds are distinguished from each other by their 'rates of vibration' is proposed by the forementioned physicists. It is a concept that has long been used by occultists and in esoteric literature, and we have previously quoted Crookall's statement that a person could learn to make the astral body 'vibrate at so high a rate that it could no longer remain "in gear" with the relatively sluggish physical body'. It is supported, too, by the testimonies of many experients that they feel a build-up of inner vibrations before an OBE, although the physical body is quite immobile.

Although the 'multiple interpenetrating universes' theorists are pushing speculation out on a limb, quite orthodox modern physics teaches that what we call 'matter' is really immaterial – 'a convenient formula for describing what happens where it isn't', as Bertrand Russell said; that the stuff of which all substantial things are made is basically empty space in which certain patterns of vibrations occur. So the proposition that man may possess one or several non-physical bodies is not inherently implausible, and a statement like the following, made by the French OB virtuoso 'Yram' might make sounder sense to a modern physicist than to the man in the street: 'Everything happens as if we had a series of different bodies, boxed one in the other by means of a more reduced dimension. As the conscious will penetrates into new dimensions, it uses a corresponding body.'

It has been widely reported over recent years that Russian scientists have succeeded in photographing the 'energy body' of living things using the techniques of electro-photography developed forty years ago by Semyon and Valentina Kirlian. When the colourful pictures purporting to be of energy discharges from leaves or people's fingertips were first published. Western scientists were quick to point out that the 'Kirlian effect' could be explained as an artifact of the experimental situation (see Plate 32). But replication experiments, notably by Dr Thelma Moss at the Neuropsychiatric Institute at the University of California, Los Angeles, and Dr William Tiller at Stanford University, California, have consistently shown correlations between the pictures and the states of emotion or of health of the subjects. The Russian hypothesis that the effect is due to emissions of 'bioenergy' would appear to be justified.

The Russians actually go much further than this, and maintain that all living things are surrounded by a second body composed of what they call 'bioplasma', an energy body that is a distinct organism which emits its own electromagnetic fields. If a leaf is photographed by the Kirlian method, it shows brilliant and colourful emanations soon after it has been plucked, but the luminescence diminishes with time and eventually disappears. If a small section is cut away from a healthy leaf, a Kirlian photograph of the mutilated leaf will still show the 'phantom' body of the cut-away portion. This latter phenomenon, it has been suggested, may help us understand why people who have limbs amputated sometimes complain of pain located where the limb had been. Perhaps the pain is in the still intact bioplasmic body.

'Have the Soviets made the breakthrough? Have they made the human double visible? And explorable?' asked Sheila Ostrander and Lynn Schroeder in their book *Psychic Discoveries Behind the Iron Curtain.* They implied an affirmative answer. The bioplasmic body, they suggested, was the etheric body of man that esoteric teachings had always said existed and that psychics and mediums professed to see in the form of an aura surrounding the living body. And they quoted the following interesting passage written by English medium Geraldine Cummins in the 1930s as 'startlingly relevant to what we were to discover in Russia':

> Mind does not work directly on the brain. There is an etheric body which is the link between mind and the cells of the brain . . . Far more minute corpuscular particles than scientists are yet aware of travel

along threads from the etheric body, or double, to certain regions of the body and to the brain. I might call them life units . . . This invisible body – called by men the double or unifying mechanism – is the only channel through which mind and life may communicate with the physical shape. Should a thread snap between the two, there is immediately a failure in control .   .   . Each animal has a unifying body made out of modified ether. It should be possible to devise in time an instrument whereby this body can be perceived.

That instrument, Ostrander and Schroeder imply, is the Kirlian 'camera'.

It will be recalled from the previous chapter that when Gustave Geley tried to comprehend the nature of the transitory matter that Charles Richet had called ectoplasm, he considered that it might be analogous to the bioluminescence of certain insects and fish. It now appears in the light of this Russian research that all living things emit bioluminescence, and perhaps this emission – in the form of bioplasma – is the semi-physical 'vehicle of vitality' that Crookall writes about as well as the transitory matter that is said to issue from physical mediums, and maybe even the 'spiritual essence' that Paracelsus said that Elementals were made of.

Biologists have long debated the question: What is life? It was long assumed that the answer must be sought in terms of chemistry, but there are fundamental problems that have not yielded to a chemical explanation. For instance, how do body cells, which are originally all alike, become specified for their particular functions? If we put the question in another way and ask: How do they know what to do? we spotlight a basic difference between animate and inanimate matter – that the former depends for its existence on a flow of information as well as of energy.

Physical systems, according to the Second Law of Thermodynamics, are subject to the process of entropy – they run down, or tend towards a state of increasing disorganisation. Biological systems reverse this tendency, are self-sustaining and capable of complex adaptations and co-ordinations. This is because they have an information component. Biologist L. Hayflick at the Wistar Institute, Philadelphia, found that if a culture of human embryonic cells is kept *in vitro* (ie in glass), the cells will continue to multiply for about fifty generations, then they will start to become amorphous and anonymous, as if they have forgotten what they are supposed to be. Eventually, they will die. If, however, a cell is restored to its original body when it is beginning to lose its 'memory' of its role and identity, it will soon become healthy and normal. It is as if being brought back into proximity with its kind has enabled it to revitalise itself by recovering the information it had lost.

Now if there is an information component in animate matter at the cell level, can this be explained entirely in terms of chemical activity?

Biophysicist Joseph Hoffman thinks not and to explain the specificity of cells, he has put forward what he calls the 'template hypothesis'. He writes:

> In each of the billions of trillions of living cells in the world today, there is a pattern, or guide, or mould, or working plan. This is an immortal molecular template because it has been reproducing itself incessantly since the beginning of life over two billion years ago.

The template hypothesis is not popular with scientists because it seems to bring back into the physiology of life the indeterminate 'vital principle' of the chemists of old, but the work of another researcher, Professor Harold Saxton Burr of Yale University, would appear to indicate that the organising principle in living systems is not a 'ghost in the machine' but simply an electrical field force.

In a book in which he gives an account of thirty years of research and theories, Burr writes:

> It has usually been assumed that all the changes in the electrical properties of a living system are the consequence of biological activity. But it is our hunch that a primary electrical field in the living system is responsible.

He calls this the field of life, or 'L-field', and explains it by analogy to the way that iron filings scattered on a card over a magnet will arrange themselves in the pattern of the lines of force of the magnet's field. He says:

> Something like this happens in the human body. The molecules and cells are constantly being torn apart and rebuilt with fresh material from the food we eat. But, thanks to the controlling L-field, the new molecules and cells are rebuilt as before and arrange themselves in the same pattern as the old.

Over his thirty years of research, Burr said, he studied almost every form of living organism and he came to the conclusion that 'wherever there is life there are electrical properties'.

Several of his discoveries were potentially of great practical value. He found that it was possible to pinpoint the monthly occurrence of ovulation in females by monitoring their L-fields and looking for a sharp rise in the voltage, that L-field measurements could help locate malignancies in the body, and that when measurements were taken of seeds, it was possible to predict how strong and healthy the future plants would grow.

But of even greater importance than these practical discoveries was his finding that L-fields are, as he put it, 'our antennae to the universe'. Over a period of years, Burr kept a large maple tree wired up in his garden. He found voltage changes corresponding with lunar cycles and sun-spot variations. Human beings, he thought, must also be subject to such influences, and he wrote:

> L-fields are links in a 'chain of authority'. This starts with the simplest living forms, runs upwards through all the life on this planet to the most complex form we know – man – and then extends outwards into space and upwards to an infinite, ultimate authority, about which we can only speculate.

Compare this with a statement by the Russian biophysicist Victor Inyushin:

> It is through the biological plasma body that we react to all cosmic occurrences. When there are disturbances of the sun, or solar flares, our biologists have charted all kinds of biological reactions in humans, plants and animals. These disturbances of the sun cause changes in the whole plasmic balance of the Universe and in turn affect the bioplasma of living organisms.

Thelma Moss remarked with reference to Burr's and the Russians' discoveries: 'Perhaps this is another example of similar discoveries by scientists working independently, like Darwin's and Wallace's theory of evolution.'

Burr entitled his book *Blueprint for Immortality*, but he left it to another author, Edward W. Russell, to bring out the full implications of this title in another book, *Design for Destiny*. Russell points out that Burr's researches imply that wherever there is life or substance, there is an invisible and intangible thing – an organising field. And as 'anything that can organise has to exist before what it organises,' human L-fields must exist before the bodies they organise. Furthermore, 'there is no reason to suppose that they cease to exist when the bodies they have organised die and decompose, any more than a magnet's field ceases to exist when the iron filings it has formed into a pattern are thrown away.' Thus the existence of a fundamental, non-physical component in human personality – a component that is independent of the physical body and may survive it – is a logical necessity, Russell argues. Moreover there is evidence that the L-field itself is controlled by a field of thought – the T-field.

The fact that thought is a form of energy and can act directly upon matter has been demonstrated many times by modern parapsychological research, and biofeedback research has shown that people can generate a T-field that can slow their heartbeat or stop a wound bleeding if they are fed back information through electronic circuitry about these physiological processes. The enduring nature of memories, too, despite the fact that the brain cells that contain them are perishable, implies that thought is a field phenomenon that determines the properties of whatever it acts upon in the physical world.

The subtitle of Russell's book is *Science Reveals the Soul*, and he justifies it as follows:

> Research has shown that the human body is built, maintained and repaired by an electromagnetic field, which can be influenced and over-ridden by another kind of field, the human mind ... Mind, like memory, must be a manifestation of what religions refer to as 'soul' or 'spirit' – it cannot be a product of the body (though it may be influenced by it) because mind and memory are permanent and the body always changing. The fact, then, that mind can produce measurable and repeatable electrical changes – Science's criterion of a valid phenomenon – is evidence that mind and its source, the 'soul', are the realities, independent of the body. There is abundant evidence ... that thought or mind can behave like a field, within the accepted definition of a field. Since fields can exist in – and transverse – space without any material manifestation, the fields of mind and memory, the essence of the 'soul', can exist and travel apart from human bodies.

Russell's conjectures, Burr's and the Kirlians' researches, Crookall's exhaustive phenomenological studies, the anecdotal evidence of people who have undergone pseudo-deaths and of OBE experients, the recent 'remote viewing' experiments of Puthoff and Targ, and the 'fly-in' experiments of Karlis Osis, all point to the conclusion that there is this component of human personality that is non-physical and, in certain circumstances, separable from the physical body. Some of this evidence further suggests that this non-physical component manifests intelligence. Moreover, the death and decay of the physical body with which it has been associated may not impair its intelligent functioning, although it does necessarily impair its ability to act upon the physical world.

If all this evidence be taken to have proved that mind is independent of matter, then the existence of ghosts or spirits, of demons and gods, of space beings – and maybe even of Olaf Stapledon's 'Cosmic Mind' and 'Star Maker' – must be admitted to be distinct possibilities not incompatible with either science or reason. They are possibilities that we shall consider in the rest of this book, beginning in the next chapter with evidence in support of the existence of the discarnate personalities of individuals known to have previously lived and died on earth.

5 Mind Beyond the End of Its Tether

A recent television investigation into spiritualism concluded that the evidence for survival of bodily death is very slender, and that the sometimes startling revelations of mediums can be attributed to their skill in eliciting information from their sitters, or to the exercise of extra-sensory perception. The investigation did not, however, take account of, or attempt to explain, the substantial evidence suggestive of survival that has accumulated over the last century, nor indeed the best evidence available today.

The period 1880–1930 has been called the age of the great mediums, and among the greatest was the British spiritualist medium Mrs Gladys Osborne Leonard, whose 'spirit control' named Feda gave many people information that convinced them that people close and dear to them had survived death.

Mrs Talbot had two sittings with Mrs Leonard in March 1917. It was the first time she had been to any medium, and at the time Mrs Leonard knew neither her name nor her address. Mrs Talbot's husband had died some time before, and during the first part of the first sitting Feda, supposedly speaking for him, mentioned many incidents in the past and referred to many of their personal belongings. Mrs Talbot found this very interesting and very convincing, and she was irritated when, as she put it: 'Feda began a tiresome description of a book.' Her husband apparently wanted her to look up something in it on page 13. It was one of his old, personal notebooks, and Feda described its size and colour and said she would distinguish it from others by the fact that there was a table of languages in the front. Mrs Talbot found the description 'wearisome', but she said that she would try to find the book, although secretly she believed it must either have been thrown away or put in storage where it would be very difficult to get at.

When she arrived home, she told her sister and niece about all the interesting things that had been said at the beginning of the sitting and briefly mentioned 'that in the end, the medium began talking a lot of rubbish about a book'. Later in the evening, her niece urged her to try to find the book, and at the back of the top shelf of a bookcase she found an old notebook which seemed to answer the description. She opened it and, as she later wrote: 'To my utter astonishment, my eyes fell on the words, "Table of Semitic or Syro-Arabian Languages".' Turning to page 13, she found an extract copied out from a book entitled *Post Mortem* which described the sensations of a man passing through death and his surprised discovery that he survived the experience.

Mrs Talbot had never opened her late husband's personal notebooks, and obviously, Mrs Leonard, who did not know who her sitter was going to be, could not have had access to them. In fact the only person who knew the contents of the books was the alleged communicator through Feda – the 'dead' Mr Talbot. The case certainly seems to constitute evidence for the survival of memory of his earth-life on the part of a communicator.

It is by no means an isolated case. The 'Chaffin Will' Case concerned the family of a North Carolina farmer, James Chaffin. He died in 1921 and a will dated 1905 was found. In it he left his entire property to his third son, Marshall, who duly inherited the estate, but died himself a year later. In 1925 the second son, James, began to dream regularly and vividly that his father was standing at his beside and talking to him. In one dream he saw his father dressed in a black overcoat which he recognised as one that he had had in life, and the apparition said: 'You will find my will in my overcoat pocket.'

James found the old coat in his elder brother's house, and in the pocket he found, not the will but a paper on which was written: 'Read the 27th chapter of Genesis in my daddy's old Bible.' The two brothers went to their mother's house, found the old Bible in a drawer, opened it at Genesis 27 and there found between the pages a new will, made in 1919, dividing the property equally between the four sons. The late father stated that he had decided to make the change after reading Genesis 27; the chapter in which the story of the supplanting of Esau by Jacob is told. Again we seem to have a case of a discarnate mind communicating information which no living person could have known: a 'message from beyond the grave'.

Another example of this type of evidence has an additional factor of interest as it appears to give evidence of survival supplied by the great writer Aldous Huxley, who died on 22 November 1963.

Just a year after Huxley's death, his wife, Laura, was asked to participate in a television interview to be filmed in her home, to which she agreed. The interviewer, a young man named Keith Milton Rhinehart, told her that he was a medium and in gratitude for the interview, he offered to give her a 'reading'. She accepted, but as she was engaged that evening and he was leaving on a world tour the next day, it was not until some three months later that they were able to have the reading. In fact they had two sessions.

In the first, a group of Mrs Huxley's friends also participated.

Rhinehart gave each of them messages supposedly from dead friends or relatives, each of which made sense to the person addressed. He said he felt Aldous Huxley's presence very strongly, but that he would not at present act as a medium for him because the sitters might think that anything he said could be derived from his own knowledge of the man or his writings.

When Mrs Huxley sat alone with Rhinehart the following day, however, after giving her a good deal of correct information purporting to come from a friend of hers who had been murdered ten years before, he said: 'Aldous says that you are going to receive what eventually is going to be considered classical evidence of survival of the personality and consciousness – not something that can be explained by telepathy or other theories.' The 'classical evidence' was not forthcoming during the sitting, but afterwards, when Rhinehart was threading film into a projector prior to showing the film of the interview, he suddenly said: 'Please give me a pencil and paper. Aldous is saying I must write this down.' Pencil and paper were supplied, and he wrote: 17th page, 6th book from left, 3rd shelf; or: 6th shelf, 3rd book from left, 23rd line.

He handed Mrs Huxley the paper and told her, 'Aldous wants you to look up those books.' She went upstairs to her late husband's study and took out the sixth book from the left on the third shelf of his bookcase. It was a report in Spanish of a literary conference held in Argentina in 1962. Opening it at page 17, she saw that the name Aldous Huxley appeared half-way down, just before line 23 on which began a sentence containing a phrase that she translated as 'the spiritual richness of this communication'. She replaced the book and went downstairs to fetch Rhinehart and some other witnesses. She asked Rhinehart to follow the instructions on the paper and he picked out the same book and turned to the same paragraph in it. Somebody translated the entire passage and it turned out that the phrase 'the spiritual richness of this communication' referred to something that Aldous Huxley had written.

They then located the second book referred to, the third from the left on the sixth shelf, and on page 17, lines 23–4 they read the sentence: 'These phenomena are not generally accepted by science although many workers are firmly convinced of their existence.'

So here were two references that could certainly be interpreted as highly pertinent in the light of the ostensible promise from the discarnate Huxley to provide evidence of the survival of personality and consciousness. The possibility that many books would yield sentences or phrases that could be interpreted as pertinent was suggested, and the group spent some time taking out books at random and looking at line 23, page 17, but none of them contained anything that could by any stretch of imagination be related to Aldous Huxley or to the question of survival.

The question of whether the discarnate Huxley thus provided 'classical evidence of survival' or not is complicated by two facts. Firstly, that while he was alive he could not have read the first book because it had been sent to him shortly before his death, when he was too ill to read. According to Laura Huxley, it 'looked and felt as if it had never been opened before'. Secondly, that he could not have taken with him into his after-life the memory of the location of the books, because the arrangement of his entire library had been changed after his death. If he had planned the evidence before his death, the change in the arrangement of the library might not have been a problem for conceivably he could still locate his chosen books, but it is difficult to conceive that he could posthumously have read a closed book or acquired knowledge of its contents by clairvoyance. One would think that if an intelligent 'survivor' like Huxley was concerned to provide 'classical evidence of survival' he would foresee such ambiguities and avoid complicating his evidence with them.

The anti-survivalists would argue that if we have to invoke clairvoyance to explain such a case, we might as well attribute it to a living person as to a discarnate one and would suggest, for instance, that Rhinehart's subconscious ferreted out the references. To this suggestion the rejoinder may be made: to what purpose? We undoubtedly have evidence that the powers of the subconscious to acquire information are far greater than orthodox psychology allows, but the evidence from parapsychology does not suggest that such powers are exercised randomly and without motivation. On the other hand, the discarnate Huxley would be highly motivated to get his message across.

Whenever an ostensible survival case comes under close scrutiny, the analysis inevitably leads to a choice between at least two sets of improbabilities, and to establish objective criteria to enable a choice to be made is very difficult indeed. The anti-survivalist will argue that body, mind, and personality constitute an integral unity, and that there is no kind of evidence that could convince him that the latter might exist independently of the former. While he may concede that some of the mediumistic evidence is very impressive, he will argue that the possession of 'super-ESP' abilities (telepathy, clairvoyance, and precognition) by the medium is a more reasonable hypothesis to explain it than the survival of personality. He may even quote Shakespeare to the effect that to die is 'to lie in cold obstruction, and to rot', and argue that the very act of seeking evidence for survival is motivated by an understandable feeling of repugnance towards this bleak but undeniable prospect.

The survivalist, on the other hand, will maintain that the type of evidence reviewed in the previous chapter greatly diminishes the improbability of the existence of a non-physical component of human personality which is separable from the body and that to put all mediumistic evidence down to super-ESP is simply to explain one unknown quantity in terms of another, thus repudiating that logicality and tough-mindedness that the anti-survivalist takes pride in. Generally, the argument will rest there, perhaps with amicable agreement that, in the words of philosopher C. D. Broad: 'We can only wait and see; or (which is no less likely) wait and not see.'

As a simple example of how the ESP hypothesis has to be stretched near to breaking point to account for some circumstances, consider the following case.

Richard Hodgson was a highly-sceptical researcher of the late nineteenth century, and when he heard from William James how impressed the latter was by Boston medium Mrs Piper he undertook his own investigation of her, expecting to be able to prove her fraudulent. His investigations lasted over a period of years and as a result he was converted to the survivalist position. One of the many incidents that gradually brought him round was the following:

One day, when Hodgson was on his way to a sitting with Mrs Piper, he happened to notice a newspaper announcement of the death of a person he called 'F' in his account of this incident. Hodgson knew that F had been a close relative of a certain Madame Elise, a friend of his who had died some time ago and from whom he had had several ostensible communications through Mrs Piper. When this day's sitting began, Madame Elise immediately came through, and said that F was with her but was not yet able to communicate. She also said that she had been present at F's death-bed and had spoken to him just before he died. She told Hodgson what she had said to F on that occasion.

Some days later, Hodgson heard, from a completely different source, an account of the death of F. Before he died he had said that Madame Elise was speaking to him – and he had repeated what she had said. The words were exactly those that Madame Elise had told Hodgson, through Mrs Piper, that she had spoken. They were, moreover, 'an unusual form of expression,' Hodgson said.

Here, surely, is a case to which it is very difficult to apply the ESP hypothesis. To do so, we would have to suppose that Mrs Piper's subconscious had been capable of invading the minds of the living people who had been present at F's death-bed and withdrawing therefrom the words they had heard him speak. Or we would have to suppose that she exercised precognition to glean from Hodgson's mind the knowledge that he would possess a few days later and incorporated it in her communication from Madame Elise, which on this theory would not have been a communication at all but a creation of Mrs Piper's subconscious. Even allowing for the fact that the ESP faculty may be able to transcend the limitations of space and time as we experience them in normal consciousness, such strained applications of the hypothesis have no better support of proven precedent than has the survival hypothesis.

The curious phenomenon of split or multiple personality is well known. There have been some 150 cases recorded over the last eighty years. Typically, a person manifests two or more quite distinct, often conflicting, personalities, each with a full complement of consistent characteristics – desires, memories, modes of speech, and so on. Usually each of the personalities knows nothing of the other or others.

This phenomenon has been of interest both to survivalists and to anti-survivalists. The former consider that sometimes a discarnate being may have taken over the body of the sufferer, while the latter consider that mediumship may be the emergence of a secondary personality in the medium's trance – a personality endowed with ESP abilities.

Psychoanalytic treatment of the multiple personality syndrome consists in rooting out the traumatic experiences in the person's past which caused the split-offs in personality, bringing them to consciousness and either eliminating them or integrating them into one coherent personality. American psychologist Walter Franklin Prince had a startlingly different method, however. He would act on the assumption that the most troublesome of the emergent personalities was an invading spirit. He would give this spirit a severe lecture, reproaching it for its mischief, pointing out that it was preventing its own development by engaging in such mischief, and exhorting it to change its ways. Surprisingly, in several cases the approach worked. That it did so, of course, was no proof of spirit possession, but psychoanalytic theory could offer no alternative explanation.

A psychical researcher who co-operated with Prince on one of his cases, James Hyslop, was also Professor of Logic and Ethics at Columbia University. Hyslop developed a means of separating material of subconscious origin from material of apparent external origin in split or multiple personality cases. He took the sufferer to a medium who knew nothing about the case. If there were any correspondences between the information given or the characteristics manifested by the medium in trance, and the other personality that the sufferer was occasionally seemingly possessed by, Hyslop considered that this must constitute powerful evidence that the other personality was of external origin. After trying this experiment with a number of people, Hyslop came to the conclusion that 'in certain cases traditionally ascribed to hysteria, multiple personality, paranoia, or some other form of mental disturbance, there were strong indications that the person had, in fact, been invaded by foreign or nonphysical agencies'.

26 Hopi Indians in ceremonial dress (*Courtesy of Western Americana*)

27 The Kachina ceremony of the Hopi (*Courtesy of Western Americana*)

26

27

Hyslop had sixteen sittings with Mrs Piper, and like James and Hodgson he became convinced of survival through the experience. Hundreds of facts came through about personal and family matters and convinced him that the medium could not possibly have had access to either by normal or supernormal means. He wrote:

> I have been talking with my father, my brother, my uncles. Whatever supernormal powers we may be pleased to attribute to Mrs. Piper's secondary personalities, it would be difficult to make me believe that these secondary personalities could have thus completely reconstituted the mental personality of my dead relatives. To admit this would involve me in too many improbabilities. I prefer to believe that I have been talking to my dead relatives in person; it is simpler.

In this passage, Hyslop brings up a telling argument against the idea that ostensible survival evidence can have been obtained by ESP on the part of the medium, or by one of her secondary personalities. ESP is, after all, extra-sensory *perception* – a supernormal way of obtaining *information* – but there is a big difference between conveying information and manifesting characteristics and idiosyncrasies peculiar to a particular individual. When the medium had not met the individual in life, and people who were close to him receive through her mediumship distinct impressions of the personality with all its idiosyncrasies, it is understandable that they should consider the ESP hypothesis quite untenable, as Hyslop did.

Another thing that the ESP hypothesis cannot easily explain is evidence of purpose or planning on the part of a communicator, as seen for instance in the Chaffin will and Aldous Huxley cases. And this point brings us to the most astonishing case of all – one which many people consider has proved survival beyond doubt: the Myers 'cross-correspondences'.

Frederic W. H. Myers was one of the founder-members of the Society for Psychical Research. Indeed, it was chiefly due to his initiative that the society was founded. At Cambridge he had won great distinction as a classical scholar and poet. He had established a firm friendship with his tutor, Professor Henry Sidgwick, and a brilliant contemporary, Edmund Gurney, and these three men were co-founders of the society, formed in 1882 (see Plates 33–35). Between then and the turn of the century, the Society published some 11,000 pages of reports of investigations, mostly written by the founder members. In addition, two massive double-volume works appeared. *Phantasms of the Living* by Gurney and Myers, and *Human Personality and its Survival of Bodily Death* by Myers.

28 Novelist, William Gerhardie (*Courtesy of Camera Press*)

This tremendous output, in which were laid the experimental and theoretical foundations of parapsychology, represented great industry on the part of the three men and of Richard Hodgson, who became an equally industrious co-worker. It is as well they did work hard and fast, because none of them was to enjoy a long life. Gurney died in 1888 at the age of forty-one, Sidgwick died in 1900 at sixty-two, Myers in 1901 at fifty-eight, and Hodgson in 1905 at fifty-five. But if the cross-correspondences evidence is what it seems, these men – and Myers in particular – did not allow death to curtail their work.

In 1903, a sister of writer Rudyard Kipling started producing automatic writing. She lived in India and was the wife of a man named Fleming, though she adopted the pseudonym Mrs Holland for her psychic work. She produced scripts signed 'F', which had been Myers' habitual signature, although she did not know this at the time. Nor had she known him in life, though she had read his *Human Personality*. One of these scripts contained the instruction: 'Send this to Mrs Verrall, 5 Selwyn Gardens, Cambridge.' As Mrs Holland had never heard of Mrs Verrall, had never been to Cambridge and did not know if there was such a place as Selwyn Gardens, she sent her scripts instead to the secretary of the SPR, Miss Alice Johnson, who filed them away.

However, there was, in fact, a Mrs Verrall who lived at 5 Selwyn Gardens, Cambridge. She was the wife of Dr A. W. Verrall and both she and her husband were lecturers in classics at the University. They had been close friends of Myers' when he was alive. A few months after his death, Mrs Verrall herself had started producing automatic scripts containing cryptic – and often quite incomprehensible – material, frequently written in Latin or Greek and signed 'Myers'.

About a year later, Mrs Piper in Boston produced some scripts also purporting to be authored by Myers. When these were compared with Mrs Verrall's, it was found that they often referred to the same subjects. The correspondences were noticed by Miss Johnson, to whom both Mrs Verrall and Mrs Piper sent their scripts, but she did not think to look for similar correspondences in Mrs Holland's writings, she just kept filing them away as they came in from India.

In Mrs Holland's automatic writing, however, Myers had been joined by Gurney and Sidgwick, (here and in the sequel I have used the names Gurney, Myers, and Sidgwick for convenience and to avoid such circumlocutions as 'the communicator purporting to be Gurney', etc) and the trio had begun to show signs of frustration and impatience. Gurney severely reproached the automatist: 'If you don't care enough to try every day for a short time, better drop it altogether. It's like making appointments and not keeping them. You endanger your own powers of sensitiveness and annoy us bitterly – G.'

Myers was more understanding: 'You should not be discouraged if what is written appears to you futile. Most of it is not meant for you . . . I do wish you would not hamper us by trying to understand every word you write.' In another script, Myers' frustration became quite anguished: 'Yet another attempt to run the blockade – to strive to get a message through . . . How can I convince them? . . . Oh, I am feeble with eagerness. How can I best be identified? . . . Edmund's help is not here with me just now – I am trying alone under unspeakable difficulties.'

At the same time as Mrs Holland was writing this in India, Mrs Piper in America was writing: 'I am trying with all the forces together to prove that I am Myers.' Eventually, in 1905, Miss Johnson noticed that in Mrs Holland's scripts correspondences with those of Mrs Piper and Mrs Verrall were appearing, and about the same time the communicators began to reveal through the scripts an ingenious plan they had devised in order to give the world evidence of their identity and their survival.

As men who had devoted a good part of their lives and their considerable intellectual abilities to the survival question, Myers, Sidgwick, and Gurney would have known how difficult it is to get unambiguous evidence – evidence that could not be alternatively put down to telepathy or clairvoyance. The plan of the cross-correspondences brilliantly takes account of and circumvents this problem. 'Most of it is not meant for you,' Myers had written through Mrs Holland. Through Mrs Verrall he wrote: 'Record the bits, and when fitted, they will make the whole,' and 'I will give the words between you neither alone can read but together they will give the clue he wants.'

The plan, then, was to use a number of automatists and to send through them corresponding or complementary communications. Mrs Verrall's daughter, Helen, had begun producing scripts independently in 1904. In 1908 another prolific automatist, Mrs Willett, also began, and corresponding motifs were sometimes found in scripts produced by all five women. Correspondences, however, were not in themselves adequate evidence to rule out the possibility of the exercise of telepathy between the automatists, and as if in recognition of this fact some of the themes came across in fragments that were meaningless in themselves, only to become coherent when a key to their relationship and meaning was supplied. It was as if two people had first been given unconnected pieces of a jigsaw puzzle and then a third person was given a piece that enabled all three pieces to be brought together to form a meaningful picture.

Furthermore, the references were often so recondite and their relationships so ingeniously suggested, that it was impossible that they should have emanated from any mind except one with a profound knowledge of classical literature and a nimble intellect. Myers, Sidgwick, and Gurney had such knowledge, but the automatists, with the possible exception of Mrs Verrall, certainly had not. And in other cases the references were to things, events, or people that were known or found to have a significant connection with one of the ostensible communicators.

One of the simplest examples was to be found in one of Mrs Verrall's scripts. There was a poem beginning with the line: 'Tintagel and the sea that moaned in pain.' It signified nothing to her, but when Miss Johnson at the SPR read it, she was immediately reminded of some verses by a poet named Roden Noel. Four days later Mrs Holland in India wrote: 'This is for AW. Ask him what the date May 26th, 1894, meant to him – to me – and to F.W.H.M. I do not think that they will find it hard to recall, but if so – let them ask Nora.'

This meant nothing to Mrs Holland, but it was a coherent communication from Sidgwick, who had been a close friend of Roden Noel's. The initials AW referred to Dr Verrall, FWHM was Myers, and Nora was Sidgwick's wife, who was still alive and would surely remember that the date given was the date of Roden Noel's death. But this was not all. Another three days elapsed, then Mrs Holland wrote something even more incomprehensible to her: 'Eighteen, fifteen, four, five, fourteen . . . Fourteen, fifteen, five, twelve. Not to be taken as they stand. See Revelation 13, 18, but only the central eight words, not the whole passage.'

Perhaps recalling Myers' injunction not to try to understand everything she wrote and not to be discouraged if it seemed futile, Mrs Holland sent her scripts off to Miss Johnson. Miss Johnson looked up the reference to the Book of Revelation and found that the central eight words were: 'for it is the number of a man.' Given this clue, she took the numbers given in the script as standing for the letters of the alphabet in order, and translated them into the name Roden Noel. Two weeks later, Mrs. Verrall produced a script which contained another reference to Roden Noel, a correct description of him, and an appropriate reference to Cornwall.

This is one of the simplest cases in the cross-correspondences literature. The more complex cases are dense with literary and classical allusions, and any summary of one of them can only disentangle a few of the closely interwoven strands. But even such a summary will give an idea of the sense of an independent mind at work that emerges from this material, so here is a brief summary of what is known as the 'Hope, Star, and Browning' case.

On 16 January 1907, a prominent SPR member, J. G. Piddington, sat with Mrs Piper and put to Myers, through her, the suggestion that when a cross-correspondence was being communicated, the fact might be indicated by the automatists' drawing a circle with a triangle inside. A week later, there came an apparent answer to this suggestion when Mrs Verrall's Myers wrote: 'An anagram would be better. Tell him that – rats, star, tars and so on . . . or again tears, stare . . . Skeat takes Kate's Keats stake steak. But the letters you should give tonight are not so many – only three: A S T.'

Mrs Verrall was not herself interested in anagrams, but her husband remembered that 'Skeat takes Kate's Keats stake steak' was one that he, Myers, and another friend had devised. When Piddington read Mrs Verrall's script, he recalled that when he had been going through Richard Hodgson's papers after his death he had found correspondence with Myers showing that Hodgson and Myers had been exchanging anagrams for years, and Hodgson had jotted many of them down on scraps of paper. He asked Hodgson's executors to send him these papers and found on one of them the anagrams that had appeared in Mrs Verrall's script – star, rats, etc.

So considering the living Myers' interest in anagrams, the fact that the discarnate Myers should use them in his cross-correspondences was an interesting consistency. Five days after Myers had given the initial anagrams, Mrs Verrall's automatic script went as follows:

Aster (Latin = star). Teras (Greek = wonder or sign). The world's wonder. And all a wonder and a wild desire. The very wings of her. A winged desire. Upopteros eros (Greek = winged love) . . . But it is all the same thing – the winged desire. Eros potheinos (Greek = love – the much desired) the hope that leaves the earth for the sky – Abt Vogler for earth too hard that found itself or lost itself – in the sky. That is what I want. On earth the broken sounds – threads – In the sky, the perfect arc. The C major of this life. But your recollection is at fault.

Following this passage, there was a drawing of a triangle in a circle – the symbol that Piddington, in his session with Mrs Piper, had suggested Myers should use.

Mrs Verrall recognised in her script a number of phrases from the work of the poet Robert Browning. She was puzzled by one misquotation, though. It should have been 'the passion that leaves the earth for the sky,' not 'the hope'. Later it emerged that this might have been a deliberate misquotation, to draw attention to the word 'hope'. She noted the anagrams, 'aster' and 'teras' and their connection with her script of the previous week, but when she tried to puzzle out the theme of the passage as a whole she guessed that it might be 'Bird'.

Next it was Helen Verrall's turn. On 3 February, she wrote a script which contained the words: 'a green jerkin and hose and doublet where the song birds pipe their tune in the early morning. Therapeutikos ek exoticon (Greek = a healer from aliens).' After this, she drew pictures of a crescent moon and a star and wrote: 'remember that and the star.' At this time she knew nothing about her mother's script. Two weeks later, in another script, Helen again drew a star, and after it wrote: 'That was the sign she will understand when she sees it.' Later in the same script came: 'No arts avail . . . and a star above it all. Rats everywhere in Hamelin town. Now do you understand?'

In these last phrases, the dominant themes of the cross-correspondences were brought together. There were the anagrams 'arts', 'stars', and 'rats', which had also come through Mrs Piper and Mrs Verrall; there was the drawing and specific mention of the word 'star', and there was a quotation from Browning's poem 'The Pied Piper of Hamelin' (who was perhaps alluded to in the phrase, 'a healer from aliens' in the 3 February script).

On 11 February, Piddington had another sitting with Mrs Piper and Myers now gave him the key to the cross-correspondences that had appeared in Helen and Mrs Verrall's scripts. 'I referred to Hope and Browning. I also said Star . . . Look out for Hope, Star and Browning.'

There were other correspondences in this particular cluster, but the above account is adequate to show how Professor Gardner Murphy came to the conclusion that 'most of the Hope, Star and Browning plan was effectively consummated, and in a fashion very much in the spirit of the Browning-lover and aspiring star-seeker, F. W. H. Myers'.

The cross-correspondences literature built up over a period of thirty years, and when Dr Verrall died in 1912, it seemed that he, too, joined the communicators, for scripts written by Mrs Willett contained material characteristic of him or referring to obscure personal matters.

'This sort of thing is more difficult to do than it looked,' wrote the discarnate Verrall, and scholars connected with the SPR who have tried to create sets of cross-corresponding texts after the manner of those that have come through the automatists have likewise found the task unexpectedly difficult.

Myers himself, through Mrs Holland, wrote: 'The nearest simile I can find to express the difficulties of sending a message is that I appear to be standing behind a sheet of frosted glass which blurs sight and deadens sounds, dictating feebly to a reluctant and somewhat obtuse secretary.'

Anti-survivalists who have attempted to explain the cross-correspondences literature have argued that it must all have emanated from the mind of Mrs Verrall, who was the only one of the automatists who possessed the necessary scholarship. But this argument is undermined by the fact that the phenomenon did not cease with the death of Mrs Verrall in 1918. It eventually ceased in the early 1930s, and sceptics have seen this as indicative that the originators of the scripts were of this world and not the next. Others have pointed out, however, that by the 1930s the communicators might well have considered that they had adequately proved their point, and if the living disbelieved the evidence, there was no point in adding to it.

Again Gardner Murphy sums up the conclusion well:

It is the autonomy, the purposiveness, the cogency, above all the individuality, of the source of the messages, that cannot be by-passed. Struggle as I may, as a psychologist, for forty-five years, to try to find a 'naturalistic' and 'normal' way of handling this material, I cannot do this even using all the information we have about human chicanery and all we have about the far-flung telepathic and clairvoyant abilities of some gifted sensitives. The case looks like communication with the deceased.

There is no stronger evidence for the survivalist position than the cross-correspondences literature, but recently some evidence that is almost as good has been accumulating through the mediumship of an Isle of Wight housewife, Mrs Margo Williams.

As Mrs Williams' material is not well known, and as I have had an opportunity to investigate it personally*, I propose to devote the rest of this chapter to it.

But first, a word about 'drop-in communicators'. The term is used for putative spirits that are totally unknown to anyone present during a sitting with a medium and who give information about themselves and their former lives which can later be verified. If they are quite obscure people, and the possibility can be ruled out that someone present could at some time have read about them, then the ESP hypothesis becomes rather strained and the survival hypothesis has to be seriously considered.

In 1972 Professor Alan Gauld of Nottingham University published an account of an investigation of thirty-seven identities claimed by drop-in communicators who had given such details as their names, former addresses, and occupations. Gauld was able to verify the information given by ten of these communicators, and his investigation has been considered highly significant because the facts that the putative spirits gave could only be checked by going to obscure sources, such as parish records and local newspapers.

Since April 1976, Mrs Williams has produced by automatic writing more than 1350 scripts comprising material from over 750 drop-in communicators. Her husband, Walter Williams, has investigated each case and been able to prove the existence of more than half of them. A curious fact is that the communicators all come from the period of about 1830–80, although there are a few from before and after these dates. They come from all classes and from a wide range of occupations. Their style of expression and the vocabulary they use is always appropriate to their stated occupation or background, and often terms are used that would be

*A book entitled *The Moving Hand Writes*, is shortly to be published by Granada Publishing Co.

considered recondite anachronisms today. One thing the communicators appear to have in common is a need to make some kind of a confession – to unburden themselves of some sort of guilt. When they have done so, the communication ceases. The confession does not come all at once, but in a series of scripts which Mrs Williams may write over a period of weeks. At any one time she may have three or four communicators.

I have been able to examine bundles of the scripts and there are noticeable variations in the handwriting, although Mrs Williams stresses that as she gets messages through clairaudience, she would not necessarily expect the handwriting to correspond with that of the communicator when alive. She writes in a state of slight dissociation, but not in trance. Her conscious mind might be bent on domestic plans and details, while in another part of her mind she is hearing the voices and taking their dictation at great speed. Afterwards, she has no recollection of what she has written. When Mrs Williams reads the script, it is a novelty to her and often contains things that she does not understand. Some scripts, purporting to come from a certain scholar, contain sentences in Latin – a language that Mrs Williams never learnt.

Most of the communicators are quite obscure. Indeed, the only one among them who had any kind of public life was Mary Todd Lincoln, the wife of the American president Abraham Lincoln. If this case stood alone, a sceptic could argue that Mrs Williams must have read a life of Lincoln at some time and could attribute her scripts to cryptomnesia ('forgotten memory'). Such a possibility could not be contradicted, although the scripts contain a tremendous amount of detail about the Lincolns' domestic life that subsequent research has verified as correct.

For instance, there are the names Nancy (Nancy Hanks was Lincoln's mother); Julia (Julia Trumbull was Mary's bridesmaid); William (William Butler was a close friend of Lincoln's); Robert, Willie, and Tad (the Lincolns' sons); Diller (the storekeeper the Lincolns' dealt with); Shields (James Shields was an enemy politician); Mead, Macdowell, Pickett, and Ewell (who were all Civil War generals); Henry and Clara (Major Henry Rathbone and Miss Clara Harris were an engaged couple who shared the Lincolns' box at the theatre on the night the President was assassinated); and Elizabeth Keckley (who was Mary's personal maid

29 The projection of the astral body: (a) slightly out of coincidence; (b) above the physical body; (c) moving away from the physical body, as indicated by the arrows; (d) upright still attached to the body; (e) returning to the body.

30 Two-page sequence of infra-red photographs showing the materialisation of Silverbell, an indian girl. An assistant holds the curtain back to reveal the medium (*Courtesy of Psychic News*)

29a

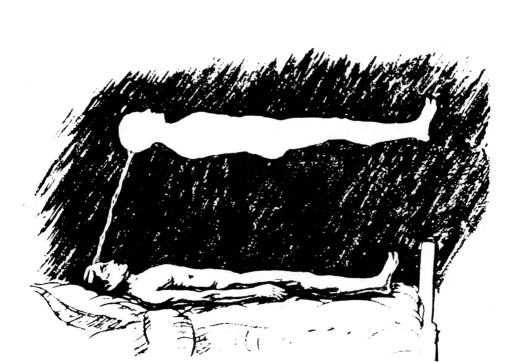

29b

29c

29d

29e

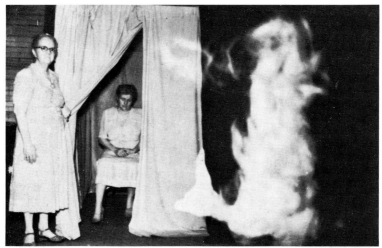

30a

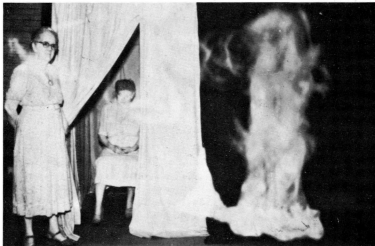

30b

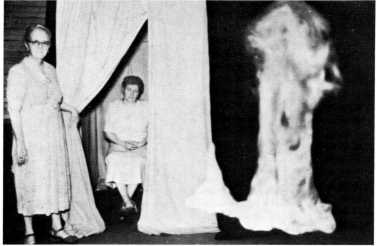

30c

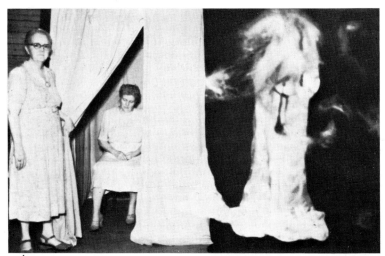

30d

30e

30f

and friend after Lincoln's death). Other abstruse but verifiable facts in the scripts are that the minister who married the Lincolns later sold them his house, and that there were sixteen horses in the cortège at Lincoln's funeral.

There was a sentence in one of the scripts that gave the Williams a great deal of puzzlement. It was 'We were going to see our American cousin.' As the Lincolns themselves were American, it was odd that they should refer to a cousin in that way. The puzzle was solved when Walter Williams came across the fact in a biography of Lincoln that the play he was watching on the night he was assassinated was *Our American Cousin*.

A rather more obscure Victorian lady was Mrs Margaret Gatty. Between 25 March and 15 April 1977, Mrs Williams wrote eleven scripts from this communicator in which they learnt that she had been the wife of a Yorkshire clergyman, had had many children, and in middle age had taken up an interest in seaweed – a subject which she had written about. The great moment in her life had been when a certain professor had named a species of seaweed after her – described in the script as 'with small, thin, tubular fronds and dichotomous stems'. The script also mentioned a friend who 'could not understand why I was so excited when a species of weed was named after me, but when a sandworm also bore my name the poor soul began to think I was demented to think it an honour'.

Research facilities in the little town of Ventnor in the Isle of Wight are limited, and in order to check details contained in his wife's scripts, Walter Williams has generally had to write away to appropriate sources. In this case, he first wrote a letter to the *Yorkshire Post*, which was published in the newspaper's correspondence column. He was fortunate in immediately getting a lead. A correspondent informed him that a Mrs Margaret Gatty had been the wife of the Revd. Alfred Gatty, vicar of Ecclesfield. She had written a *History of British Seaweeds*, which had been published in 1863, and had also published books of children's stories. Walter Williams pursued his research on the basis of this information, and found several other points in the scripts confirmed. The professor Margaret mentioned was Professor William Henry Harvey, and he had named an Australian species of algae, *Gattya pinella*, after her, also another, *Cladophora gattyae – harv.*, which has thin, dichotomous stems. The sandworm named after her is *Gattia spectabilis*. In the scripts, Margaret mentioned spending time on the Sussex coast and in a biographical note on her, Walter discovered that she had spent five months in Hastings in 1848 after her seventh child was born.

As Margaret Gatty was a woman of some distinction and as there was material in print about her, a thorough-going sceptic might say that Mrs Williams could have got the information by exercising super-ESP faculties. But as Professor Raynor C. Johnson has written in the context of a discussion of a similar case:

Clairvoyance, and a faculty of telepathy which can sweep like a searchlight into the odd corners of libraries and gather information which is almost always right, is certainly a possible hypothesis. But is it comparable in its plausability with the ostensible one which presumes the survival of personality? . . . We cannot help but think that there is a disposition on the part of some commentators to extend the range of the psi-faculty and the measure of its precision far beyond the point where experiment shows it to be, in an effort to avoid the hypothesis of survival.

Let us take as another example a man of no distinction at all – even his name is in doubt. Between 8 and 17 April 1977, seven scripts were written telling of the death of a coalminer in a pit disaster in the 1870s. The communicator gave his name as Edward Rose and the name of the colliery as Swaithe. The vocabulary and style were simple, direct, and graceless, and there were phrases that suggested a Yorkshire dialect, such as: 'Me mam said she didn't want me in't pits.' 'Swaithe, it were called.' 'We could do nowt but sit and wait.' There was a reference to 'the two Allen men,' and to 'a blinding explosion before the rotten beams gave way'.

The National Coal Board librarian was helpful when Walter Williams wrote to him saying that he was involved in historical research and inquiring initially if there were records of a colliery named Swaithe where there had been a disaster in the 1870s. He replied that indeed there was. Swaithe Colliery was near Barnsley in Yorkshire, and on 6 December 1875, a fire-damp explosion had killed 143 people. Further investigation turned up the fact that two brothers named Allen were listed as killed in the disaster in the Mines Inspector's report, and a canister belonging to an Edward Rhodes was found down the mine.

Mrs Williams thinks that the discrepancy in the name can be put down to the fact that she receives the communications clairaudiently and could have misheard 'Rhodes' as 'Rose'.

Let us take one last example – a case that in some repects is the most interesting of all. Between 9 and 15 July 1977, Mrs Williams produced nine scripts by a communicator identified as 'Robert', a ship's surgeon. The scripts dramatically refer to the terrible conditions aboard a ship named the *Ardent* during a sea battle. The last one names the battle as Camperdown, an action off the coast of Holland in 1797 between the British and Dutch fleets. 'Robert' writes about his long hours of work in a small and ill-lit operating room with inadequate help and of his attempts to get the captain, whose name he mentions was Captain Burgess, to give him extra lanterns, helpers, and rum for the injured. He mentions having to perform many amputations, and that the captain himself was killed in the action. Sometimes he uses medical terminology – for instance, 'femoral artery bleeding, ligatures not holding' – and in the last script he mentions a journal in which he kept a record of his work and which was in the possession of the Admiralty.

To check the details in these scripts, Walter Williams obtained the help of the librarian at the Royal Naval College, who sent him some photocopies of pages from naval records. One page listed the fleets in action at Camperdown and gave the numbers of casualties for each ship. The *Ardent* was included on the list, her captain was named as Richard Randle Burgess, and her casualties were 41 dead and 107 wounded – the heaviest toll suffered by any ship of the fleet. In the scripts 'Robert' had not mentioned his surname, but in the official history of the battle, the *Ardent*'s ship's surgeon was named as Robert Young. There was also confirmation of the fact that he had kept a journal, which could be consulted at the Public Records Office. An extract had been included in the official history. It contained several points corresponding with those arising in the scripts – for instance, specific mention of stanching the blood from the femoral artery of one casualty; of Captain Burgess being killed in the battle; and Robert Young working himself to exhaustion and having to perform numerous amputations without the assistance of a mate.

To read the extract from Robert Young's journal and then the automatic scripts written by Mrs Williams is an uncanny experience. It is as if it is the same man speaking, although nearly two centuries separate the penning of the two documents.

Most of us will have at least residual doubts about the survival question until the day comes when we find out the truth of the matter for ourselves, but the cross-correspondences literature and the Williams scripts certainly constitute strong evidence for the existence of discarnate mind.

Part III: Non-terrestrial 'Persons'

6 The Space People

'How many kingdoms do not know us!' cried Pascal, agonising about the gap that he believed kept intelligent creatures throughout the universe incommunicado and unaware of each other's existence. Belief in the existence of a plurality of inhabited worlds pre-dates Pascal, and is to be found, for instance, in Buddhist and Jainist scriptures and in the works of some ancient philosophers. 'Nature is not unique to the visible world,' wrote Lucretius, 'we must have faith that in other regions of space there exist other earths, inhabited by other peoples and other animals.' In Lucretius' day, as in Pascal's, the existence of other inhabited worlds and intelligent creatures could only be a matter of faith, for there was no conceivable way that the hypothesis could be tested. But with the development of radio technology at the beginning of the present century the situation changed dramatically, for man now had a means of sending messages at the speed of light into the farthest reaches of space.

He also had the capability to receive messages from extraterrestrial sources. Two of the pioneers of radio technology, Nikola Tesla and Thomas Edison, believed that in the course of their researches they received intelligent, if not intelligible, signals from space. Tesla wrote of his experience:

I was familiar, of course, with such electrical disturbances as are produced by the sun, Aurora Borealis, and earth currents, and I was as sure as I could be of any fact that these variations were due to none of these causes . . . The feeling is constantly growing on me that I had been the first to hear the greeting of one planet to another.

That was nearly eighty years ago, and in the intervening time many anomalous signals have been picked up by radio receivers on Earth; signals indisputably of extraterrestrial origin that appeared to have an order and a patterning suggestive of an intelligence at work. Many people have wondered whether these signals might not be messages or call-signs from the inhabitants of other worlds.

Although popular fantasy fiction and films have concentrated on the theme of a direct physical contact between human beings and extraterrestrials, the probability is that in reality the initial contact would be by means of radio. It is an intriguing fact that some of the anomalous radio signals received over the years have seemed to be of a type consistent with the expected manner of first contact predicted by scientists.

For over half a century the puzzle of the LDEs (long delayed echoes) has fascinated astronomers. In 1973 a young Scotsman, Duncan Lunan, caused considerable excitement when he announced that he had decoded the information contained in some LDEs recorded at Eindhoven in Holland in 1928 as charts of known star constellations, presumably indicating where the senders of the message came from.

When radio operators send out normal communication signals they receive back an echo one-seventh of a second later. This echo is a rebound from the earth's ionosphere. If a radio signal is directed at an astronomical object – the moon or one of the planets, for example – the echo will take longer to rebound. The duration of the delay will depend on the distance the signal has to travel, but it must obviously always be the same for signals aimed at the same astronomical object. If an echo were to come back after varying intervals of time, one might well suspect that it was something other than an echo. A hunter shooting in the mountains would expect to hear an echo a split second after each of his shots. If the 'echo' came at any time from one to twenty seconds after his shot, he would naturally think that there was someone else shooting in the vicinity.

The inference that there was somebody or something 'up there' was one that had often been made about the Eindhoven LDEs. In the early 1960s Professor Ronald Bracewell suggested that they might have emanated from an alien probe vehicle programmed to seek evidence of intelligent life on our planet, and he asked a question that put Duncan Lunan on the track of his discovery. 'Should we be surprised,' he wrote, 'if the beginning of its message were a TV image of a constellation?'

Pulse sequence No	1	2	3	4	5	6	7	8	9	10	11	12	13	14
Echo delay time(seconds)	8	11	15	8	13	3	8	8	8	12	15	13	8	8

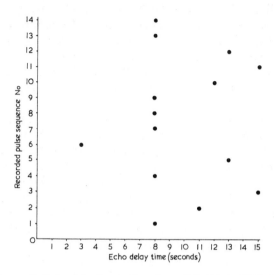

Duncan Lunan's graph of the delaying radio echoes of Boötis in 1928 (*Courtesy of Duncan Lunan*)

The sequence of intervals recorded by Professor Van der Pol at Eindhoven in 1928 was as follows: 8, 11, 15, 8, 13, 3, 8, 8, 8, 12, 15, 13, 8, and 8 seconds. Lunan tried graphing these echo intervals, plotting the signal sequence on the vertical axis and the delay times on the horizontal. The predominance of 8s made a vertical barrier in the diagram, dividing it into two halves; in one half there were six points, and in the other just one. He noted that the six points, formed a pattern with a striking but incomplete resemblance to the star constellation Boötis, known as the Herdsman, a system two hundred light years away. Moreover, when the one isolated point was moved over to a corresponding position on the other side of the diagram it occupied the position of the star Epsilon Boötis and thus completed the constellation pattern. 'It would seem then that Epsilon Boötis was the star the probe came from,' Lunan wrote, 'and had we returned the completed map to it, it would have "known" it had contacted intelligent beings.'

There was one other anomaly in the diagram, namely that Epsilon's neighbour star, Alpha Boötis, known as Arcturus, was a little above and to the left of its true position. At first Lunan thought that this fact might invalidate his star map interpretation, but then he realised that Arcturus was shown in the position it would have occupied some thirteen thousand years ago. He concluded that the probe could have arrived in our system that long ago, settled into orbit somewhere between the Moon and Earth, and then waited patiently until radio was invented on Earth.

When Lunan announced his theory, Professor Bracewell reacted enthusiastically. 'The map of Boötis constructed by Lunan's analysis could be interpreted as a method of communication from another planet,' he said in an interview. 'If I wanted to tell you where I came from, and I couldn't speak your language, I could show you with a picture. Naturally, I am pleased to hear that the British Interplanetary Society is investigating these echoes. Their investigation could result in a shattering discovery.'

Working with other sequences of LDEs recorded at Eindhoven in the 1920s, Lunan graphed other star maps, and although he had to assume a few errors in the original timings or records in order to obtain correct correspondences, the results certainly appeared to suggest that the sequences of delay intervals were not random. Lunan answers one obvious objection to his theory, namely that the LDE sequences it is based on were received fifty years ago and have not been repeated since, by pointing out that the radio wavelengths originally used soon became cluttered with man-made noise, and he suggests that 'the probe may have varied its efforts and be trying to attract our attention in other ways'. He cites reports of radio operators receiving long-delayed speech echoes, of a TV station test card reappearing on the screen years after it was last broadcast, and of the spacecraft Sputnik I reappearing a year after it was launched and months after it had burned up in the atmosphere. Such phenomena, he proposes, might be attributable to the alien probe from Epsilon Boötis.

Naturally, other scientists critically examined Lunan's data and theories and began to cast doubts upon them. Professor F. Crawford of Stanford University solved the mystery of how the delays could have occurred by pointing out that there are clouds of plasma, or highly ionised gas, in space, and when a radio wave passes through such a cloud it will be slowed down; and British astronomer, Professor G. C. McVittie, bluntly accused Lunan of manipulating the data. So the mystery of the LDEs remains unsolved and a matter of dispute. The possibility that they emanated from an alien probe may have been diminished but has not been ruled out by the criticisms of Lunan's work.

The same can be said of the anomalous radio signals received at the Radio Institute at Gorki in Russia in 1973. These took the form of regular sequences of pulses, and the astrophysicists who first picked them up, Drs Vsevolod Troitsky and Nikolai Kardashev, both went on record as saying that they emanated from an artificial and intelligent source.

31 The swaying of the astral body

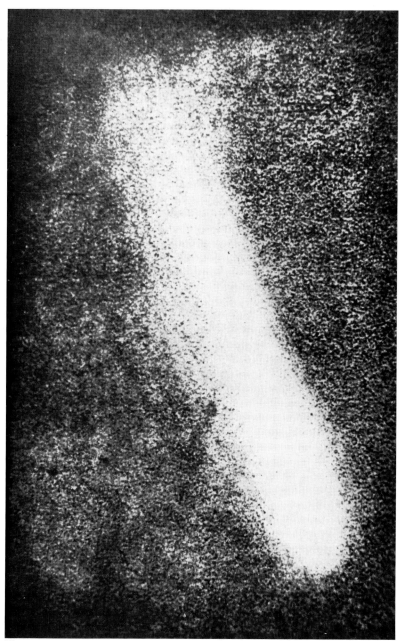

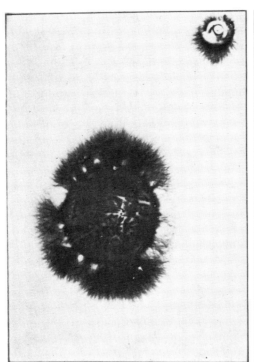

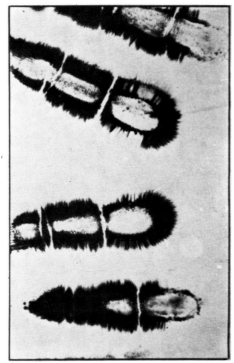

Kardashev said:

> We have been receiving radio signals from outer space in bursts lasting from two to ten minutes. Their character, their consistent pattern and their regular transmissions leave us in no doubt that they are of artificial origin – that is, they are not natural signals, but have been transmitted by civilised beings with sophisticated transmission equipment.

Troitsky was no less positive. 'They are definitely call-signs from an extraterrestrial civilisation. This is only the beginning of some very exciting discoveries.' But some months later, addressing a conference of his scientific peers, Troitsky said that further research had suggested that the radio emissions did not come from outer space but apparently arose in the atmosphere and might in the final analysis, be traced to solar activity. Another theory put forward at the time was that they might have come from a US spy satellite that had gone out of control and was transmitting out of phase coded information that it should only have transmitted when in position over the United States. However, this was considered highly unlikely for a number of reasons, and the possibility that the signals came from an alien probe satellite was proposed as an alternative explanation. Subsequently the Russians fell silent about the Gorki signals, much to the annoyance of Western scientists, who did not know whether to interpret the silence as indicating that they considered the mystery solved or that they were withholding new evidence from the rest of the world.

Among the numerous radio emissions from extraterrestrial sources, says Carl Sagan, 'there are a large number of other incompletely understood phenomena . . . which might just conceivably be due to ETI [extraterrestrial intelligence]'. But astronomers have learnt caution. In 1965 a radio source known as CTA 102 was found to have regular periodicities in its emissions and some astronomers jumped to the conclusion that it was artificial, but when it was identified as a quasar (quasi-stellar object) and others like it were found, its emissions were thought to be probably a natural phenomenon. Then in 1967 the first pulsar – a star that emits radio frequency pulses at very regular intervals, creating a 'lighthouse effect' – was observed, and although its discoverers half-jokingly called it LGM 1 (the initials standing for 'little green men'), astronomers on the whole suppressed any excitement they may have felt until further searches revealed that it was far from a unique object and obviously not artificial.. There are many unsolved mysteries of the universe, and astonishing discoveries are still being made, so the problem of distinguishing artifacts from natural phenomena is complicated. All

32 Kirlian photographs of auras around a coin, a leaf and fingers (*Courtesy of Psychic News*)

that can be said at present is that a number of phenomena have been observed that are consistent with the interpretation that an alien intelligence has been seeking to make its existence known to the latest recruit to what Professor Bracewell has called 'the galactic club' of advanced technological civilisations.

We have been making our presence known, too. As Arthur C. Clarke has repeatedly pointed out, our own radio emissions have by now travelled more than fifty light years out into space and an advanced civilisation could have detected them. From the point of view of a distant observer using a radio-telescope, our planet's brightness would on some wavelengths exceed that of any other object in our solar system, including the sun itself – a sure indication of the presence of intelligent life. The waveband used for our television broadcasts is one that is being transmitted into space, and it is conceivable that our television programmes are being watched by our galactic neighbours, which some people may find a dismaying thought.

Before the radio age various suggestions were put forward as to how we might signal our presence to any neighbours. They were all utterly impractical and involved the creation of vast geometrical designs on the earth's surface, for instance by laying out wheatfields and forests in Siberia in a particular pattern. With the development of lasers, however, the possibility of sending an optical signal far into space has become a reality. It would be a kind of interstellar heliography – a flashing of light at controlled intervals such as is achieved in the heliograph by a mirror and shutter system using the reflected light of the sun. Laser beams powerful enough to focus on a narrow area of the moon's surface are within the scope of today's technology, and their power levels are being increased so rapidly that Carl Sagan has said that the majority of astronomers 'are convinced that Lasers, after optimal improvement, will be entirely suitable for interstellar contact'.

Anthony Lawton, a British scientist, has suggested a means by which a technology not greatly in advance of ours could signal its existence over a distance of hundreds of light years by using lasers to create anomalies in the spectrum of its sun. He has made the intriguing observation that no less than fifteen stars have been discovered within a hundred light-years of Earth with unexplained anomalous radiation in their spectra. The anomalies may have a natural cause, but if any of them has been artificially induced, Lawton says, 'that could mean only one thing – extraterrestrial intelligence', and he proposes that they should be given very careful scrutiny.

Scrutinising the universe for signs of intelligent life presents many problems, as Professor Frank Drake of Cornell University points out: 'Although we have the power to discover civilisations, we know neither where to look nor on what frequency.' It was Drake who, in 1960, undertook the first prolonged radio monitoring of stars with the specific purpose of ascertaining whether any radio signals of artificial origin were coming from them. He chose for intensive study two stars situated about eleven light-years from Earth – Tau Ceti and Epsilon Eridani – and he humorously titled his research programme 'Project Ozma', suggesting that it was as quixotic as setting out to contact the mythical land of Oz and its bizarre inhabitants. Working with the 85-foot receiver disc at the National Radio Astronomy Observatory at Green Bank, Virginia, Drake and his colleagues kept tuned to these two stars for six months on the 21-centimetre waveband. (This waveband was chosen because it corresponds to the frequency with which the hydrogen atom, the most abundant constituent of the universe, emits radiation.)

The probability that even if there were other advanced technological civilisations in the universe, neither Tau Ceti nor Epsilon Eridani had evolved one, and the possibility that if a satellite of either star was sending out radio signals they would be some other frequency than the one to which the Green Bank antenna was attuned, made the odds against success seem truly astronomical. Drake and his colleagues were astonished therefore when they got a strong positive signal obviously of artificial origin as soon as they pointed the receiver at Epsilon Eridani. The equipment was carefully checked, and although the possibility that the signals emanated from a terrestrial source was investigated, no such source was at first discovered. It was weeks before Drake found that the signals came from radar apparatus aboard military aircraft. Fortunately he had not made any premature announcement of contact with alien intelligence on a planet of Epsilon Eridani.

Project Ozma was conceived as a pilot project, a practical way of working out some of the problems involved in what is known as the search phase – as distinct from the communicative phase – of extraterrestrial contact. In 1971 Drake was one of forty distinguished participants in a study programme which produced 'Project Cyclops', a much more ambitious project requiring an observatory of over a thousand large radio telescopes arranged in a circle with a ten-mile diameter. The Cyclops system would be able to 'listen in' to millions of stars over a wide range of wavelengths in a decade, allowing a thousand seconds, or nearly seventeen minutes, to each star, and could cover a distance of several hundred light-years. Its estimated cost is between six and ten billion dollars: a fact which brings the question of the value of contacting our galactic neighbours literally down to earth (see Plates 42–43).

There are those who argue that if they exist we should not let them know that we do, and who cite the unfortunate Incas as an example of what happens to the least evolved of two alien civilisations that suddenly come into contact with each other. Others maintain that our technological escalation has been so rapid that it has got out of control

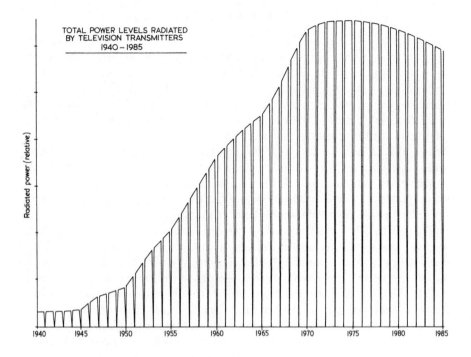

TOTAL POWER LEVELS RADIATED
BY TELEVISION TRANSMITTERS
1940 – 1985

Radiated power (relative)

1940   1945   1950   1955   1960   1965   1970   1975   1980   1985

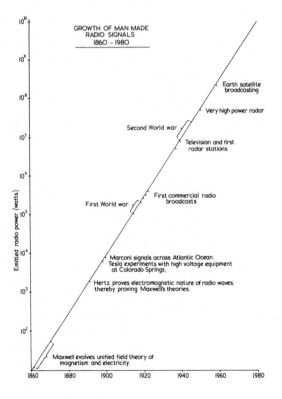

GROWTH OF MAN MADE
RADIO SIGNALS
1860 – 1980

Emitted radio power (watts)

10^{10}

10^{9}

10^{8} Earth satellite
                  broadcasting

10^{7} Very high power radar
          Second World war
                          Television and first
                          radar stations

10^{6}

10^{5} First commercial radio
                         broadcasts
        First World war

10^{4} Marconi signals across Atlantic Ocean.
               Tesla experiments with high voltage equipment
               at Colorado Springs.

10^{3} Hertz proves electromagnetic nature of radio waves,
               thereby proving Maxwell's theories.

10^{2}

        Maxwell evolves unified field theory of
        magnetism and electricity.

1860   1880   1900   1920   1940   1960   1980

The Radio 'Brightness' of the Sun over the last 100 years as seen from outside the Solar system. (Courtesy of A. T. Lawton)

If an alien civilisation on a planet circling the star Eta Cassiopeia (almost a twin of the Sun) has been monitoring the Sun over this period, they will have observed the increasing radio emission. The 'Cassiopeians' would soon deduce that they were of artificial origin since to produce an equivalent brightness by natural means the Sun would have to be several million degrees hotter than it is – or ever will be. Although Eta Cassiopeia 'looks down' on the Solar system, a small but detectable Doppler shift superimposed on the signals would show that they emanated from a planet orbiting the Sun. Further analyses would determine the orbital period of the planet (its year) and, by identifying particular signals, the rotational period (its day) could be ascertained.

If the Sun has been so monitored, then the alien group would be able to determine various phases in the growth of radio communication on Earth. From 1900 onwards they might occasionally have heard recognisable artificial signals. But it would not be until after the late 1930s that really powerful signals would have been heard. These would be radar and television transmissions. Because of their short wave nature, these can easily penetrate the Earth's ionosphere with very little loss, and hence would produce a more powerful signal in the alien receivers. Previously they would only have heard intermittent signals as the ionosphere changed its characteristics during a possible solar flare period. By the late 1940s and early 1950s, very powerful signals were being produced from early warning radars.

Eta Cassiopeia is almost twenty light years from the Sun so those powerful signals generated in the 1950s will have been received for approximately the last six years.

The downward trend in broadcast power may continue with a further move to Earth satellite transmitters and the use of fibre optic land lines. If so the *total* transmitted power from Earth may level off, and possibly decrease over the next century. Up to the present it has increased approximately ten times every fifteen years. This trend could not continue on Earth's surface without disturbing amenities and environment and by the end of the twenty-first century the radio power requirements (allowing for conversation losses) would be approaching 10^{-6} of the total output of the Sun! It is possible therefore that as a civilisation acquires radio communication skills, it goes through a 'noisy phase, and then becomes quieter.

We may therefore be the only noisy infant civilisation in this part of the Galaxy. The others have grown up and 'calmed down'!

and on to a self-destruction course, and that we could use some help from other members of 'the galactic club' who have successfully passed the technological climacteric in their evolution. Yet others would say that if there is a club which we are eligible to join, we ought to do so no matter how high the admission fee, for the benefits that would accrue are inestimable. But people who allocate public funds are unlikely to be persuaded by such speculative considerations to support Project Cyclops. They would certainly first require answers to a number of specific questions, such as: what is the statistical probability of the existence of life on other worlds? What is the probability that it would have evolved as intelligent life? What physical forms might it take? Where might such intelligent beings be located? What kinds of technology might they have evolved? And finally: why should they be interested in us? So let us now consider these questions.

Before the Viking I probe was sent to Mars, a MIT physicist, Philip Morrison, remarked that the discovery of life on the planet would convert the origin of life from a miracle to a statistic. In other words, if even micro-organisms were found on our nearest neighbour, the discovery would permit the inference that life at various stages of evolution must be abundant throughout the universe. But no evidence of life has so far been detected on Mars, and so the age-old debate continues as to whether life on Earth was a freak and unique occurrence or an inevitable and common one. There is of course the third view that it was a unique and divinely ordained occurrence, but as this is even less accessible to scientific verification than the other alternatives it has rather fallen into disfavour.

Although science has been called upon to settle the debate, its evidence is equivocal and each side can claim some scientific justification for its position. The question comes down to the definition of life itself and the determination of how it originated on Earth. When we try to specify the unique defining properties of organic life we soon become entangled in difficulties. We say that living things grow, and then realise that so do clouds and stars. We then propose that they grow by taking material from the environment and re-organising it to a predetermined shape, but this is precisely what a crystal does, so is a crystal a form of organic life? No, we might argue, a crystal is not because it is unable to reproduce itself. But if the ability to reproduce itself is the definitive property, viruses must qualify, for when a virus invades a bacterial cell it can multiply a hundredfold in minutes; although inert viruses are indistinguishable from crystals and can be ground to a powder.

If in desperation we abandon the ambiguous border areas between life and non-life and seek to define life as determined by a combination of properties, we might expect to be on firmer ground. Scientists have proposed that a living organism has three essential properties: irritability, or the ability to react to environmental influences; conductivity, or the ability to pass information from one part of itself to another; and contractility, or the ability to draw itself in. Until recently this definition applied, but with the development of computer-controlled robots with all these properties – not to mention the ability to reproduce themselves – the debate has taken a new turn. In fact, the question of whether life is necessarily and exclusively a biological phenomenon has been raised. It is a question that we shall return to. For the present I just want to draw attention to the fact that before we can answer the question of whether there is life elsewhere we have to have a clear idea of what we mean by life, which is not such a simple matter as it at first appears.

We can, however, by-pass these difficulties by qualifying the term 'life' and considering the probability of the existence elsewhere of organic life as we know it on Earth. Which raises the question of how life originated on Earth, and involves us in biochemistry. This is a promising approach, however, for the science of spectroscopy has established that the chemical compounds of which living systems are composed are basic elements that exist throughout the universe, although of course in different proportions in different locations.

Life as we know it is a property of natural systems composed of hydrogen, carbon, nitrogen, oxygen, sodium, magnesium, phosphorous, sulphur, chlorine, potassium, calcium, and iron. Of these elements carbon is fundamental and predominant in living organisms, because it is able to form complex bonds with other elements. The question of the origin of life can be reduced to the question of how such bonds might have been formed on Earth in primordial times.

Until German chemist Friedrich Wohler synthesised urea in his laboratory in 1828, scientists had believed that organic and inorganic chemical compounds were quite different, and that it was impossible to synthesise substances found in, and produced by, living organisms. Other organic chemicals were synthesised in the nineteenth century, and by the 1920s the science of biochemistry had developed to the point where a general theory of the origin of life on Earth could be attempted.

Working independently in that decade, English scientist J. B. S. Haldane and the Russian I. A. Oparin produced general theories so strikingly similar that they became known as the Haldane–Oparin theory. The theory proposed that in primordial times there existed on the Earth's surface a 'hot, dilute soup' of chemicals which went through a series of reactions. The reactions would have been kept going and the mixture prevented from settling in equilibrium or a low state of energy by a number of circumstances different from those prevailing on Earth today. The primitive Earth's atmosphere would have been composed mainly of carbon dioxide (suggested Haldane) or methane (suggested Oparin), and would have lacked the ozone layer which protects us from the sun's short-wave ultra-violet radiation. Although such radiation is inimical to evolved life, it catalyses chemical reactions and can stimulate the formation of organic molecules. On the primitive Earth, the chemical 'soup' would also have been kept in disequilibrium through the action of volcanoes and rivers, deluges from the atmosphere, and electrical storms, and eventually the continual process of chemical reactions would have produced the compounds basic to all life – the amino acids.

The Haldane–Oparin theory stimulated laboratory research, and a number of biochemists working with simulated primitive Earth environments produced complex organic compounds including amino acids through the action of ultra-violet radiation upon or electrical excitation of the 'soup'. Such research has continued to the present day, and the American biochemist Arthur Kornberg has recently announced success in synthesising a kind of DNA. This molecule is the essential component of living organisms. Carl Sagan has said of such experiments:

There is nothing in them special to the earth, either in composition or in energy source. In fact, we have done experiments simulating the present atmosphere of Jupiter comprising the same gases under somewhat different conditions and to no one's surprise we can still make lots of amino acids . . . This experimental result inclines some of us to think that the probability of the origin of life is rather high.

Sagan sustains his optimism in full knowledge of the school of thought which the French biologist Jacques Monod leads, which maintains that the occurrence of life on Earth was a chance event of such infinitesimally small probability that it was probably unique. In his book, *Chance and Necessity*, Monod wrote:

> Before life did appear its chances of doing so were almost nonexistent. The universe was not pregnant with life nor the biosphere with man. Our number came up in the Monte Carlo game. Is it surprising that, like the person who has just made a million at the casino, we should feel strange and a little unreal?

The argument that supports this point of view rests on the fact that the probability of a simple protein molecule coming into existence through a process of random chemical reaction and shuffling is inconceivably remote. Protein molecules have different properties depending on the way in which their amino acids are located in relation to each other. The insulin molecule, for example, consists of a chain of twenty-one amino acids interwound with a second chain of thirty. There are 280 million million possible permutations of the amino acids in the first chain, and 510 million million million possible permutations in the second chain, and insulin is not produced unless the structure and ordering of the component amino acids is exactly right.

The self-replicating DNA molecule is much more complex than insulin and its occurrence on the primitive Earth was an event which would not be likely to be repeated even if there are billions of planets in the universe potentially hospitable to biological life. So argues Jacques Monod, but the recent successes of biochemists such as Kornberg in synthesising protein macromolecules rather undermine his position, and a majority of scientists today would agree with Sagan that the probability of the origin of life under certain physical conditions is rather high. If we accept this point of view, we then have to consider what these physical conditions are and how commonly they might occur.

The first essential condition for the evolution of biological life is a temperature that is not too low to prevent chemical reactions, nor so high as to destroy the complex chemistry of life. This suggests that life might exist on planets occupying a habitable zone at a comfortable distance from their suns. Secondly, the solar system that a promising planet belongs to will have to be of a certain age, to allow time for the gradual process of the evolution of life to have taken place. It will probably also have to be a single star system, for planets in a binary system would be unlikely to have sufficiently stable orbits to support life, at least not unless the two suns were very far separated. A promising planet will also have to be of a certain mass, for too large a body would not have been able to develop an atmosphere and one too small would not be able to retain an atmosphere. It will also have to possess a suitable surface chemistry.

These conditions obviously reduce the number of possible locations of life in the universe, but they still leave enough to support the hypothesis that life may be abundant. The astronomer Harlow Shapley has done some interesting probability calculations taking into account some of these conditions. He suggests taking a conservative estimate – that there are 10^{20} stars in the visible universe. Let us suppose, he says, that just one in a hundred of these is a single star, which would allow a stable planetary orbit; that one in a hundred of these stars actually has planets; that one in a hundred of these planets is of similar mass to our Earth; that one in a hundred of these Earth-like planets is located in the habitable zone in relation to its sun; and that of this residue only one in a hundred has a suitable surface chemistry. How many habitable planets would you imagine we are left with when we have made all these reductions? The answer is ten thousand million. Which sounds a lot, but in fact there are an estimated ten thousand million galaxies in the universe so Shapley's calculations would leave only one speck of life in each galaxy. We would be it in our Milky Way galaxy so our nearest living neighbours would be two million light-years away in the Andromeda galaxy.

Frank Drake, too, has made some probability calculations, applying less severe reduction principles, and has estimated that in our galaxy alone, which contains something in the order of 250 billion suns, there may be over 100,000 habitable planets. Freeman Dyson, a mathematician of the Institute of Advanced Study, Princeton University, has suggested that advanced technological civilisations could have established colonies on comets, and says: 'I propose . . . an optimistic view of the Galaxy as an abode of life. Countless millions of comets are out there, amply supplied with water, carbon and nitrogen, the basic constituents of living cells.' The 'astroengineering' necessary to establish such colonies may be scarcely conceivable to us although Dyson himself has conceived a scheme for dismantling Jupiter and creating a number of smaller habitable planets from its substance. We have to bear in mind, however, that as a technological civilisation we are but a few decades old and other technological civilisations could well be hundreds of thousands of years in advance of us and quite capable of 'astroengineering'.

There is clearly a wide gap between simple biological life and the kind of life we would be interested in finding elsewhere, namely life exhibiting intelligence equal to or surpassing our own. It is relevant, therefore, to ask whether the development of life forms endowed with higher and higher degrees of intelligence is an inevitable part of the evolutionary process.

The answer is by no means as obvious as a vitalist or 'creative evolutionist' would have us believe. For one thing, we do not really know how or why the human brain developed the capacity that it did. We know that our distant forebears, the hominid apes, had brains of about 350cc capacity and that this remained unchanged for millions of years. There followed a gradual development through *Australopithecus* (average 550cc), *Homo habilis* (750cc), and *Homo erectus* (850–900cc). Then, all of a sudden, *Homo sapiens* appeared with a brain of 1400–1600cc, which, however, made no difference to his way of life until some tens of thousands of years after acquiring the extra capacity he actually began to use it. This suggests that the massive human brain was not a product of evolution through natural selection, which makes its sudden growth rather mysterious.

Various theories have been put forward to explain the mystery, from Osker Maerth's that human brain-growth was stimulated by sexuality and cannibalism, to Robert Ardrey's that it was a mutation caused by Earth's collision with an asteroid some 700,000 years ago, but nobody really knows whether human intelligence was a natural evolutionary development or a freak one. The development of social modes of life and organisation, of hunting, or of competition with other species, and particularly the development of language, have been proposed as primary causes of the growth of human intelligence, but the exponential growth of about the last eight millennia, which has taken man from the cave to the space module, remains a mystery. To argue from the mystery and antecedent improbability of the event to the conclusion that it could not have happened elsewhere is, however, a kind of human species chauvinism. Fortunately, we have on our own planet, in the whales and dolphins, specimens of other big-brained and highly intelligent creatures that have followed an evolutionary pathway different from that of *Homo sapiens*. On other worlds, Carl Sagan has said, 'there may be many, many pathways to an organism which is functionally equivalent to a human being but which looks nothing like a human being'.

Fred Hoyle has some fun at the expense of human species chauvinism in his novel, *The Black Cloud*. The Cloud of the title is an intelligent organism with a brain consisting of layers of appropriate molecules which it synthesises itself. A gas functions like blood, feeding and cleansing the organism, and the Cloud travels interstellar distances, stopping occasionally to recharge itself from the energy of a star. Its brain components are interconnected by radio and unlike biological brain cells can be replaced if they are destroyed, so both the lifetime and brain capacity of the Cloud are virtually unlimited.

When human beings manage to establish communication with the Cloud, it explains that it is very unusual to find intelligent animals with technical skills inhabiting planets, for planetary gravitational forces limit brain size and neurological activities. The scarcity of basic food chemicals, it says, 'leads to a tooth-and-claw existence in which it is difficult for the first glimmering of intellect to gain a foothold in competition with bone and muscle'. Generally, explains the Cloud, 'one only expects intellectual life to exist in a diffuse gaseous medium, not on planets at all'. *The Black Cloud* may be a fun fantasy, but the point it makes, that intelligent life-forms may conceivably be abiological, is valid and one that has to come into any discussion of life in the universe. The evidence reviewed in Part Two may dispose the reader to seriously consider the possibility, difficult though it is to conceive.

If, however, some extraterrestrial life-forms are biological, what are they likely to look like? There are two diametrically opposed schools of thought on this question: one maintaining that a wide diversity of biologies might exist throughout the universe; the other holding that any intelligent life-forms on any other planet would probably be humanoid. Superficially, the former view would appear the most plausible and the obvious one for an open-minded person to adopt. So let us review the argument for the latter.

It is known as the argument from convergent evolution, and goes as follows: life has evolved two distinct types of symmetry – radial and bilateral – and it is no accident that all the most successful and most intelligent forms of life have bilateral symmetry. It is generally agreed that life must have originated in a viscous medium, and in such a medium a creature with a streamlined body has the advantage of speed in pursuit and escape. Life-forms with radial symmetry have a relatively stationary way of life and very simple nervous sytems. A necessary precondition for the development of complex nervous systems is an active, mobile, predatory way of life. Clearly high intelligence cannot be present in a biological organism without a complex nervous system, and in such systems the nerve centre, or brain, must be located near the primary sensory organs – the eyes and ears – in order that the connecting nerve pathways will be short and the animal's response times correspondingly quick. The active predator must also have its sensing and grasping organs at the front of its body and near to the mouth that it has to feed, and if it possesses the sense of smell in order to check the suitability of the food it ingests, the organ for this sense must be located above its mouth.

Bilateralism and the possession of a large ganglion of nerves located at the front of the body and near the principal sense organs are, then, essential characteristics of intelligent creatures. On our planet, birds, fish, and mammals all conform to this pattern – they have evolved convergently. But birds and fish are not likely to evolve high intelligence.

Birds must be light and have a large surface area in order to fly, and therefore could not afford to carry a large brain and a heart capable of pumping the quantity of blood that such a brain needs. The development of birds' brains may be more constricted than that of creatures living in a watery medium, but it is arguable that life in the water does not facilitate the brain's development through use. The brain's higher functions of conceptualisation are generally associated with three things: the use of tools, the development of language, and the existence of a social environment and mode of life; and only land-based mammals fulfil all three of these conditions.

Another notable feature of terrestrial convergent evolution is the development of jointed legs, which afford the best way of moving over varieties of terrain. Large numbers of legs make for slowness of movement, and an odd number would create a balance problem, so the swift predator will have not more than three pairs and not less than two pairs of appendages. The adaptation of one pair to arms for climbing, and at a later stage of evolution for tool manipulation, will be a development favoured by the process of natural selection.

Intelligence could not evolve without information input, and in any physical environment the modes of such input – the sense organs – must evolve similarly in all creatures. On Earth, creatures as disparate as mammals and advanced molluscs have evolved an eye of basically the same structure, and on any planet that receives light from a central sun advanced life-forms would have evolved eyes. In a movable head two eyes facilitate adequate vision; information from more than two would tend to confuse the brain. The same is true of the organs of hearing. As for the senses of smell and taste, these would evolve for survival purposes in a creature living in a world where chemical reactions occur. So we would expect extraterrestrial creatures to possess the same sensory modalities as human beings, although they may have different degrees of relative sensory acuity like the humanoids in Stapledon's *Star Maker* in whom the senses of smell and taste are most acute. They might also possess extra senses, the magnetic sense that some terrestrial animals have, for instance, or a faculty for sensing radioactivity, or the functions such as telepathy and clairvoyance that we categorise as extra-sensory perceptions. But although they may be further evolved than we are in some ways, they will still be basically humanoid. Thus argue the supporters of the convergent evolution theory.

It is obviously, as the theologian would say, an argument *ad hominem* – an example of human species chauvinism. However, the fact is that the argument from convergent evolution can only be countered by somebody who can propose a different plausible model of an intelligent life-form and also a plausible evolutionary process leading up to it. It is not an answer to say with Sagan that there may be many alternative pathways to creatures functionally equivalent to, but physically unlike, human beings.

The only alternative model that would appear plausible, because analogies to it have developed on our planet, is a life-form comprising myriads of small components that lack individuality but function in concert to a particular purpose, like a nest of termites or a flock of birds (see Plate 36). If different parts of such an organism became specialised for different functions, as cells do in the body, and one part functioned as a brain with its components linked by bio-electrical pathways, such a composite creature could perhaps evolve in intelligence beyond man as Hoyle's Black Cloud was supposed to have done, since it would be virtually immortal and indestructible. But as we saw in the discussion of robots and artificial intelligence, non-human intelligence might operate on quite other data and to quite different ends than that of human beings. Thus comparisons of degree between the two would be meaningless.

A parable illustrating the latter point is developed in the novel *Solaris* by Polish science fiction writer Stanislaw Lem. Life on the planet Solaris takes the form of a 'sentient ocean'. The 'primordial soup' from which the diversity of life-forms gradually evolved on Earth did not develop analogously on Solaris. The planet belonged to a binary star system, and had an erratic orbit and in order to survive on it the 'soup' had to evolve rapidly to the stage where it could influence its planet's orbital path. Life on Solaris had not had time to diversify, and 'thus it had reached in a single bound the stage of "homeostatic ocean" without passing through all the stages of terrestrial evolution, by-passing the unicellular and multicellular phases, the vegetable and the animal, the development of a nervous and cerebral system'.

Man establishes a research station above Solaris with a view to studying the ocean and if possible establishing contact with it. The ocean reacts to the human presence by synthesising for each of the scientists on the station a living female the form and character of whom it has somehow 'read off' from each man's memory: a precise and vital replica of a woman he had in his past injured in some way. The ocean's purpose in creating these simulacra is as baffling to the scientists as the technology it employed to do so. The females, though formed of neutrinos instead of atoms, feel and think like human beings and mutual attachment develops betwen them and the scientists. In a conversation between the hero, Kris Kelvin, and the synthesised double of his former wife, Rheya, the following exchange occurs:

Rheya, I don't know what your fate will be. It cannot be predicted any more than my own or any other member's of the Station's personnel. The experiment will go on, and anything can happen . . .'

'Or nothing.'

'Or nothing. And I have to confess that nothing is what I would prefer. Not because I'm frightened – though fear is undeniably an element of this business – but because there can't be any final outcome. I'm quite sure of that.'

'Outcome? You mean the ocean?'

'Yes, contact with the ocean. As I see it, the problem is basically very simple. Contact means the exchange of specific knowledge, ideas, or at least of findings, definite facts. But what if no exchange is possible? If an elephant is not a giant microbe, the ocean is not a giant brain. . . .'

What Kelvin is saying is that the alien intelligence that is the Solaris ocean is probably so alien that no purpose would be served and no profit accrued from contact with it. We have to concede the possibility of the existence of such utterly alien life-forms in the universe, but since to establish contact with them would probably be both impossible and pointless, we can only hope that they would keep to their world and leave us to ours. So let us return to the theory of convergent evolution and consider whether any other modes of convergence would follow logically from the fact of general biological convergence. Would we have any reason to expect extraterrestrial humanoids to have values, motives, purposes, instincts, or beliefs corresponding to ours, or might they be as totally alien as the Solaris ocean? If a likely answer to this question can be arrived at by dint of reasoning, it should certainly be attempted. In any foreseeable contact between human beings and extraterrestrial humanoids we would probably be the inferior and weaker party, and if our reasoning tells us that those we are prone fondly to think of as cosmic brothers might really be cosmic enemies with no fellow-feelings for us at all, then we would be well advised to forget about project Cyclops and – as they say – keep a low profile.

The argument from convergent evolution regards the development of intelligence as contingent upon the predatory mode of life and upon socialisation. Another inseparable condition would appear to be that the young of an intelligent species must have a relatively long period of maturation and parental dependence. Although man's religions hold that moral obligations and prohibitions are God-ordained, basic ones are in fact biologically ordained and only reinforced by divine law. The three factors – predatory mode of life, socialisation, and parental dependence – which must be universally cognate with the evolution of intelligence, are powerful influences in determining moral concepts and behaviour. Terrestrial mammals of widely different species have in common innate inhibitions against aggressive and destructive behaviour, appeasement formalities for ending confrontations, tendencies towards mutual aid (both inter- and intra-specific), manifestations of tenderness towards the young, and, in certain circumstances, the ability to sacrifice self for the sake of dependents or of the social group.

Whether such behaviours are moral, or whether to qualify for the name they not only have to be done but also be known to be done, and be done according to law, precept, or prohibition, is a semantic question. The point is that mammals consistently manifest behaviours which, although they may not be consciously goal-oriented, subserve the goals of mutual survival and peaceful co-existence. Many tales are told of dolphins saving the lives of human beings, for instance, and as the dolphin is a large-brained mammal, a predator, and a socialised animal that raises its young, its example may, in this as in other ways, prefigure the type of behaviour that man might expect of extraterrestrial humanoids. The most convincing argument against such optimism is regrettably that in his dealings with other species man himself has not behaved considerately and morally, and it is indeed a weighty objection. But in this respect man is an exception, and the answer may be, as Arthur Koestler has argued, that he is an anomaly, that there is 'some construction fault in the circuitry' of his brain, some failure to integrate the urges of the old brain and the dictates of the new; or as the ethologist Konrad Lorenz has put it that 'the long-sought missing link between animals and the really humane being is ourselves'.

It is a platitude to say that the human species is at present in a situation of crisis, in danger of being destroyed by its own runaway technology. Complacency answers that every age fancies itself to be an age of crisis and transition, but this is not an adequate reply. We have learnt time and again in the present century that when technology reaches take-off point its rate of escalation becomes exponential, and human pyschology and social institutions are simply not equipped to cope with such a rate of change. It is probable that any technological civilisation will have experienced a similar crisis, in which any one of a number of consequences of its technological explosion – nuclear war or accident, ecological breakdown, depletion of energy resources, or overpopulation – could have brought about its destruction. Civilisations that have not transcended the crisis will obviously thereby be disqualified as potential contactees. Those that have transcended it, however, will probably have done so by making up the lag in psychological and social evolution.

One of the things that will have to be central in the new psychology and social institutions is a recognition of the subtle inter-connectedness and interdependence of all things; another is the elimination of the instincts towards aggression and dominance and of the institutions and modes of life that foster them. So if advanced technological civilisations exist, I think we might expect their representatives to have the characteristics of that 'really humane being' in whose evolution Lorenz sees man as a half-way house; for they will need to have developed to that point in order to have survived.

Those who cry, 'For God's sake don't let them know we're here', will not be convinced by such reasoning, but the reasoning behind their fears is, I think, less plausible. It is true that any civilisation we contact will be ahead of us, for the technologies that would make us eligible for membership of the galactic club are only a decade or two old and still underdeveloped, and we are infinitely less likely to contact another cosmic embryo than a fledged adult. But to attribute to such adults motives of aggression and exploitation like those that human beings have manifested towards each other when one group has been technologically superior to the other is surely insupportable. Any advanced technology will have learnt how to synthesise protein and would never travel light-years to procure human meat, so ideas of this planet being a sort of immense cattle farm are laughable. So are ideas that extraterrestrials would want to exploit any of our planet's natural resources, for to transport them would be uneconomical and an advanced technology would in any case be able to synthesise such materials. The one sinister possibility, which cannot entirely be ruled out, is that a civilisation might seek to escape from a dying planet or to establish colonies for an overpopulated one. If such a situation did exist, we would certainly be at a grave disadvantage in competition for *Lebensraum* with beings so technologically advanced as to be able to transport themselves over interstellar distances. Apart from this possibility, the likelihood is that extraterrestrials would be interested in us for similar reasons as we are interested in them: because advanced beings have become advanced by virtue of being endowed with an insatiable curiosity and thirst for knowledge, and because their need for a sense of meaning in life and the universe would be gratified by the discovery that they are not an accidental and bizarre anomaly.

The question of what kinds of technology might have evolved elsewhere in the universe poses problems for the argument from convergence. At the primitive level of tool-using there is evidence of considerable convergence in the practices of societies widely dispersed throughout our world, but when we come to technology in the service of advanced science we have only one example, that of post-Renaissance Western man. That one example is not enough to extrapolate suppositions about alien civilisations from, so we cannot be certain that science would have evolved along the same lines in an extraterrestrial civilisation. As Louis Pauwels and Jacques Bergier pointed out in *The Morning of the Magicians*, during the twelve years that Nazi Germany went entirely its own way its science flew off at a tangent from that of the rest of the world.

33

34

35

36

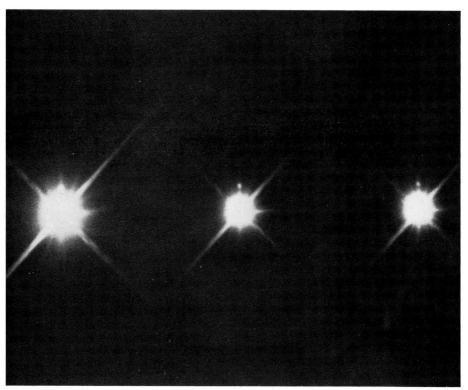

37

There does not appear to have been any inevitable step-by-step progression in the development of our sciences; indeed the characteristic anecdote of scientific discovery is of some chance event that gave an individual scientist a leading clue. Frank Drake attributes the recent rapid growth in laser technology to the fact that the laser happened to be invented long after the world's technology was ready for it. Several contemporary speculative writers, such as Pauwels and Bergier, and John Michell in his *View over Atlantis*, have sought to explain mysterious artifacts of ancient civilisations in terms of forgotten technologies, and their case is plausibly argued. In the last hundred years we have surely seen enough unanticipated scientific and technological innovations to make any dogmatism about what is and what is not scientifically conceivable very presumptuous. So while we are trying to communicate with extraterrestrial intelligence by the most sophisticated means we know – radio and laser technology – extraterrestrial intelligence may be sending signals that we are not able to receive or to recognise. We may be, as Carl Sagan has said, 'like the inhabitants of isolated valleys in New Guinea, who communicate with their neighbours by runner and drum, and who are completely unaware of a vast international radio and cable traffic over them, around them, and through them'. There may be civilisations much closer to us than we think but 'so smart we can't detect them'. But even Sagan's open-minded speculation does not go far enough for some contemporary scientists, and physicist Jack Sarfatti has accused Sagan of 'electromagnetic chauvinism' and implied that communication with extraterrestrial intelligence through other channels may be a more common phenomenon than we would suppose, which is a point we shall take up in Chapter 8.

To conclude this chapter, we are left with the question, where might extraterrestrial intelligent beings be located?

Until fairly recently it was widely supposed that our neighbour planets Mars and Venus might be inhabited, and indeed there are still a number of people, particularly among the UFO contactees, who speak familiarly of Martians and Venusians. But the consensus scientific opinion today is that intelligent life is unlikely to exist on any other planet in our solar system. Mars was the most likely candidate, for it is just within the habitable temperature zone, but it has low gravity so that any creatures that evolved on it would be tall and spindly, and instrumental probes of Mars have not even produced evidence of micro-organisms let alone

36 The corridors of a nest of termites (*Courtesy Bruce Coleman*)

37 Three exposures of Sirius with the companion Sirius B (*Courtesy of Lick Observatory, University of California*)

spindly giants. Venus, with an atmospheric pressure twenty times that of Earth and with fifteen-mile-thick clouds containing a 75 per cent concentration of sulphuric acid, is hardly the inviting lady that the name suggests.

Of the other planets, Mercury is devoid of water and oxygen, has a very thin carbon dioxide atmosphere, and a surface temperature of 400°C on its sunlit side. Jupiter is surrounded by clouds of frozen crystals of ammonia at about −100°C, and the outer planets – Saturn, Uranus, Neptune, and Pluto – also have gaseous surfaces under high pressure. As biological organisms are vulnerable to extremes of heat and cold, to high pressures, and to radiation or chemical contamination, it is generally agreed to be extremely unlikely that there are any intelligent life-forms in our solar system except on Earth.

The possibility of the existence of silicon-based rather than carbon-based life has been entertained by some scientists, since silicon also has the property of easily forming chemical bonds. However, a creature so constituted would have to breathe sand and excrete concreté and would probably be too preoccupied with these processes to develop and exercise intelligence.

Leaving aside possible bizarre life-forms like silicon creatures and various forms of abiological life, with which contact would probably be both impossible and unprofitable, and working on the hypothesis that humanoids might exist elsewhere in the universe, we have some guidelines as to where we might seek our cosmic counterparts. Obviously our interest will initially be in planets orbiting stars in our own galaxy. Such planets cannot be seen, but their existence can be inferred from measurements of the movements of their parent stars. We would look for stars of a size and age similar to those of our sun, for much smaller stars will not have a broad habitable zone and much larger ones will be too short-lived for biological evolution to occur on their planets. Too young a star system would not have had time to manifest such evolution. Applying these and other criteria, the American astronomer Stephen Dole has come to the conclusion that of the nineteen stars within a distance of twelve light-years from Earth there are seven that could have Earth-like planets. Dole's calculations are cautious, and even within an extended distance of twenty-two light-years he only estimates a 43 per cent chance of finding another Earth. Twenty-two light-years is, however, relatively close and on this basis the probability for the galaxy as a whole must approach certainty, even if it falls short of Frank Drake's estimate of 100,000 habitable worlds.

One of our neighbour stars which Dole in his caution eliminates as a possible parent to a habitable planet is Sirius, the brightest star in the constellation *Canis Major* (the dog). But in 1976 American astronomer and scholar Robert Temple's fascinating book, *The Sirius Mystery*, was published presenting facts which are difficult to explain on any other hypothesis except that contact between human beings and inhabitants of a planet in the Sirius system has already taken place. If Temple is right, the space people whose possible existence we have been discussing not only certainly exist but have already been to Earth.

In 1834 the astronomer Johann Friedrich Bessel observed that the star Sirius appeared to wobble, and to explain the movement he proposed that there must be a very massive and heavy star in orbit around Sirius. No such object was observable, although in 1862 a tiny speck of light was noted where the companion star should be and was named Sirius B (see Plate 37). Only in the present century has the mystery of how the tiny Sirius B could affect Sirius A been solved, for astronomers now know that there is a rare type of star – a white dwarf – which does not emit much light but is tremendously powerful gravitationally because the matter of which it is composed is super-dense, so dense in fact that a match-box full of it would weigh more than a ton. Sirius B has been studied by astronomers and has been found to describe an elliptical orbit around Sirius A every fifty years. Its movement is consistent with the principles of celestial mechanics established by Johannes Kepler, who worked out that when one celestial body orbits another it does so elliptically and the body it moves around is not situated at the centre of the ellipse but at one of its two foci.

This is all rather recherché knowledge, but apparently every detail of it has been known for centuries by the Dogon, an African tribe who live in Mali in the southern Sahara. The Dogon have traditions, preserved in their tribal lore and illustrated in their art, that they were long ago visited and instructed in the arts of civilisation by beings from a planet that orbits Sirius B. The belief could easily be dismissed as fanciful, except that the Dogon have a theory of the Sirius system which fits all the known scientific facts. Temple summarises:

They know that the star is invisible, but they know it is there nevertheless. They know that the star's orbital period is fifty years, which it really is. They know that Sirius A is not at the centre of its orbit, which it is not. They know that Sirius A is at one of the foci of Sirius B's elliptical orbit, which it is. They know that Sirius B is the smallest kind of star, which it is (barring totally invisible collapsing neutron stars). They know that Sirius B is composed of a special kind of material which is called sagala, from a root meaning 'strong', and that this material does not exist on the earth. They know that material is heavier than all the iron on earth, etc., all of which is perfectly true.

"It's not one of ours."

(Reproduced by courtesy of Michael ffolkes)

How did the Dogon discover all this, if not as they claim, by contact with extraterrestrial visitors? That is the Sirius mystery. And the mystery deepens when we learn how the Dogon describe the visitors, for they say that they were amphibious beings, and in drawings they represent them with fish-like tails. The reader may recall that in Chapter 3 we discussed an identical tradition concerning an amphibious culture-bearer associated with the origins of the oldest known civilisation on Earth, that of Sumer. Temple follows up this hint and discovers other remarkable correspondences between Sumerian and Dogon traditions, and also evidence that the ancient Egyptians and Greeks were contacted and instructed by extraterrestrials. The proposition would seem preposterous if Temple's presentation were not utterly cool and level-headed and his scholarship impeccable.

The Sirius mystery is the most persuasive evidence that we have of the existence of the space people and of prehistoric contact with them, and if Project Cyclops is ever mounted the Sirius system certainly should, as Temple urges, be investigated thoroughly even though exobiologists consider the possibility of life existing within it to be slim.

7 The UFO Phenomenon

Of all the tales of alleged close encounters with extraterrestrial beings, that of Betty and Barney Hill may be the best known but it remains one of the most intriguing, for at first the Hills were not aware that they had had a close encounter and never sought to exploit it. The full story emerged only by chance some time after the incident, and subsequent research turned up a number of facts that seemed to authenticate it.

The Hills, a racially mixed couple, were returning from a holiday in Canada in September 1961. It was night and they were driving along a lonely road in New Hampshire when they noticed a brightly luminous object in the sky ahead of them. The object came nearer, and in order to observe it better Barney stopped the car and got out, taking with him a pair of binoculars. He became alarmed when the object came closer still and swooped down towards them. He could see that it was some sort of craft. It had flashing lights and two rows of portholes through which uniformed figures with strange eyes were peering down at him. Barney rushed back to his car and drove away as quickly as he could. Two hours later he was thirty-five miles further along his route and neither he nor his wife had any recollection of what had happened during the intervening period.

The Hills reported the sighting of the UFO to the nearby Pease Air Force Base and to the independent UFO research organisation NICAP (National Investigations Committee on Aerial Phenomena). Some days after the experience, Betty Hill started having disturbing dreams, and for some time both she and Barney manifested symptoms of physical and mental distress which eventually led to their being referred to a Boston psychiatrist, Dr Benjamin Simon. Dr Simon, who was well known for his success with amnesia cases, hypnotised Betty and Barney in order to find out what had happened during the two hours between their fleeing from the UFO and finding themselves thirty-five miles nearer home. Under hypnosis the couple produced accounts, with many corresponding details, of how they had been abducted aboard the UFO, subjected to a medical examination, and then released after being given a post-hypnotic suggestion that they should forget all about the experience.

Describing the creatures that had abducted them, Betty said they were about five feet tall, had large chests, long noses, broad foreheads, eyes like those of cats, dark hair, and greyish skin. Barney described them as having large heads tapering down to the chin, eyes that were elongated round the sides of their heads, thin and straight lips, slits in the face for nostrils, and 'grayish, almost metallic-looking', skin. Betty said she had the impression that there were two different types of being, and that the leader and medical examiner were distinct from the crew members, which may explain why her description differed from Barney's in some details. Their accounts corresponded, though, in stating that they had had a medical examination which apparently included some kind of sex test. Barney said that the aliens had done something in the region of his groin and lower abdomen, and Betty reported that she had had a long needle inserted into her navel.

The fact that under hypnosis the Hills independently recalled the same sequence of events and many corresponding details from the 'lost' two hours of their lives has been taken by believers in the extraterrestrial visitation hypothesis as positive proof that the landing and the abduction actually took place. Dr Simon, however, was not persuaded of this and took the view that the entire episode was a creation of Betty Hill's subconscious mind. Barney, in Dr Simon's view, had acquired the details of the event through Betty's telling him about the nightmares she had started having a few days after their experience. This would appear to be a rational explanation of the correspondences between their two accounts, and it could be argued that the Hills' need for psychiatric treatment was not a product of their experience but existed prior to it and that the reported incident was a shared hallucination. On the other hand, their accounts corresponded remarkably in some details with other close encounter reports with which they could not have been acquainted. Furthermore, as Jacques Vallée discovered when he investigated the case, military radar had picked up an anomalous object in the sky at precisely the time and place of the Hill's reported experience. As usual with UFO sighting or encounter tales, when all the facts and theories are taken into account we find ourselves left with irreducible ambiguity.

The reader will recall that other bizarre abduction case briefly related in Chapter 3, of the Brazilian farmer Antonio Villas-Boas who was taken aboard a UFO and seduced by a strange female. Here again we have a case that can easily be dismissed as an erotic fantasy but with features that are irreconcilable with such an explanation. The doctor who examined Villas-Boas after his experience reported that the ulcers and recurrent sickness that caused him to seek medical aid were caused by exposure to radiation, and that there were two marks on his chin where he said that a specimen of his blood had been extracted. Also, when Villas-Boas's description of his seductress is compared with Barney Hill's description of the beings that abducted him, there are clear correspondences. 'Her eyes,' he said, 'were more elongated than round, being slanted outwards . . . the

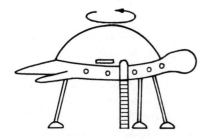

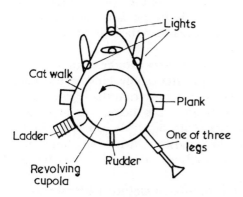

Sketch by Villas-Boas of the craft he saw and of the hieroglyphs on the side of the craft

cheekbones were very high, making the face very wide; but then, immediately below, the face narrowed very sharply, terminating in a pointed chin . . . Her lips were very thin, hardly visible.' These features, the elongated eyes, the triangular face, and the thin lips, are no doubt ones that might be attributed to an imaginary alien, but the fact that they should all three occur in the descriptions of two alleged abductees in two widely separated areas neither of whom could have seen or heard the other's report, is a coincidence so remarkable that one might well wonder whether it is attributable purely to chance.

Early in the morning of 1 July, 1965, a French Provençal farmer, Maurice Masse, had an experience of a close encounter with creatures similar to those described by Villas-Boas and Barney Hill. He came upon them in a field of lavender, where they were bending over a plant. Masse thought at first that they were mischievous boys and were deliberately spoiling his plants, but close to them there was a vehicle shaped like a rugby football and standing on six legs. When Masse drew close to the trespassers one of them turned and pointed a pencil-shaped instrument at him which somehow immobilised him. He had time to observe the creatures, which he described as about four feet tall, with large eyes that slanted away round the sides of their faces, slit mouths without muscular lips, high cheeks, and very pointed chins. Masse could not have read any account of the Hill or Villas-Boas encounters, so the similarity of his description of the aliens to the ones they gave is remarkable.

When the French UFO researcher Aimé Michel interviewed Masse in Valensole he found another interesting correspondence with a reported UFO landing a year before at Socorro in New Mexico. A policeman, Lonnie Zamora, had come across two 'small adults or large kids' beside a strange machine which they had quickly entered when they saw him, and which, like the one Masse saw, then took off and flew away silently at great speed. Michel had taken with him to Valensole a photograph of a model constructed from Zamora's description of the object he had seen, and when he showed this picture to Masse the farmer was astonished and thought at first that it was an actual photograph of the craft he had found standing in his lavender field.

In the UFO literature there are numerous tales like these, manifesting remarkable correspondences which imply that some kind of objective reality must be involved. Many of the tales suggest that the Earth and its flora and fauna, including human beings, are being systematically studied by somebody. There are stories of strange little men being found stealing vegetables, flowers, barks and mosses, farm tools, and even clothes from wash lines, and making off in flying machines as soon as they were seen.

In 1897 a Kansas farmer, Alex Hamilton, together with two other witnesses, reported seeing one of his cows winched up into a flying machine hovering about fifty feet above ground level. Such tales are preposterous, but they are extraordinarily common and consistent. An American scientist and writer, Ivan T. Sanderson, has accepted the extraterrestrial visitation hypothesis and posed the question why, if the visitors are so competent technically as to be able to travel interstellar distances, they have to resort to such primitive methods of collecting. 'I have only one answer to this conundrum,' Sanderson writes. 'This is simply . . . that this lot is only one of many different intelligences that have

38 One of three 'flying-saucer nests' found in Northern Queensland in the mid 'sixties (*Courtesy of Associated Press*)

39 Photograph taken by a young girl in North-Eastern Bohemia in September 1965 (*Courtesy of Syndication International*)

40 In 1961 a UFO was reported to have landed on a Wisconsin Chicken farm – Joe Simonton, the farmer, apparently received a strange oatcake from the unidentified travellers (*Courtesy of Philip Daly*)

41 Barney and Betty Hill (*Courtesy of Philip Daly*)

42 Artist's impression of a high altitude view of the lunar Cyclops array (*Courtesy of NASA*)

43 Three Arecibo type spherical antennas constructed within natural craters on the far side of the moon (*Courtesy of NASA*)

38

39

40

41

42

43

visited this planet . . . and they seem not to have been quite ready to do a proper job . . . ' It is a wild conjecture, but if the internal correspondences of the numerous tales of abductions and thefts by strange creatures in flying machines are taken as evidence that such visits really have taken place, no conjecture can be stranger than the facts it seeks to explain.

Most people will not be so convinced as Sanderson was of the extraterrestrial visitation hypothesis, and will prefer to seek a psychological explanation of the phenomenon. The view that accounts of sightings and encounters are all hoaxes or lies does not stand up to long scrutiny. The idea that there exists what has been called a 'flying saucer psychosis', that tales told in newspapers or books excite people's imaginations and thus generate more tales, and that the generation of such tales is symptomatic of the stresses, fears, anxieties, and frustrated aspirations of modern man, would appear more plausible. If this is the case, however, one would expect to find that psychological and sociological analysis of significant numbers of people who claim to have seen or encountered UFOs or their occupants reveal common characteristics. For instance, one would expect the majority of reports to emanate from areas where the incidence of psychosis is relatively high, namely areas of high population density, and one would expect the typical person involved to be unstable, highly imaginative, and probably rather irresponsible. If such common characteristics were found among reporters of UFO sightings, the probability that the phenomenon was purely psychological would be enhanced.

There have been too few scientific studies along these lines, but one has been undertaken and published by Jacques Vallée. Based on 200 reported landings in 1954, the majority of them in France, the analysis produces some very interesting findings. Vallée plotted the reported French landings on a map, and found that they tended to be in sparsely populated areas. Indeed, Paris and its environs, where one-third of the population of France lived and where the incidence of psychosis would be expected to be relatively high, did not contribute a single report. There was a total of 624 persons connected with the sightings, with a roughly equal distribution of men, women and children. Most witnesses were family men or women who held steady jobs and often positions of social responsibility. Less than half of the observations were made by only one witness, and in eighteen of the cases people who had no connection with each other independently reported observing the same phenomenon. Furthermore, sightings tended to cluster in groups of three or four within fairly small areas over

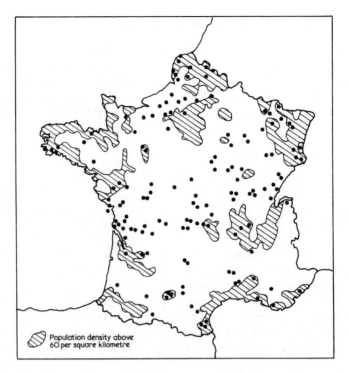

Vallée's map of France which shows the plots of UFO landings reported in 1954

specific periods of time, and there were notable correspondences in the witnesses' descriptions of the UFOs and their occupants. All descriptions of the latter were of human or humanoid creatures, and one-third of them made the point that they were of exceptionally short stature. Vallée does not canvass the extraterrestrial visitation hypothesis in his report, but he does rather effectively demolish the psychological hypothesis and establish the existence of a cluster of hard facts that are not to be so glibly explained away.

The observations of landed UFOs and their occupants and the reports of their experiences given by contactees would be the most interesting and important documents of our time if the extraterrestrial visitation hypothesis were true, but on the whole the writings produced by *soi-disant* contactees have not been such as to carry the conviction that they emanated from a higher intelligence. One fact that argues in favour of the authenticity of the experiences of such people as the Barney Hills, Villas-Boas, and Maurice Masse is that they made no attempt to publicise or exploit their bizarre experiences. But in the 1950s scientists and intelligent people generally were deterred from giving the UFO phenomenon serious consideration by the outrageous claims and jejune fantasies promulgated by a number of contactees, some of whom might have been quite sincere pseudo-religious cranks, although others were undoubtedly opportunists cashing in on the human appetite for signs and wonders.

The typical story was that the contactee had met some Ufonauts in some remote place, had been taken aboard their craft, and had been given a quick spin around the solar system while his new-found friends told him about their own utopian civilisation and expressed their concern about the way things were going on Earth. He was then returned to the spot where the encounter had taken place and charged with the mission of conveying to the world a message which, if heeded, would avert the impending collapse of civilisation. The appeal of tales told after this formula was itself a phenomenon of psychological interest, although the only distinguished psychologist who saw it that way was Carl Jung; others, probably mindful of their reputations, preferred to regard it as an ephemeral fad and the literature itself as cynical and mendacious commercialism. But not only did books with such titles as *Flying Saucers Have Landed*, *Aboard a Flying Saucer*, *The Secret of the Saucers*, and *From Outer Space to You*, become best-sellers, but also their authors became cult figures with a following of eager believers, and were able to augment the income from their considerable book sales with rich pickings on the lecture circuit and such spin-offs as albums of 'Saturnian' music.

The whole phenomenon was certainly of psychological and sociological interest, but it did not help the cause of serious research in Ufology, for the ill odour in which the contactees were held by the intelligentsia rubbed off on any of the latter who ventured to profess a scientific interest in the subject. Consequently the important question of whether or not there really were things in our skies that were not of terrestrial origin was generally considered to be disqualified from serious investigation by its very preposterousness.

The defence forces of the advanced nations could not, however, afford to be so dismissive. During World War II many Allied pilots had reported strange disc-shaped objects which followed or flew alongside them. At first it was thought that they might be enemy secret weapons, for the Allies did not know that German and Japanese pilots were having the same experiences and entertaining the same suspicions. However, it soon became clear that the 'foo-fighters', as they were called, were not hostile, so no thorough investigation of the phenomenon was undertaken. Soon after the war American intelligence became curious about a number of reports of mysterious cigar-shaped objects seen in the skies over Scandinavia, for they thought that these might be developments of Russian military technology, but again investigations were curtailed when the phenomenon seemed not to constitute any threat to security. But when people started seeing unidentified flying objects in the skies over the United States, the interest of the Defense Department was definitely aroused.

The strange bright green creature spotted by a family in Hopkinsville, Kentucky in 1955
The creature is reported to have appeared with several others and to have terrorised the
family by clambering onto their roof and remaining there all night

In June 1947 Kenneth Arnold, a businessman, reported that on a solo
flight in his private plane he had seen nine disc-shaped objects flying in
close formation at a speed he estimated at 1,700 mph. He described their
movement as undulating and like 'a saucer skipping over the water'. The
newspapers took up his analogy and coined the term 'flying saucer,'
which stuck – probably because to believers it suggested an artifact and to
non-believers it was derisory. When Arnold's sighting was publicised
people all over the country began to report similar experiences, many of
which had occurred months before. By the end of the year newspapers
had published accounts of some 850 sightings. At the beginning of 1948
the US Air Force set up a special investigatory body, code-named Project
Sign, with a brief to 'collect, collate, evaluate and distribute . . . all the
information concerning sightings and phenomena in the atmosphere
which can be construed to be of concern to the national security'.

There has been a great deal of controversy about the part that
government agencies have played in UFO investigations. It is widely
believed that vital information has been withheld from the public; that
'they' know full well that UFOs are extraterrestrial vehicles; and even that
a landing has occurred and been filmed at a secret Air Force base. These
rumours circulate at high levels. I heard the one about a landing having
occurred from a well known scientist connected with the Stanford
Research Institute. Recently I have heard another rumour, said to be top-
secret information disclosed by a famous astronaut, that an alien
spaceship has crashed in Mexico, killing two of its crew but leaving one
survivor, who is in custody. The site of the crash is said to be heavily
guarded, and it is alleged that an international cover-up operation is

under way. It is impossible to know what to make of such hearsay, but since the publication, in 1975, of Professor David Jacobs' study, *The UFO Controversy in America*, it has been clear that it has long been US official policy to explain away or debunk UFO phenomena. It would be a natural extension of this policy to conceal or misrepresent any hard facts that came to light.

In 1948, Project Sign produced a report on 243 of the best documented sightings. It reported that 'simple and understandable' causes had been found for most of the phenomena, but concluded that there was no definite evidence whether or not UFOs constituted a security threat to the US, and recommended continued study. The project's code name was then changed to 'Project Grudge', and the following year a report on a further 244 cases was published, which came to the conclusion that 'The phenomena present no threat to the security of the United States and the vast majority of sightings are misrepresentations of conventional objects'. However, 23 per cent of the cases investigated could not be explained by the Project Grudge staff and these were dismissed as probably attributable to psychological factors.

Many of the cases that were explained were very dubiously dismissed. For intance, there was the case of an Air Force pilot who had seen a light in the sky and approached to investigate it only to find it take 'evasive action'. The pilot had manoeuvred for ten minutes to get close to the object, and it too had manoeuvred, apparently deliberately to avoid him, although he had once got close enough to see that it was a 'dark gray and oval-shaped'. After the ten minutes of aerobatics, the UFO sped away and the pilot landed his plane. When he reported his experience it was found that four other Air Force personnel had witnessed precisely the events he described from their position on the ground. Project Grudge reported the case and explained that the object had been a weather balloon, despite the fact that the witnesses testified that its movements had been relative to the pilot's manoeuvres and that the Air Weather Service had stated categorically that it was 'definitely not a balloon'. This kind of glib dismissal of anomalies was to be typical of official reports of UFOs for the next twenty years.

Since 1947–8, UFO sightings have tended to come in waves, the biggest being that of 1952, by which time Project Grudge had become rather dormant. Its consultant on matters astronomical, Professor J. Allen Hynek of the University of Ohio, who had originally accepted his post in a spirit of levity, underwent a dramatic change of attitude as a result of the torrent of reports that he was required to assess in 1952. He even began to consider seriously the extraterrestrial visitation hypothesis which a number of writers had already put forward as an explanation of the phenomenon. A total of 1,501 cases were entered in Air Force files in 1952, and after investigation no less than 303 of these remained unexplained.

The type of case that shook Hynek's original scepticism was one which was witnessed by individuals familiar with anomalous aerial phenomena and in which visual sighting of the UFO was corroborated by simultaneous radar detection. In July 1952 there occurred a dramatic series of such sightings in the vicinity of Washington, DC. A number of reports of sightings of unusual objects had been made by commercial airline crews in the days prior to 19 July, when a group of UFOs appeared on two radarscopes at Washington National Airport. Reports by airline crews of erratically moving lights in the skies, which corresponded with the radar returns, caused the Chief Radar Controller to recommend an interception, but when the jets approached their targets the UFOs just seemed to disappear, both out of sight and off the radarscopes. Their erratic peregrinations were not over, however. Throughout the night ground observers and radarscopes continued to register corresponding observations of luminous objects in the sky, and on one occasion the Washington National Airport radar detected an object which appeared to be located directly above the radio tower at Andrews Air Force Base in Maryland.

When the radio operators at the Andrews Base were informed of this they rushed outside and saw what one of them described as 'a huge fiery-orange sphere' hovering above them. The UFOs put on a similar performance the following week, in the course of which interceptor jets played a kind of game of tag with them while radar operators watched, but none of the pilots got close enough to see anything more substantial than lights in the sky.

The location of these sightings, and the fact that the objects had several times entered the restricted air space above the White House and the Capitol, really worried the security people and caused the press to call for the disclosure of all the facts of the case. The Air Force held a press conference at which scientists calmly explained that the phenomena were attributable to abnormal atmospheric conditions and, somewhat inconsistently, the director of Air Force intelligence assured reporters that the responsible authorities were confident that UFOs did not constitute a threat to national security.

The CIA, however, apparently did not share this view, for they got together a distinguished panel of non-military scientists to investigate the UFO data. The Robertson Panel, as it was called after its chairman, reviewed a selection of UFO reports and came to the conclusion that UFOs themselves were not a threat to national security. But it warned that 'the continued emphasis on the reporting of these phenomena does, in these parlous times, result in a threat to the orderly functioning of the protective organs of the body politic', because there was a danger of mass hysteria which an enemy could exploit. There was also a possibility that 'actual enemy artifacts' might be ignored if people misidentified them as UFOs.

The Panel recommended a programme of public education with two aspects: 'training and "debunking" ', in other words, teaching the public to recognise natural effects which could produce spurious 'UFOs' and disposing them to regard the ones that could not easily be explained away as the hoaxes or hallucinations of 'nut cases'. The CIA conveyed the Robertson Panel's recommendations to the Air Force, who then adopted them as official policy.

Professor Jacobs relates a fascinating anecdote about CIA involvement in the UFO controversy. In 1959 a woman psychic who claimed to be in touch with space people was brought to the attention of the CIA. A Canadian government UFO expert had investigated her and had been astonished to find that in trance, by means of automatic writing, she could produce highly sophisticated and technical details about space flight.

Two US Intelligence officers were sent to investigate her, and the woman suggested that the best way they could confirm her claims would be for one of them to go into trance himself and contact the space people. One of them tried, without success, but later, at CIA headquarters, he was persuaded to try again and this time apparently was able to establish contact with space people. His CIA colleagues, six of whom were in the room at the time, were naturally sceptical, and asked if any sort of proof could be given. The entranced officer, through whom the space people were supposed to be communicating, said that if they looked out of the window they would see a flying saucer. The witnesses rushed to the window and indeed, to their astonishment, saw a UFO. Simultaneously, it was later discovered, the Washington National Airport radar had been blocked out in the direction of the sighting. This incident was never satisfactorily explained, and the CIA men involved were reprimanded by their superiors and transferred to other positions, which suggests that it caused the Agency some embarrassment, as indeed it would since the Robertson Panel's views were the official truth about UFOs.

Newspaper editors, on the whole, were persuaded of the truth of the official line, and they ably abetted the Air Force programme of 'training and "debunking" ', a task which was made easier for them by the rise of the contactees with their tall tales. Private UFO organisations contested the official views and harassed the Air Force to disclose all the information that its investigative body, which now went by the code name 'Project Blue Book', had amassed. Prominent among these was NICAP (National Investigations Committee on Aerial Phenomena), which was energetically led by Donald E. Keyhoe, a retired Marine major who championed the view that 'living, intelligent observers from another planet' were responsible for the UFO phenomena.

NICAP's campaign was assisted by the occurrence of another wave of sightings in 1957, and for some eight years thereafter the Air Force and the private UFO organisations did battle, although the controversy

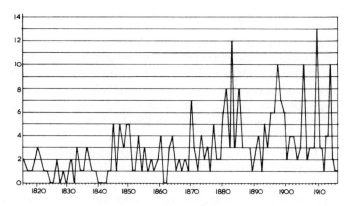

Annual reports of UFO sightings 1815–1915

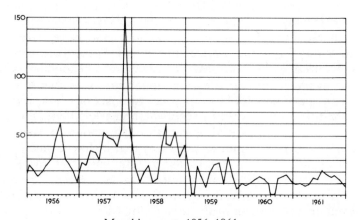

Monthly reports 1956–1961

received little publicity. It was not until a prolonged wave of sightings occurred between 1965 and 1968, that the scientific community really started to show interest in UFOs. When this happened the Air Force turned over the investigations to the University of Colorado and a committee chaired by the distinguished physicist Edward U. Condon.

It was hoped that there would now be a really thorough and objective investigation of the UFO evidence. Unfortunately the hope was not fulfilled, for the Condon committee acted as if its purpose was to continue the Air Force policy of explaining away and debunking UFO reports. The majority of the reports that it investigated were therefore of a kind that lent themselves to such treatment, and when it confronted a phenomenon that defied explanation it came up with pronouncements of transparent evasiveness, such as : 'This unusual sighting should be assigned to the category of some almost certainly natural phenomenon which is so rare that it apparently has never been reported before or since'.

Condon himself had made no secret of his negative attitude to UFOs, and in interviews just after his appointment he had stated: 'My attitude right now is that there's nothing to it,' and 'there's just no evidence that there is advanced life on other planets'; so it was not really surprising that the committee's Report should have been negative. On the one hand it is understandable that responsible and intelligent men should have been concerned not to give unstable people any encouragement to focus their fears or their hopes on UFOs, but on the other hand it is clear that the Condon committee did not employ strictly scientific and impartial principles in its investigations and was therefore deceiving the public in presenting its conclusions as the considered verdict of Science on the UFO question.

Scientists of other persuasions were not slow to criticise the committee's methods and conclusions. Condon's most vehement critic was Dr James McDonald, Professor of Atmospheric Sciences at the University of Arizona. McDonald returned to some of the original source materials that the Committee had assessed, and he found that in their Report there had been so many *non sequiturs*, omissions of relevant data, and instances of highly conjectural conclusions being presented as proven facts as to render the Report 'quite inadequate' as a scientific document. At a symposium on UFOs held under the auspices of the American Association for the Advancement of Science in 1969, McDonald re-examined four cases which he claimed that the Condon committee had inadequately investigated and explained, and he stated:

it is difficult for me to see any reasonable alternative to the hypothesis that *something in the nature of extraterrestrial devices engaged in something in the nature of surveillance lies at the heart of the UFO problem.*

Having thus gone out on a limb, McDonald went on to deplore the fact that

while a large body of UFO evidence now seems to point in no other direction than the extraterrestrial hypothesis, the profoundly important implications of that possibility are going unconsidered by the scientific community because this entire problem has been imputed to be little more than a nonsense matter unworthy of serious scientific attention.

McDonald canvassed his views energetically, and although he drew the fire of some fellow scientists (Condon called him 'a kook'), others were persuaded by him that the UFO phenomenon was real and constituted a challenge to science.

People trained in scientific disciplines are loath to deal with anecdotal evidence or to entertain theories which it is impossible to disprove experimentally. Carl Sagan has pointed out that the extraterrestrial hypothesis is only one of many equally plausible explanations of UFOs, and he asks: 'What is the critical test for disproving the hypothesis that UFOs are angels' halos?' The implication is that there is no conceivable test, and therefore that the hypothesis – and the extraterrestrial hypothesis likewise – is unscientific, a matter of faith upon which science can say nothing.

What science can concern itself with, however, is the question of whether there exists a class of phenomenon among the UFO reports that defies explanation in terms of known science. If there is, and even if it is as little as 1 or 2 per cent of the cases, this irreducible residue is something that responsible scientists ought to keep an open mind about. The majority of scientists who have looked into the question would admit that there is at least such a percentage of utterly inexplicable phenomena. In fact if only a fraction of a per cent of UFO sightings were authentic the extraterrestrial hypothesis would be strengthened, for a telling argument against it is that there could surely be no cost-effective rationale for an alien civilisation to have so many spacecraft whizzing about our skies, whatever their purpose.

One way in which scientific method can help probe the UFO enigma is by statistical studies. In many areas where ambiguities are rife, application of information theory and statistical methods has facilitated the separation of 'signal' from 'noise' and distinct patterns have emerged indicative of a non-random and objective reality. In UFO studies Jacques Vallée has pioneered this approach. The suggestive patterns that emerged from his analysis of 200 reports of observations made in 1954 have already been noted. In another very interesting study he took reports of 100 close encounter cases from Spanish sources and compared their contents statistically with 1,176 cases reported from other parts of the world. He found a number of correlations. For instance, in 60 per cent of the non-Iberian cases and in 53 per cent of the Iberian cases the object was observed on the ground. In 35 per cent and 38 per cent respectively it was observed near the ground; in 32 per cent and 25 per cent respectively occupants of the vehicles were observed. As Hynek said of this study in his 1972 book, *The UFO Experience*: 'A correlation such as this would be accorded high significance in recognised disciplines such as sociology or economics. It points strongly to the existence of "invariants" in sightings of a given category.'

In 1973–4 there occurred another wave of sightings and encounters which gave the public and scientists more data to work on and kept the UFO debate going. Among them, Professor Jacobs summarises, were high-level and distant sightings, low-level sightings, car-chasing incidents, sightings causing electrical and/or mechanical effects or interference, sightings affecting animals, sightings affecting people physically, sightings causing psychological and mental effects on people, landings with traces left behind, and occupant cases.

There were also, no doubt, a number of hoaxes, such as the report by two fishermen from Pascagoula, Mississippi, that they had been abducted aboard a flying saucer and medically examined by five-foot tall creatures that had cone-shaped appendages for nose and ears, slits for eyes and mouth, gray and wrinkled skin, and that moved by floating through the air. The publicity given the Pascagoula fishermen case did not help the cause of serious research into the phenomena, but some of the other categories of sighting listed by Jacobs included cases of unquestionable authenticity which are very puzzling.

There was, for instance, the case of the army helicopter with a crew of four men which, on the night of 18 October 1973, was apparently involved in a near-collision with a UFO. Flying near Mansfield, Ohio, the pilot, Captain Lawrence Coyne, noticed a bright red light which appeared to be flying parallel with his helicopter. He asked his crew chief to keep an eye on the light. He did, and soon reported that it was getting brighter and appeared to be converging on them on a collision course. The pilot put the helicopter into a dive, but still the glowing red object seemed to be headed straight towards them. The crew had given up hope of avoiding collision when, as Coyne later explained:

We looked up and there was this object, right over us. Stopped! The best way I can describe the object is it was approximately fifty to sixty feet long . . . The leading edge of the craft was a bright-red light. The trailing edge had a green light, and you could delineate where the light stopped and the gray metallic structure began . . . The trailing light on the aft end of the craft . . . flooded the cockpit with a green light.

He estimated that the strange craft was about 500 feet above them. After remaining stationary for a few seconds, it sped away, made a climbing turn and disappeared. Coyne consulted his cockpit instruments and was astonished to see that the helicopter was climbing at a rate of 1,000 feet per minute, as if it was being drawn up in the wake of the UFO. When eventually he and his crew landed safely, Coyne immediately made a report to Federal Aviation Administration officials, who later testified to investigators that he had 'sounded emotionally shaken'.

The army helicopter case is one that the staunchest critic of the extraterrestrial hypothesis, Philip J. Klass, has ingeniously analysed in his book *UFOs Explained*. He explains that the UFO was probably a meteor-fireball, and cites examples to illustrate how even experienced meteorists can be very far out in their judgements of the distances and movements of these objects. The helicopter's sudden climb he attributes to automatic and unconscious action on the part of the pilot in order to avoid crashing into the ground. He does not suggest that Coyne and his crew were lying or deliberately inventing any details of the sighting. However, he believes that the description of the craft was supplied by their imaginations and that the whole story can be quite logically explained as an understandable malobservation of a rarely-encountered natural phenomenon which, because of its rarity, is the more alarming on the odd occasion when it is met with. In support of his hypothesis he points out that a major meteor shower, the Orionids, occurs annually and reaches its peak activity during the week when this incident occurred.

Klass is a very persuasive critic of the UFO idea, and readers of his two books (*UFOs Identified* is the other) might easily be convinced that to use the term unidentified flying object is to confess ignorance of science and of anomalous aerial phenomena. Yet James McDonald was a Professor of Atmospheric Sciences, and when Hynek discreetly canvassed fellow astronomers he found that 5 per cent of them had seen a UFO. Such men could hardly be considered naive about aerial phenomena. Another problem with Klass's analyses is that when it is necessary to explain physical effects associated with reported UFO sightings or landings he generally has to fall back on the fraud or hoax hypothesis, and cases that cannot be so explained, for instance when a person has suffered hurt or injury from an encounter, do not fall within his purview.

Let us consider some of these physical effects cases, for such evidence is germane not only to the question of whether UFOs exist but also to the question of what they are up to.

In early October 1973, at about dawn, a truck driver was driving near Cape Giradeau in Missouri when he noticed in his rear-view mirror an object with red and yellow lights which he estimated was about a mile behind. The object seemed to be about four or five feet off the ground. It rapidly gained on him, and when it was not far behind the truck he observed that it was turnip shaped, about thirty feet in diameter, and was constructed in three sections, the top and middle of which were spinning.

The driver put his head out of the window and looked back, and when he did so the UFO began to rise and a spotlight came out of it. He also noticed a humming noise which rose in pitch as the object gained height. Then suddenly there was a bright white flash and the driver was struck in the face by something. He screamed that he was blinded and pulled the truck to an emergency stop. His wife, who was beside him but had seen nothing, noticed that his brow was red and hot, the frames of his glasses were melted, and a lens had fallen out. She called an ambulance and the driver was taken to hospital. Five days after the incident he still had only

20 per cent vision. A physicist who examined his glasses said that the frames had apparently been melted from the inside.

There are a considerable number of cases similar to this in the UFO literature, a selection of which has been written up by Brad Steiger and Joan Whritenour in their books *Flying Saucers are Hostile* and *The New UFO Breakthrough*. People have been injured, maimed, blinded, even killed, in mysterious circumstances which they or witnesses to their misfortune have associated with UFO activity. People have also manifested psychological aberrations at the time or subsequent to UFO sightings or encounters, and although it is easy to allege that the aberration must have been the cause rather than the effect of the sighting no correlation between psychological instability and UFO-sighting has been found. To assume on the basis of this type of evidence that UFOs are spacecraft from an alien world which has hostile designs upon planet Earth and its inhabitants is not justifiable, but the evidence certainly has to be taken into account in any attempt to assess the UFO phenomenon.

The evidence afforded by so-called 'trace cases', ie cases in which an observed UFO has left behind some trace of its visit, must also be considered. There have been many cases of scorched vegetation, marks on the ground such as might have been made by a craft's landing-gear, or readings of a high level of radioactivity being found at sites where landings have been observed. Mysteriously, in a number of cases, grass roots have been scorched but not the grass itself. In the previously-discussed Socorro case – the landing witnessed by policeman Lonnie Zamora – which Philip Klass argues was a fraud perpetrated to draw some attention and some money to the depressed town in central New Mexico, it is said that traces of a metal supposedly scraped from the craft when it hit against a rock proved on analysis at NASA laboratories to be of an alloy unknown on Earth. NASA, however, denied this and said the substance was silicon, but even so the question remains how silicon got there.

White rings, which some researchers have identified with the fairy rings of folklore, have been found at many sites, as have masses of particles and small strips and shreds of aluminium and other metals. Queer artifacts have apparently fallen out of the sky all over the world. There have been metal balls and discs in profusion, and even objects with hieroglyphic-type script on them. Markings in similar script have been made by contactees who have tried to reproduce what they allegedly saw on their visit to the alien craft. The physical evidence for the reality of UFOs is substantial, but like all the other evidence it is ambiguous.

It is also sometimes quite absurd, as in the case of Joe Simonton (see Chapter 3), the chicken farmer who said he had been given three pancakes by the occupants of a flying saucer. Simonton suffered such ridicule that he told a reporter that if the incident occurred again he would not tell anyone about it. However, his preposterous story was, in part, later corroborated by insurance agent Savino Borgo, who reported a sighting of a flying saucer about a mile from Simonton's farm at about the same time as the farmer claimed that the incident had occurred. Such is the kind of ambiguity with which the investigator of the UFO phenomenon is confronted.

What to make of it all? Scientists accustomed to dealing with data that may be elusive but are not utterly preposterous and inconsistent with each other are disposed to dismiss the whole phenomenon as nonsense. The one thing that they know is capable of producing preposterousness and inconsistency in the human mind, so they say 'It's all in the mind', and, contented with that explanation, get back to the type of researches that they are equipped for and that they believe to be useful. But, as Hynek has pointed out, many aspects of modern science would be utterly incomprehensible to a nineteenth-century scientist, and there is going to be a twenty-first century science and probably a thirtieth-century science which is at present utterly incomprehensible to us and to which the UFO phenomenon may provide a key. Peremptory dismissal of the evidence because of its inherent ambiguity is scarcely scientific.

The question we are concerned with in the present context is whether reported UFO behaviour is a manifestation of alien intelligence. Chasing cars and blinding people, intimidating aircraft or playing tag or hide-and-seek with them, stealing plants and animals, and giving people pancakes and other bizarre souvenirs, are certainly intelligent actions, although hardly the type we would expect of higher intelligences. So much reported UFO activity is mischievous or simply silly, and is irreconcilable with the idea that they are spacecraft from another world accomplishing a mission on Earth. Nobody would go to all the trouble and expense of sending spacecraft to a world just for the fun of mystifying its inhabitants, would they? Or would they? There are, in fact, hypotheses that account for this type of behaviour, but most of the theories that have been put forward to explain the UFO phenomenon tend to ignore it or to attribute it to something else. They all tend to the view, though, that there is a non-human intelligence of some kind behind it.

Let us briefly review some of the most popular theories. Probably the best known is the one put forward by Erich von Daniken in his several books. Originally formulated by Russian physicist, Professor Agrest, the view is that we have clear evidence of extraterrestrial visitation in ancient times and therefore the possibility that it has occurred more recently, or is occurring today, is by no means preposterous. The evidence comes in various forms. There are works of ancient art, for instance, in the Sahara and in Mexico, that seem to depict spacemen, and there are ancient religious traditions that speak of gods or the sons of god descending to Earth. There are also mysterious ancient structures, such as those at Baalbek in Lebanon, that are evidence of an advanced

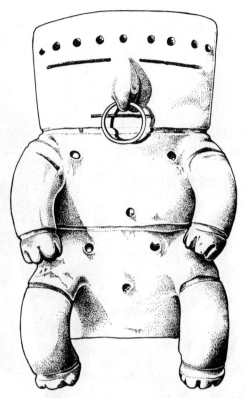

An unusual ancient ceramic figure found in South America, the kind of object used by researchers to suggest that alien intelligences visited Earth in antiquity

technology, and some ancient scientific ideas are not congruous with the level of development attained by the people who possessed them. Possibly the best evidence in this category, which neither Agrest nor von Daniken was aware of when the theory was first formulated, is the knowledge that the Dogon have of the Sirius system. Von Daniken has discredited the theory with his tendentious and unscholarly treatment of the evidence, which is unfortunate because some of the evidence merits serious thought.

A writer who has given serious consideration to the possibility that many events reported in ancient scriptures refer to interactions between human beings and extraterrestrials is Frenchman Paul Misraki. In his book *Les Extraterrestres* (published under the pseudonym Paul Thomas), Misraki interprets many mysterious events in the Bible and other scriptures in terms of such interactions. He points out correspondences between ancient scriptures, and also parallels with modern UFO reports, which suggest that contact with aliens occurred in many parts of the world in prehistoric times and is still occurring. He maintains that angels were extraterrestrials and points out that the Church did not teach that they were purely spiritual beings until the sixth century AD. Interestingly,

Compare this artist's impression of the humanoids described by various contactees with the creatures in Fig 7

he compares the Fatima apparitions and prophecies, which occurred in Portugal in 1917 and were witnessed by thousands of people, with both scriptural and modern accounts of encounters with UFOs, which is evidence strongly supportive of this theory that contact has been continuous throughout human history and has a religious significance.

People with a more scientific cast of mind have tended to interpret UFO activity in terms of exploration or surveillance of Earth by aliens. The theory was more plausible in 1954 – when it was first put forward following a wave of sightings all over the planet – than it is today because our own technology is now capable of detailed surveillance from great distances with a single automated vehicle that is virtually undetectable. So aliens, who must have a superior technology if they have managed to get into our vicinity, would surely not require multiple craft and low-level or direct contact in order to study us and our world. On the other hand, it might be maintained that the purpose of the study may not be objectively scientific, but may be preparatory to an attack on, and possible take-over bid for, our planet, and that the aliens do not mind us suspecting their existence because we are powerless to do anything about it. Indeed, their purpose may be helped by the state of nervousness and confusion such a suspicion can induce in us.

A variation on this theme has been put forward by two Christian writers, John Weldon and Zola Levitt in a book titled: *UFOs: What on Earth is Happening?* and sub-titled *The Coming Invasion*. These authors maintain that UFOs are not of extraterrestrial origin but the creations of demons from a parallel world performing a mission to prepare for the coming of Antichrist.

The parallel world or other dimension idea of the provenance of UFOs has in recent years become more popular with many Ufologists than the extraterrestrial hypothesis. Many advanced physicists entertain the idea that there may exist multiple worlds parallel to the one we know and therefore not separated by physical distance, and that, in certain circumstances, interactions between these worlds and ours may occur. Recent developments in quantum theory (known as 'Quantum Geometrodynamics') would permit such existences and interactions.

The UFO phenomenon can be interpreted in the light of these theories. Such an interpretation not only disposes of the difficulty of explaining why so many spacecraft would have travelled light-years just to fool about in our atmosphere, but also explains some of the puzzling behaviour of UFOs, particularly their way of apparently materialising and dematerialising at will. They do not really dematerialise, they just flip back into their own dimension.

It used to be poets and fantasists who produced ideas like that, but today it's professors of physics. Such men are also often involved in what is known as the consciousness movement, and have no difficulty with the idea that different realities are accessible to people in different states of consciousness. The most intriguing UFO theory, to my mind, is one put forward by such a man, Jacques Vallée, whose work has been referred to previously and who is an astrophysicist as well as a computer scientist.

The idea that UFOs are spacecraft from another planet, Vallée contends, is naive and fails to account for the diversity of their manifestations and behaviour. But the fact that people think of them in these terms is significant, and the belief may be an intended product of the phenomenon. 'With every new wave of UFOs', Vallée writes, 'the social impact becomes greater. More young people become fascinated by space, with psychic phenomena, with new frontiers in consciousness'. The congeries of diverse ideas and practises that people in the consciousness movement take up, from UFOs and extraterrestrial life to magic and meditation – a muddle that is anathema to the rational, lateral thinker – constitute a change in our awareness of reality which is already producing profound effects upon our culture. 'A subculture now exists in every country, based on the idea that humanity has a higher destiny', Vallée rightly observes, and he attributes the emergence of this subculture in part of the UFO phenomenon. 'UFOs are the means through which man's concepts are being rearranged,' he says. 'We are faced with a *technology* that transcends the physical and is capable of manipulating our reality, generating a variety of altered states of consciousness and of emotional perceptions. The purpose of that technology may be to change our concepts of the universe.'

To speak of a technology having a purpose implies, of course, that there is an intelligence behind it, an intelligence capable of conceiving the purpose and devising the technology. Vallée argues that reported UFO manifestations and behaviour, far from being random, preposterous, and unpredictable, are precisely the kind of effects that an intelligence seeking to bring about a fundamental change in a living species would create. Our behavioural scientists employ similar methods in experiments with animals, modifying their behaviour by reinforcing certain actions by rewarding them in various ways. They have found that 'the best schedule of reinforcement is one that combines periodicity with unpredictability', and, of course, the UFO phenomenon exhibits exactly this combination of features. The absurdity of many of the manifestations and their incompatibility with others has resulted in the rejection of the UFO phenomenon by the higher echelons of our society and culture, but this rejection has only precipitated the process of gradual modification of human consciousness at the subconscious level; and of course it is only at this profound level that enduring change can be effected.

Vallée's ideas may seem a case of *post hoc, propter hoc* reasoning, but of course if they are correct this is the only mode of reasoning by which man could arrive at them. Indeed, it is the way he would be *intended* to arrive at them, after a long period of exposure to ambiguity and anomaly had prepared his mind to be fertile ground for the nurture of such ideas. Vallée does not offer any speculations as to where in the universe, or multiverse, the controlling intelligence behind these subtly purposeful manifestations may exist, but he makes the point that the question may be irrelevant, that it may exist in a parallel dimension or in *time*. As the evidence we reviewed in Part Two implied, intelligence and purpose may exist independently of a corporeal vehicle, so such speculations are not inherently outlandish.

The idea that human consciousness is being manipulated, even though it be by a well-intentioned higher intelligence and to accomplish a further evolution of the species, is not one of unmitigated appeal. But of all the ideas that have been advanced to explain the UFO phenomenon it is the only one capable of accounting for all the facts, including the most puzzling one – that a putative higher intelligence should sometimes behave like a mischievous prankster. What we have been witnessing, perhaps, is an attempt to emancipate the human mind from its conceptual bonds of linearity and logicality and to make it capable of understanding and participating in a meta-logical reality. It is arguable that our terrestrial and human species chauvinism has cut us off from the sense of the cosmic and therefore from our own psychic wholeness, and that the UFO phenomenon is having the effect of putting people back in touch with the cosmos and with the profounder levels of their own being. If the point is conceded, it is only a small step to the assumption that the effect was intended and has been controlled.

Which brings us to our final chapter on the evidence for the existence of Higher Intelligence, or Supermind.

8 Supermind

There are hundreds, perhaps thousands, of people who believe they are, or have been, in communication with extraterrestrial Higher Intelligences, and they are not all in mental hospitals. In fact, many of them are very active and highly placed in our society. The American physicist Saul-Paul Sirag has said that he knows of more than a hundred scientists who have experienced such communications. John Lilly, whose investigations of dolphin intelligence were reviewed in Chapter 1, is one of them. In his 'autobiography of inner space', *The Centre of the Cyclone*, Lilly writes:

> Man's future lies with aware, courageous, informed, knowledgeable, experienced individuals in a loosely coupled exploratory communicating network. Such a network exists and functions ... throughout this planet. *I suspect it extends farther than our earth*, but this is yet to be publicly demonstrated unequivocally *beyond the private experience of myself and others*. (My italics.)

It is difficult to imagine how an objective test could be applied to the proposition that an intelligence that communicates telepathically or through a trance medium is really an extraterrestrial; for whatever is allegedly channelled through a human mind could theoretically have emanated from that mind. Yet people who have this experience generally become convinced of the objectivity and independence of the mind that they are communicating with. In some cases the communicator manifests over a period of time a distinct personality, and the content of the communications is so consistent, and themes are developed with such coherence, that there comes across a distinct sense of a powerful mind at work; a mind possessed of greater knowledge and wisdom than any human person participating in the communication has.

This is the case with the 'Seth' material channelled by the medium Jane Roberts and the communications from 'the Nine' channelled by Phyllis Schlemmer to scientist and psychic researcher Andrija Puharich and Englishman Sir John Whitmore. I recently published a long book on the latter material, in researching which I participated in some communication sessions when Phyllis Schlemmer went into trance and a *soi-disant* extraterrestrial spoke through her, and I therefore know from experience how impressive and convincing such communications can be. Although I remained doubtful about the extraterrestrial angle, I could not but be convinced that the communicator was a person quite distinct from Mrs Schlemmer or from any other person present.

Before I became involved in psychic research I used to have a very negative attitude to mediums and the phenomena of mediumship. I believed that most mediums were bogus and that their craft consisted in the heartless and despicable practice of bamboozling the bereaved. I also thought that they only channelled messages from so-called spirits, and that the content of such messages was invariably banal. I mention these preconceptions because others probably have them, and they are a block to serious consideration of the subject of this chapter. The main evidence that we have for the existence of higher intelligences is in the writings or utterances of mediums, and, if the sceptic maintains that this material must emanate from the mediums' own subconscious, he will have to concede that the subconscious minds of a number of people, most of them women, who under normal conditions show no great powers of thought or range of knowledge, are so creative, original, and broadly knowledgeable that they can plausibly simulate a more-than-human intelligence. Either these mediums are, as they believe, 'channels', or they are creative geniuses of the first order. I think that the evidence weighs heavily in favour of the former view.

The phenomenon has, of course, long been known. Socrates had his *daimon*, and many of the scriptures of the world's religions, not to mention many works of literature, have been written in circumstances which suggested that the writer was but an amanuensis and that the work was generated by another and higher mind. The psychoanalytic view is that the phenomenon can be explained as a 'downrush from the super-conscious', but I doubt whether anyone who has written or uttered this type of material would go along with that; for invariably the person has the sense of having been *used*. And it does seem that the incidence of the experience of contact with Higher Intelligence has increased tremendously in recent times. A psychoanalyst might explain this in terms of the survival of the need for a God-figure at a time when orthodox religions are in decline, although there are other explanations. Robert Anton Wilson has expressed the two alternative views rather well:

(1) It is all done by our own nervous systems. As we advance towards Higher Intelligence, our brains can increasingly affect the universe by quantum inseparability, creating first coincidences, then Jungian synchronicities, then seemingly external Superhuman Beings, who are really masks of the greater selves we are evolving into. (2) It is *not* all done by our nervous systems. As we advance towards Higher

Intelligence, our brains can increasingly contact other Higher Intelligences . . . This includes contact with advanced adepts who are both human and inhuman, terrestrial and extraterrestrial, and located temporally throughout what we call past, present and future.

Wilson, who is co-author of the three-volume SF novel *Illuminatus!*, believes that he has been in contact with Higher Intelligence, and, in his book *Cosmic Trigger*, he gives a fascinating account of his experiences, and those of a number of other contemporary contactees, notably his friend Dr Timothy Leary. Wilson's case is particularly interesting in the light of Temple's *The Sirius Mystery*, for before that book was published Wilson had experienced communications which he believed came from Sirius and had discovered that some of the key figures in modern occult philosophy, Helena Blavatsky, George Gurdjieff, and Aleister Crowley, all had connections with Sirius.

On 23 July 1973, Wilson awoke, as he says, 'with an urgent message from Dreamland', and scribbled quickly in his diary the words, 'Sirius is very important'. He did not know why it was important, but he did a bit of research. He was engaged in some occult studies at the time, and in a book on Aleister Crowley he read that Crowley had identified the source of his magical current as the star Sirius. He also found out that that very day, 23 July, was, according to Egyptian tradition, the day when the occult link between Earth and Sirius is most powerful. From that time on, odd things started happening. Wilson found himself saying or thinking things that turned out to be prophetic or clairvoyant, and he had a distinct sense of an entity who spoke to him and gave him all this information in 'a melodious and angelic voice' which he heard in his head. He wondered: 'Was it possible . . . had he actually . . . turned on and tuned in to an Earth-Sirius channel used by adepts since ancient Egypt?'

It was nearly three years later that Wilson discovered Temple's *Sirius Mystery*, and read with fascination his evidence that contact with beings from the Sirius system had occurred about 4500 BC. He admired Temple's scholarly tracing of connections with Sirius in the mystery religions of ancient Babylon, Egypt, and Greece, but he wished that the astronomer had also studied modern occultism; for his own discovery of the connections of Crowley, Gurdjieff, and Blavatsky with Sirius had convinced him that the contact had not been a once-for-all event but 'that methods of interstellar telepathy between Earth and the Sirius system had been discovered back then [4500 BC] and that many have been tuning in on that channel ever since'. Crowleyian 'magick', incidentally, Wilson regards as a 'system of contacting Higher Intelligence', and he has himself employed Crowleyian rituals for that purpose.

In July 1973, when Wilson had the first experience that he interpreted as a contact with Sirius, his friend Dr Timothy Leary, who was in prison at the time, formed 'a four-person telepathy team in an attempt to contact Higher Intelligences elsewhere in the galaxy'. The experiment comprised periods of meditation and discussion and resulted in the reception, ostensibly from an extraterrestrial intelligence, of a long message to the effect that mankind was now 'capable of communicating with and returning to the Galactic Network'. The message also contained a promise of a sign: 'We are sending a comet to your solar system as a sign that the time has come to look to the stars.' A few months later, Wilson relates,

> Comet Kohoutek, as predicted in the Transmissions, arrived in the solar system and sped inward toward the sun, while astronomers announced an unprecedented spectacle and Leary's disciples chortled at the confirmation. Then the comet fizzled, leaving us wondering.

Many people have been left wondering after predictions apparently made by an alien intelligence have come true or partly true. In his book, *The Mothman Prophecies*, John Keel tells of some very strange events that occurred in Virginia between 1965 and 1968. There were hundreds of UFO sightings, many of them supported by the evidence of radar returns. There were also poltergeist disturbances, cattle mutilations, sightings of the traditional Virginian flying bogey, 'Mothman', and many cases of contactees receiving messages. Among these messages there were a number of predictions. Three of them being reported independently by different contactees. The first was that the Pope would be stabbed on a visit to the Middle East; the second that Robert Kennedy would be in danger in a hotel kitchen; and the third that at noon on 15 December 1967, there would be a nationwide power failure.

What happened? The Pope went on a trip to the Middle East and no attempt was made on his life, but three years later, on a visit to Manila, he was attacked by a man dressed like a priest who leapt out of the crowd with a long knife in his hand. The second prediction was exactly fulfilled when Robert Kennedy was assassinated in a hotel kitchen. The third was not fulfilled, but at precisely the time when the power failure was to happen a traffic-laden bridge collapsed in West Virginia, right where the UFO sightings and other phenomena had been most intense, and many people were killed. The correctness of the second prophecy and the fact that the other two were near misses, could hardly be put down to chance coincidence.

Keel took the events as evidence for the theory he had developed in his earlier book, *Our Haunted Planet*, that there exists a category of beings, whom he calls 'ultraterrestrials', who were the original inhabitants of this planet. These 'nonphysical beings from the world of higher frequencies' may resent man's take-over, Keel suggests, and such phenomena as the

'Mothman prophecies' may be mischief attributable to their vindictiveness. Robert Wilson has another explanation, however. Maybe, he proposes, 'all their predictions came true, in one universe or another. Keel just happens to be in one of the universes at a tangent to theirs, where only a part of the prophecies came true'.

These are wild conjectures, but then the facts are also wild, and difficult to fit into any model of reality except perhaps the teaching of the Church that there exist demons and 'principalities and powers' of darkness. The Church, of course, also teaches that revelation was given only in the Bible and through Jesus Christ, and that since the biblical canon was closed there have been no more revelations, although the illumination of individuals through participation in the biblical revelation is a continuing process. In other words, Highest Intelligence, or God, has spoken once and once only to His creatures, and all other so-called revelations are the work of the Devil or of lying spirits.

This orthodox view is very difficult to uphold. Firstly, as nineteenth-century German scholars established with characteristic thoroughness, the New Testament is full of inconsistences and even of conflicting teachings, and lacks the homogeneity that one would expect if it were the revealed word of God. And secondly, there are other revealed teachings that *are* homogeneous, wise, and profound, and which cannot be regarded as serving any diabolical purpose unless it be to subvert the claims of the Church to the uniqueness of the biblical revelation.

In his very useful study, *Revelation: The Divine Fire*, Brad Steiger has examined the writings and experiences of people who claim to have experienced revelation and to have been in spiritual communication with Higher Intelligence, and he comes to the conclusion

> that the soul-igniting mechanism of the gifts of Spirit did not cease with the prophets and saints of antiquity . . . that the Divine Fire – the transfer of thought, spirit, and power from an Infinite Intelligence to a finite, human intelligence – is a vital, continuing process which observes no denominational boundaries and employs a spiritual-psychic mechanism that is timeless and universal.

In his *Legend of the Grand Inquisitor* Dostoevsky pointed out the irony that whereas Jesus had supposedly rejected miracle and mystery as means of compelling belief, and considered them the Devil's counsels, the Church was not so scrupulous and in fact sought to buttress its claim to divine authority by invoking the evidence of miracle and mystery. In fact, miracle and mystery are not good guarantors of the unique authenticity of any revelation, for they are far too common. This is perhaps the reason Jesus rejected them and not because – as Dostoevsky suggests – their use was incompatible with his mission of promoting human freedom and dignity.

We find tales of miraculous happenings in the lives of several individuals who have had the revelatory experience and produced scriptures. The classic case is that of the Prophet Muhammad, who in his fortieth year had a vision of the angel Gabriel, who held before him a silken cloth with writing on it and bade him read, whereupon Muhammad read the decrees of God which he later wrote down in the Koran. In 1821, Joseph Smith, an American farm boy, had a similar experience. A being that introduced himself as the angel Moroni appeared to him and told him where he would find some buried gold plates. Joseph Smith later dug them up and found that they were covered with strange writing. He was able to translate the plates, which were dematerialised as soon as he had done so, and the translation was published as the *Book of Mormon*, which became the bible of a new religion. Another parabiblical text, the immense *Oahpse*, was written by a New York dentist, Dr John Newbrough, in 1880. He awoke one morning to find his room filled with beings in the form of pillars of light, who instructed him to buy a typewriter and sit for an hour each day with his fingers on the keys. He complied, and although he did not know how to type he turned out, at the rate of 1,200 words an hour, a book that is at once a history of the human race and a cosmology, and which contains some facts, such as the existence of the Van Allen belt of radiation around the Earth, which have only recently been confirmed.

So what price miracle and mystery? The *Book of Mormon* and the *Oahpse* would both appear to have the endorsement of miraculous events attendant upon their creation, yet their contents are fundamentally different and in some respects incompatible; so if they are the work of some transmundane being it is not His Omniscience. Signs and wonders, and correct prophecies, are, however, rather convincing evidence that the communications have an external rather than a psychological provenance. The most plausible hypothesis that emerges from a study of revelatory literature is that there exist a considerable number of communicators, themselves at different levels of spiritual evolution, some of whom employ miracle and mystery to support their claims while others eschew such means and rely on the content of their communications itself to carry conviction. And at the lower end of the scale there would appear to be a category of mischievous, lying entity that is endowed with superpowers by human standards but is bent upon sowing confusion and discord on Earth.

In my book on the communications from 'The Nine' there is a quotation from the great Italian pyschologist Roberto Assagioli, the creator of 'psychosynthesis'. Before he died in 1974, aged eighty-six, Assagioli became acquainted with the early communications, and in a taped conversation about them he said:

. . . As regards the New Wave from 1975 on, and the coming of higher beings, I think it will be a gradual thing, but the main point is the realisation by humanity that there are higher beings, which they are strangely reluctant to admit. I think that to help them to recognise that is good . . . The time has come for the recognition of the Hierarchy that is there . . . The only point of caution is that there are dark forces that try to prevent all this happening, and one of their ways is to insinuate false teachings in the communications. It is not difficult for them for they are sly and under the guise of something fine they can be misleading. So we must always be on guard . . .

When I first heard Assagioli's gentle, high-pitched voice uttering these words I was myself struggling to make sense of the phenomenon of the communications, and the fact that the great psychologist apparently found nothing intrinsically preposterous in the idea of their emanating from a higher and non-human intelligence impressed me. I am equally impressed today – having become acquainted with a far wider range of revelatory literature – by Assagioli's reference to the sly beings that insinuate false teachings into communications in order to mislead. This explains many of the discrepancies and much of the sheer nonsense that we find in some of the revelatory literature and possibly also explains much of the nonsensical behaviour reported of UFOs and their occupants. It still takes some getting used to though, to hear a man like Assagioli speaking about unseen worlds and alien communicators in such a matter-of-fact way.

In Assagioli's reference to 'the Hierarchy that is there' I have capitalised the word 'Hierarchy' because it is always so written in the esoteric literature that the psychologist was indirectly referring to. Esotericists believe that there exists a 'Spiritual Hierarchy' which guides and guards our planet, and which is gradually providing mankind, through various channels, with a body of knowledge and teaching known as the 'Ageless Wisdom'. The first stage of this communication was accomplished through Mrs Helena Blavatsky between 1875 and 1890, and is contained in her books *Isis Unveiled* and *The Secret Doctrine*. A second stage was accomplished through Mrs Alice A. Bailey, who between 1919 and 1949 wrote a series of books telepathically communicated to her by a certain Master Djwhal Khul – 'the Tibetan'. One of the repeated teachings in these books is that in the Aquarian age, which began in the present decade, there will occur 'the Externalisation of the Hierarchy', that is to say, the appearance on the physical plane of the spiritual guides and guardians of the planet, the progenitors of the 'Ageless Wisdom'.

There are obvious and great obstacles to anyone's accepting these esoteric teachings on first acquaintance, and it would seem more reasonable to attribute the creation of the 'Ageless Wisdom' to Mrs

Blavatksy and Mrs Bailey than to the rather nebulous Spiritual Hierarchy. Yet when one begins to read the literature and learns how it came into existence, one begins to wonder, particularly in the case of Alice Bailey; for she had a profound antipathy to psychic work and occult literature before she started producing 'the Tibetan's' books. The story goes that in 1919 the Master Djwhal Khul contacted Mrs Bailey telepathically and asked her to act as his amanuensis. At first she refused, but when the Tibetan urged her and agreed to her condition that the writings should go out without making any claim to authority and simply stand on its merit, she consented to try. The result was the production, over the thirty years, of eighteen books, most of them running to six or seven hundred pages, telepathically dictated by the Tibetan; in addition Alice Bailey wrote seven books independently.

The Tibetan explained that he was a senior executive in a large lamasery situated in the Himalayas, and he had chosen Mrs Bailey as his amanuensis because they had worked together several lives ago, so the books do not strictly speaking purport to be communications from an extraterrestrial intelligence. Their content, however, particularly the details of the Hierarchy's plan for accomplishing the further evolution of man, is presented as a revealed teaching that the Tibetan himself is channelling from a higher source. Explaining how the actual writing was done, Mrs Bailey said in her autobiography: 'I had to write at regular hours and it was clear, concise, definite dictation. It was given word for word, in such a manner that I might claim that I definitely heard a voice.' Obviously this is not the manner in which normal literary composition occurs, and Mrs Bailey's testimony, combined with the tremendous scope, profundity, and consistency of the writings, is evidence enough to convince most sceptics of the objective origin of the material she penned.

Although many tales of miraculous events are related about Muhammad, the Prophet himself only claimed one miracle: the writing of the Koran. The same could be said of the Alice Bailey books. The amanuensis admitted that often she did not understand what she wrote, and the consistency and high quality of the writings are miraculous. This is true also of another and more recent series of texts that purports to come from a non-human intelligence – the 'Seth' material channelled by American medium Jane Roberts. It is worth discussing this material in some detail, both because of its intrinsic quality and also because it is of our time. Jane Roberts is an informed woman who had written about her mediumship intelligently and in the light of modern knowledge of psychology and parapsychology.

One autumn evening in 1963, Jane Roberts, a young writer who had just published her first novel, settled down after dinner to work on her poetry. Sitting at her work table, with a cup of coffee and a cigarette she suddenly had a revelatory experience. She later wrote:

A fantastic avalanche of radical, new ideas burst into my head with tremendous force. I was . . . connected to some incredible source of energy . . . It was as if the physical world were really tissue-paper thin, hiding infinite dimensions of reality, and I was suddenly flung through the tissue-paper with a huge ripping sound.

Her hand scribbled furiously, and when she eventually returned to normal consciousness she found that she had written a batch of notes on ideas quite unfamiliar to her under the title *The Physical Universe as Idea Construction*.

The ideas thus elliptically expressed were later elaborated by Seth when Jane, in trance, began to channel his voice and ideas directly while her husband Rob took notes. Seth soon established himself as a distinct personality, and Jane and Rob started to have two regular sessions a week to enable him to communicate. In one early session Seth described himself as 'a sensitive but disciplined and sensible – if somewhat irascible – gentleman', and Rob has testified that when she is in trance and functioning as the Seth channel, Jane's voice becomes deep and her movements masculine. Seth has explained, however, that these characteristics are adopted by him simply to facilitate the communication and acceptance of his teaching. 'I translate myself into an event that you can understand to some extent,' he says. He maintains that personality is 'multi-dimensional', that is to say that each individual exists in other realities and dimensions and a complete identity is very much more than the self that we normally identify with. He calls Jane 'Ruburt' and refers to her as a man. This is not a mistake; he is well aware that in our reality she is a young woman, but 'Jane Roberts' is only a fragment of a total personality. 'Ruburt' is another fragment and the one that Seth finds it most appropriate to communicate through.

Psychologists have participated in some of the Seth communication sessions. One highly-distinguished psychologist who was very familiar with the phenomena of mediumship declared that Seth had a 'massive intellect' and certainly did not appear to be a secondary personality of Jane's that emerged in her trance state. Dr Eugene Barnard of North Carolina State University, who had a long philosophical conversation with Seth, wrote:

The best summary description I can give you of that evening is that it was for me a delightful conversation with a personality or intelligence or what have you, whose wit, intellect, and reservoir of knowledge far exceeded my own . . . In any sense in which a psychologist of the Western scientific tradition would understand the phrase, I do not believe that Jane Roberts and Seth are the same person, or the same personality, or different facets of the same personality . . .

Seth is well aware of the difficulty that human beings have in accepting the existence of non-physical beings, and has said: 'if I succeed in convincing you of my reality as a separate personality, I will have done exceedingly well.' In order to help carry the conviction, he gave some successful demonstrations of telepathy and clairvoyance. He described, for instance, what was written or drawn on a piece of paper enclosed in a thick sealed envelope taken at random from a pile of such envelopes so that nobody present knew its content. Such feats were apparently child's play to Seth, but he engaged in them in order to offer some evidence of his independent existence. He was, however, aware that it would not be taken as conclusive evidence, and that psychologists have attributed some of the most puzzling phenomena of mental mediumship to the emergence of a secondary personality possessed of 'super-ESP' powers.

'I am not a secondary personality,' Seth has said. 'I make no attempt to dominate Ruburt's life, nor indeed would I expect him to allow it. I do not represent any repressed portions of Ruburt's own being . . .' These statements were made in a talk Seth gave to a college psychology class, and he put forward some other interesting arguments on this occasion:

You may, if you wish, call me a subconscious production. I do not particularly enjoy such a designation, since it is not true. But if you do call me a subconscious extension of Ruburt's own personality, then you must agree that the subconscious is telepathic and clairvoyant, since I have shown telepathic and clairvoyant abilities. So, may I remind you, has Ruburt on his own . . . However, unless you are willing to assign to the subconscious those abilities – and most of your colleagues do not – then I cannot be considered to have such a subconscious origin.

If you *are* willing to concede the point, then I have other arguments. My memories are not the memories of a young woman. My mind is not a young woman's mind. I have been used to many occupations, and Ruburt has no memory of them. I am not a father image of Ruburt's, nor am I the male figure that lurks in the back of the female mind. Nor does our friend Ruburt have homosexual tendencies. I am simply an energy essence personality, no longer materialized in physical form.

. . . I was not artificially 'brought to birth' through hypnosis. There was no artificial tampering of personality characteristics here. There was no hysteria. Ruburt allows me to use the nervous system under highly controlled conditions. I am not given a blanket permission to take over when I please, nor would I desire such an arrangement. I have other things to do.

A distinct sense of the Seth personality comes across in these brief extracts. He is knowledgeable, vigorous in thought and expression, and inclined to be amused at the psychological explanations that human beings have thought up to account for something otherwise unaccountable in their view of reality. His formulation,' I am simply an energy essence personality, no longer materialized in physical form', is, Jane Roberts thinks, as good a brief definition as anyone could give.

Seth is not a spirit, although he says that he has lived and died many times over, and in some previous lives he inhabited a physical body. His environment, he says, 'is a reality of existence created by myself and others like me, and it represents the manifestation of our development'. Behind this definition there is an understanding which he often tries to communicate: that all realities, physical and non-physical, are the creation of mind, or consciousness. As Seth says:

> You think that objects exist independently of you, not realising that they are instead the manifestations of your own psychological and psychic selves. We realise that we form our own reality, and therefore we do so with considerable joy and creative abandon. In my environment you would be highly disoriented, for it would seem to you as if it lacked coherency.

It certainly cannot be said of Seth that he lacks coherency. His function, he says, is that of teacher, and he performs it in other systems of reality as well as ours, using in each one an appropriate portion of the larger Seth identity, and teaching the same lessons in many different ways. In order to get his teaching across to our world, he has written a book. That is, through Jane Roberts he has uttered the text of a book, which Rob has written down.

In 1970 Jane published her book, *The Seth Material*, telling her story of Seth's appearance and giving long quotations from his teachings with her own comments on them. In the same year Seth announced that he would write a book. He planned out the chapters, and dictated a concise, carefully structured, and eloquently expressed text in sessions spread over the next eighteen months. He could stop abruptly and take up his theme days later at precisely the point he had left off without any prompting, and throughout almost five hundred pages of his text – published in 1972 under the title *Seth Speaks* – he develops and integrates his themes with complete consistency and impressive authority. The book is indeed the work of a 'massive intellect'.

Addressing the reader at the beginning of his book, Seth said:

> All of your attention is focused in a highly specialised way upon one shining, bright point that you call reality. There are other realities all about you, but you ignore their existence, and you blot out all stimuli that come from them. There is a reason for such a trance, as you will discover, but little by little you must wake up. My purpose is to open your inner eyes.

Seth Speaks does, in fact, open the reader's eyes to a number of novel concepts and ideas strikingly and originally expressed. Much of the material is consistent with other philosophical, religious, or esoteric teachings, but always the language and imagery are fresh and vital and the material reads as quite underivative. The insights it gives are by turn philosophical, metaphysical, theological, cosmological, psychological, and historical; and to be able to generate fresh ideas in all these areas is surely a mark of a very remarkable mind. The ostensible fact that it is a disembodied mind that has generated all this is given credence by the fact that much of the information vouchsafed has to do with non-physical realities, and that all that Seth says about these realities is cogent and internally consistent. I think that most readers who give the Seth material a chance, and put its teachings to the test of their own experience, logic, and intuitions, will be convinced of the validity of the material and of the existence of Seth as a personality quite independent of his channel, Jane Roberts. As he puts it: 'Personalities who do not exist do not write books.'

In the last chapter of my presentation and discussion of the communications from 'The Nine' I quote at length passages from two other contemporary sources that claim to have been in communication with an extraterrestrial intelligence, and draw attention to some quite remarkable correspondences, in points of detail as well as in general theme. There are correspondences, too, between the Seth material and that of 'The Nine'. Such correspondences between texts otherwise unconnected and produced by mediums unacquainted with each other and each other's work does argue strongly in favour of the objective existence of the communicators.

Brad Steiger has drawn attention to the basic similarities between 'revealed' teachings from Pythagoras down to the present day, and he asks: 'Was it in that millennium before Jesus that a Higher Intelligence began to transmit its basic messages?' John Keel, too, has studied the literature, and he writes:

> It seems to me as if all these people, widely separated by time, have been getting communications which are being broadcast over and over again by some giant phonograph in the sky. The slight alterations probably are made in the percipients' minds to tailor the messages to contemporary situations.

Robert Temple and Robert Wilson have independently identified the 'giant phonograph in the sky' as belonging to the Sirius system, and have also drawn attention to some of the philosophical and esoteric traditions cited by Steiger as evidence of a continuity of revelation. Most revelators, however, would probably be disappointed to discover that the source of their revelations was another physical civilisation elsewhere in the galaxy.

And they would surely feel that the 'giant phonograph in the sky' was an inadequate, if not a blasphemous description, of He who in His wisdom and beneficence granted them their life-enhancing vision.

Yes, we have to come in conclusion to the point that the ultimate alien intelligence, the one that the majority of mankind has always believed in, is God. When this book was first proposed I suggested to the publisher that it should conclude with a chapter entitled 'The Intelligence of God'. He thought that a bit presumptuous for a mere mortal, but whether we refer to God or Supermind or the Highest Intelligence the discussion must be broached. The question of whether or not there exists in the universe a non-human, non-physical, and non-terrestrial intelligence ultimately comes down to the question of whether God exists.

Not having been favoured with any direct and definite information on this question, I am obliged to approach it indirectly. The debate has, of course, been going on for centuries, indeed for millennia, and it would certainly be presumptuous to propose to wind it up in these few pages. To propose probabilities, though, is a reasonable truth-seeking procedure, and I think it is possible to do this by considering some of the contributions made to the debate in modern times.

In the last century the traditional 'proofs' of the existence of God fell apart. The 'argument from design', which maintained that just as the existence of a watch implied the existence of a watchmaker so did the existence of order and design in nature imply a Divine Designer, was undermined by evolution theory, which held that the order of nature was attributable to the operation of the laws of natural selection and the survival of the fittest. The objections to the 'cosmological proof', which held that everything must have a cause and therefore there must have been a First Cause, or Divine Creator, were well put by Bernard Shaw when he wrote, that in view of the evidence of evolution theory and of the new science of bio-chemistry it was easier to believe that the universe made itself than that a maker of the universe made himself, because 'the universe visibly exists and makes itself as it goes along, whereas a maker for it is a hypothesis'. The 'ontological proof', which maintained that as the mind of man can conceive of a Being that possesses all imaginable qualities in perfection, that Being must have among its qualities the quality of existence, was proof that had never carried much conviction except to believers. And Immanuel Kant demolished it by pointing out that existence was not a quality like goodness, knowledge, or power.

Many nineteenth-century intellectuals considered the hypothesis of the existence of God not only non-proven but positively repugnant to reason. Shelley declared himself an atheist, Thomas Huxley coined the term 'agnostic', John Stuart Mill argued that considering all the evil and suffering in the world God could not be both all-powerful and all-loving, and Nietzsche announced that God was dead. Philosophers, anthropologists, and psychologists addressed themselves to the task of explaining how such a preposterous idea as the existence of God had ever arisen.

Herbert Spencer, taking his basic ideas directly from the Greek philosopher Euhemeros, argued that belief in God was nothing but ancestor worship. Professor E. B. Tylor, in *Primitive Culture* (1871), demonstrated with formidable scholarship that religion arose out of a primitive belief in spirits animating all aspects of the natural world, and that 'the instinctive craving of the mind after simplification and unification of its ideas' caused man, as he progressed from primitivism to civilisation, to proceed to a belief first in a hierarchy of godlings and finally in an omnipotent, omniscient, and ethical Supreme Being. Tylor's pupil, James Frazer, further developed this kind of argument in his monumental study, *The Golden Bough*, demonstrating how man had progressed from primitive, craven superstition to modern, clear, scientific thinking which had dispensed with the gods for all time. Sigmund Freud contributed the idea that God was nothing but a substitute father, a figure projected out of man's fundamental sense of insecurity and dependence. These theories and arguments were all tremendously influential, and of course they were all reductionist; they all sought to disembarrass the rational man of a belief in God, and their collective effect was very great.

It is significant that the one book which presented evidence incompatible with the theories of Spencer, Tyler, Frazer, and Freud, indeed which invalidated all their weighty arguments, went virtually unnoticed. This was Andrew Lang's *The Making of Religion* (1898). In a key chapter entitled 'High Gods of Low Races', Lang presented anthropological evidence that the monotheistic, ethical, 'higher' religions did not evolve by degrees as man became more civilised, but on the contrary, belief in an ethical Supreme Being was characteristic of primitive religions. The evidence was drawn from studies of tribal traditions in Africa, the Pacific islands, and Australia. In the religions of all these tribes, Lang wrote,

> An all-knowing being observes and rewards the conduct of men; he is named with reverence, if named at all; his abode is the heavens; he is the Maker and Lord of all things; his lessons 'soften the heart' . . . the moral element is conspicuous, the reverence is conspicuous: we have here no mere ghost, propitiated by food or sacrifice, or by purely magical rites.

But as cultures became more advanced, this High God tended to become redundant, a *deus otiosus*, and to be supplanted by gods that could be bribed and propitiated and whose ethics were highly dubious.

Some people would no doubt regard the 'high gods of low races', – the gods who came from the sky and gave men their laws and their cultures and then returned whence they came – as evidence of world-wide contacts between human beings and extraterrestrial aliens in primordial times. I think the most we can say is that the evidence is suggestive rather than supportive of such a hypothesis. The important point about Lang's disclosures was that they repudiated the fashionable evolutionary view that mankind had graduated from a belief in spirits to a belief in a Supreme Being and would eventually attain the mature commonsense of believing in nothing except what approved scientific methods could prove existed. They demonstrated that the One God, the ethical Supreme Being, the Highest Intelligence, was not a concept that the human mind developed as it emerged from barbarism, but a concept inherent in the mind of man since the earliest times. The question Lang could not answer was whether the concept was based upon direct knowledge and experience.

The psychologist Carl Jung had an answer to that. 'The idea of an all-powerful divine being is present everywhere, if not consciously recognised, then unconsciously accepted, because it is an archetype,' he wrote. He defined an archetype as 'an irrepresentible, unconscious, pre-existent form that seems to be part of the inherited structure of the psyche and can therefore manifest itself spontaneously anywhere, at any time'. According to this definition, then, God could not be an invention of human consciousness because He 'already has a place in the part of our psyche which is pre-existent to consciousness'. The argument may appear a highly sophisticated variation on the 'ontological proof', but Jung did not leave it at that. He was fascinated by the discoveries of modern physicists which showed the naive realist's idea of the separateness of the subjective and objective worlds to be insupportable, and that a 'connection necessarily exists between the psyche . . . and the objective space-time continuum'. This implied, he wrote, 'that archetypes must have a nonpsychic aspect'. As God is an archetype, the further implication must be that He has a nonpsychic, that is to say an objective, existence.

The 'Father in Heaven' God-concept (or 'old Nobodaddy aloft', as William Blake put it with the appropriate irreverence of a man who knew better from experience) was never considered by any theologian of the least subtlety as anything but the simplest analogy to and image of God, or a convenient means of conceptualising Him. The good news of Christianity was that a personal relationship subsisted between the Creator and His creature, and the simplest way of conveying this message was by representing the Creator as a person. The trouble was that simple-and literal-minded people tended to take the representation literally. Consequently the concept of the identity of the Creator with the whole of His creation – a concept fundamental to the Hebrew Kabbalah and to mystical Christianity as well as to Hinduism – was neglected and the subject of the relationship of the individual human person to his God was overemphasised. But a very curious thing has happened in the twentieth century. Science which was supposed to have dealt the death-blow to religion, rediscovered God: not 'old Nobodaddy aloft' but the Intelligence manifest in all creation.

Jung's intuition was right when he looked to physics for endorsement of his fundamentally religious concepts. Einstein had said that he discovered the principle of relativity because he was 'so strangely convinced of the harmony of the universe', and he declared: 'I cannot believe that God plays dice with the cosmos.' The physicist and philosopher Sir Arthur Eddington neatly summarised the findings of modern physics when he said that the universe was beginning to look more like a great thought than a great machine, and that 'the stuff of the world is mind-stuff'. The relativity equation $E = Mc^2$ had shown that matter and energy are the same thing, and quantum physics recognises that thought is a form of energy. So the idea of an intelligent, dynamic principle continually at work in the universe (remember Facius Cardan's sylph's statement that God created the universe from moment to moment) is entirely compatible with the findings of modern science.

It would be ironical if it turned out that religion was wrong about God and some of our science fiction writers were right. Our terrestrial religions, which can all be traced back to some historical persons or events, and which all embody supposedly God-ordained traditions and practices that are palpably local in origin and relevance, would surely be profoundly embarrassed by the discovery of extraterrestrial intelligent life. The ingenuity of their theologians would be severely taxed to reconcile such a discovery with their claims to universality. No doubt the theologians would rise to the challenge with all the casuistry at their command, but however they argued the matter it would be very difficult for them to explain why God had not, through His prophets and scriptures, revealed the existence of extraterrestrials, when He had allegedly revealed so many other facts about His universe. Of course it could be answered that He was under no obligation to do so, but that is a rather lame apology, particularly since among the things He *had* chosen to reveal were some that were incompatible with the fact of the existence of extraterrestrials.

The Christian religion would be particularly compromised by the discovery, since it makes so much of the Incarnation as an historical event and of knowledge of the good news of Jesus Christ's Passion, Ascension, and Atonement as the *sine qua non* of salvation. It would either have to maintain that the incarnation and crucifixion of the Son of God has occurred on innumerable worlds, or embark on a vigorous missionary campaign of broadcasting the good news throughout the universe. The latter would be a vain effort, for the distant galaxies are receding from us faster than the speed of light and could never be contacted, so their inhabitants presumably would be eternally damned: a fact surely irreconcilable with any idea of Divine Providence.

Buddhism might fare better, for its scriptures do contain occasional references to Bodhisattvas inhabiting innumerable worlds, but the references are rather symbolic and do not amount to an assertion of the existence of extraterrestrial physical civilisations and their inhabitants. Oddly enough, the only revealed teachings in which there is a specific allusion to extraterrestrials are those that God conveyed to Joseph Smith. Smith was vouchsafed a vision of Moses, who, he wrote, 'beheld many lands; and each land was called earth, and there were inhabitants on the face thereof'. Scientific discoveries have had some curious and unforeseen consequences, but all precedents of the kind would be surpassed if the discovery of extraterrestrials resulted in the conversion of the peoples of the Earth to Mormonism.

God and His Creation and the nature of Divine Intelligence have undoubtedly been misconceived by millions of human beings who have believed themselves, by virtue of their faith, to be privy to revealed Truth. The mystics have generally known better, and so, I would venture to suggest, have some writers of science fiction. Let us consider briefly one work in this genre which contains some interesting reflections on the intelligence of God.

In the penultimate chapter of Olaf Stapledon's *Star Maker* the author describes a metaphysical dream-vision of how God, the Star Maker, created cosmos after cosmos, and 'advanced from stage to stage in the progress from infantile to mature divinity'. Here is a God-concept which at once shows some conception of the immensity of creation and which expresses the idea of the dependence of the Creator upon His creation, of His maturing through the creative work that He does. The origin of Stapledon's visionary metaphysics may have been the kabbalistic idea that by a series of emanations God made aspects of His nature manifest in the physical world. Stapledon writes:

> The infant Star Maker, teased . . . by his unexpressed potency, conceived and objectified from himself two qualities. With these alone he made his first toy cosmos . . . Presently, through contemplation of his creature's simple form, he conceived the possibility of more subtle creating. Thus the first of all creatures itself bred in its creator a need that itself could never satisfy . . . Thereafter, cosmos upon cosmos, each more rich and subtle than the last, leapt from his fervent imagination.

When the Star Maker has completed a cosmos, he sets it aside among his works and begins to contemplate another. And when he came to create the cosmos to which we belong he created a special substance to work with.

He conceived from the depth of his own being a something, neither mind nor matter, . . . a medium in which the one and the many demanded to be most subtly dependent upon one another, in which all parts and all characters must pervade and be pervaded by all other parts and all other characters . . . a cosmical substance in which any individual spirit must be, mysteriously, at once an absolute self and a mere figment of the whole.

This was rather abstruse language for 1937, when the novel was written, but it would make sense to a contemporary physicist acquainted with developments in quantum theory. 'All things are interconnected in the microcosmos', writes Bob Toben in his presentation of the new physics, *Space-Time and Beyond* (1974). 'Every part is connected to every other part . . . The description of any part is inseparable from the description of the whole.' The language is very like Stapledon's, which is interesting since the two writers had such different points of departure: the one speculating about the nature of a cosmical substance that is an emanation of divinity; the other describing what the stuff of the universe looks like from the viewpoint of modern quantum physics.

Our cosmos was only an intermediate creation of the Star Maker's maturity. But:

as he contemplated this the loveliest and subtlest of his works with exultation, even with awe, its impact upon him changed him, clarifying and deepening his will. As he discriminated its virtue and its weakness, his own perception and his own skill matured . . . Then, seemingly with a conflict of reverence and impatience, he set our cosmos in its place among his other works.

And he went on creating universes, 'each in its fullest attainment more awakened than the last', until he had created 'the ultimate and most subtle cosmos, for which all others were but tentative preparations'. Then: 'the Star Maker, that dark power and lucid intelligence, found in the concrete loveliness of his creature the fulfilment of desire.'

I would not suggest that Stapledon's dream-myth constitutes a basis for an alternative theology. However, I do think that his stress on the interdependence of creator and creature, and his point that the Star Maker himself can evolve, and particularly that the stuff of which our cosmos is made is – to paraphrase Eddington – God-stuff, and also the implication that to seek to create and to evolve is to participate in the divine purpose and nature, are important and relevant concepts for a modern theology.

In the Introduction I suggested that we might define the spectrum of animal-human intelligence as ranging from the low order of a sensory-motor information processing system manifesting an ability to modify behaviour in accordance with experience, to the highest order of a feeling-ratiocinative system manifesting an ability to modify behaviour in accordance with abstract principles. And I also suggested that if higher ranges of the intelligence spectrum existed they might manifest in our world in apparently random events. Let us now see how these concepts relate to the present discussion.

One of the creation myths of the *Rig Veda* tells how the Primal Being, Purusha, was dismembered and how the universe was formed from his parts. Mircea Eliade has remarked on the 'extremely wide distribution' of similar themes throughout the world's mythologies:

A single being transforms itself into the Cosmos, or takes multiple rebirth in a whole vegetable species or race of mankind. A living 'whole' bursts into fragments and disperses itself in myriads of animated forms. In other terms, here we find the well-known cosmogonic pattern of the primordial 'wholeness' broken into fragments by the act of creation.

Or again, we have the theme that the fundamental stuff of the universe is God-stuff: a theme which, as we have noted, is quite compatible with modern physical theories of the 'quantum interconnectedness' of all parts of the universe and all things in it.

Let us propose, with this support from both mythology and science, that the universe is an organism, and it is this organism that we call God. In relation to God we would be in an analogous position to, for example, a single body cell, or perhaps a single organ, in a human body. The body cell or organ is unable to perceive the whole of which it is a part, and yet its behaviour is generally governed by the interests and purposes of the whole organism. Although the more complex an organ becomes the more freedom it acquires to subvert the interests and purposes of the whole, as the human brain can subvert the body. Things can go wrong, but when they are going right the functioning of the smallest and simplest part of the organism is in harmony with the functioning of the most conscious and complex part and with the purposes of the whole.

In other words, we have an intelligent universe, a universe in which mind is manifest in the component parts, and in which, ideally, all intelligences in the hierarchy serve the purposes of the universe as a whole. If we maintain that the universe is an organism, then we can plausibly propose that its purposes are those common to all higher organisms: homeostasis and evolution, that is the maintenance of the state of organisation already attained and the pursuit of a still higher state. Ideally, intelligence on all levels serves these purposes, but the autonomy with which the higher intelligences must be invested if the system is to achieve evolution as well as homeostasis introduces an element of instability into the system; an instability which may require the occasional intervention of the Highest Intelligence in order to effect an adjustment. So God is both manifest in the universe in a manner that generally goes unnoticed because the manifestation takes the form of what we consider to be its normal and natural functioning, and also He has the potentiality to manifest in the universe to effect a necessary adjustment. Such manifestations might take the form of what we consider paranormal or supernatural events. The events upon which religions are generally based may be construed as interventions of this nature.

If this is the state of affairs in the universe, it would be entirely plausible that in certain circumstances the mind of man should participate in the mind of God, or that man should have experiences of enlarged consciousness, of mystical revelations, of precognitions, and of clairvoyance, for such experiences would be contacts with aspects of omniscience. There is definite evidence that such experiences can be sought and induced, by meditation, yoga, biofeedback, or the use of mind-altering drugs, and there is evidence, too, that the experiences often occur spontaneously. When they occur spontaneously, many experients feel that they are God-induced, and they may be right; giving human beings this type of experience may be one of the ways that God makes adjustments in the order of the universe.

Nearly a century ago, William James wrote of psychic phenomena: 'Every other sort of fact has some context and continuity with the rest of nature. These alone are contextless and discontinuous.' He was worried about the seeming triviality of paranormal events. The philosopher-scientist Michael M. Hare has expressed a possible answer to James's problem very clearly:

> This action [the paranormal event] may be one step in the long process of training man, as it were, to gain an understanding of the nature of God, a necessary inducing of this understanding. Keep in mind that this training is becoming more and more an essential to the preservation of the Universe as man gains greater and greater control over his environment. If we come to accept this explanation it could result also in an increased effort by man to perceive the mind of God, and the consequent building in understanding could mean that God's action had been far from trivial.

The point that as man gains greater control over his environment he needs also to gain an understanding of the mind of God is well made, for with his increased control man has increased power to subvert the interests and purposes of the whole of which he is a part. 'The ultimate ethical action is action to maintain a balanced ecology', Hare states; this is a relevant point. It is in the ecology – in the establishment and maintenance of the subtle interrelations, interactions, and interdependences of natural systems – that the intelligence of God is most patently manifest in the natural world. And, as people have increasingly come to realise in the last decade or so, man's actions in the world have begun to disrupt this ecology and threaten ultimately to destroy it.

The situation has certainly come to the pass where change is imperative and where it is necessary that the Highest Intelligence should intervene directly and make some adjustments in the system. A great deal has been happening in our world in the last decade or so that could be construed as such intervention. There has been, of course, the UFO phenomenon, and the reader will not have missed the parallel between Vallée's interpretation of that enigma and Hare's interpretation of apparently trivial paranormal events. There has also been a tremendous development of public interest in the occult, the supernatural, the spiritual, and the religious, and there has been the emergence and growth of the ecology movement itself. There can be no doubt that human consciousness is changing; the theory proposed here is that it is *being changed*, and that the change is a manifestation in our world of the intelligence of God, as defined above.

So we come to our conclusions: that intelligences alien to that of physical human persons of the planet Earth exist; that they exist in forms both lower and higher than man; and that man should acknowledge their existence and attempt to comprehend and participate in their functioning, for such acknowledgement and effort will contribute to his education for survival on his threatened planet and may also contribute to his further evolution. We conclude, too, that there exist alternate realities, or dimensions, inhabited by non-physical intelligences and that there are ecological relationships between these realities and the sensory and physical realities that are the primary data of our experience. And finally we suggest that the term alien intelligence as we understand it and apply it may be a misnomer; that there is evidence for the existence of mind, meaning, and purpose in the universe and in our world; and that we human beings in the pride of our superior intelligence have often subverted that mind, meaning, and purpose: in other words that in some of our thought and conduct *we* have been, with disastrous effects, an alien intelligence.

Notes and References

The following is a chapter by chapter list of books referred to in the text and the primary sources used by the author.

INTRODUCTION

Abbas, K. A., *Till We Reach The Stars: The Story of Yuri Gagarin*, (Asia Publishing House, NY, 1961)

Lilly, John, *The Centre of the Cyclone*, (Julian Press, NY, 1972; Bantam, 1973)

—— *The Mind of the Dolphin*, (Doubleday, NY, 1967)

—— *Programming and Metaprogramming The Human Bio-computer*, (Julian Press, 1967)

Plank, Robert, *The Emotional Significance of Imaginary Beings*, (Charles C. Thomas, Springfield, Illinois, 1968)

Puccetti, Roland, *Persons*, (Macmillan, 1968)

Stapledon, Olaf, *Star Maker*, (Methuen, 1937; Penguin 1972)

1 'THEY'RE ALMOST HUMAN'

Alpers, Anthony, *Dolphins*, (John Murray, 1960)

Eiseley, Loren, *Darwin's Century*, (Victor Gollancz, 1959)

Lilly, John, *Lilly on Dolphins*, (Anchor Books, 1975)

Linden, *Apes, Men and Language*, (E. P. Dutton & Co., Inc., NY, 1975; Pelican, 1976)

Marais, Eugene, *The Soul of the Ape*, (Anthony Blond, 1964)

McIntyre, Joan, *Mind in the Waters*, (Charles Scribner's Sons, NY, 1974)

Rose, Steven, *The Conscious Brain*, (Weidenfeld & Nicolson, 1973)

Sagan, Carl, *The Cosmic Connection*, (Hodder & Stoughton, 1974)

2 'COMPUTERS AND ARTIFICIAL INTELLIGENCE'

Clarke, Arthur C., *2001: A Space Odyssey*, (Arrow Books, 1968; Hutchinson, 1973)

Evans, Chris, 'Computers and Artificial Intelligence', in *Science Fact*, ed Prof. F. George, (Topaz Books, 1977)

Raphael, Bertram, *The Thinking Computer*, (W. H. Freeman & Co, San Francisco, 1976)

Weizenbaum, Joseph, *Computer Power and Human Reason*, (W. H. Freeman & Co, San Francisco, 1976)

Wiener, Norbert, *God and Golem, Inc*, (Chapman Hall, 1965)

3 'ALIENS AMONG US?'

Conway, David, *Magic: An Occult Primer*, (Jonathan Cape, 1972)

Geley, Gustave, *Clairvoyance and Materialisation*, (T. Fisher Unwin, 1927)

Hall, Manly P., *The Secret Teachings of all Ages*, (The Philosophical Research Society, Inc, California, 1973)

Jacobsen, Thorkild, *The Intellectual Adventure of Ancient Man*, (University of Chicago Press, 1946)

Keel, John, *Our Haunted Planet*, (Neville Spearman, London, 1971)

Medhurst, R. G. ed. *Crookes and the Spirit World*, (Souvenir Press, 1972)

Musés, Charles, & Young, Arthur M., *Consciousness and Reality*, (Avon Books, NY, 1972)

Richet, Charles, *Thirty Years of Psychical Research*, (W. Collins Sons & Co, 1923)

Sagan, Carl, & Shklovski, J. S., *Intelligent Life in the Universe*, (Delta Books, NY, 1967)

Shah, Idries, *The Secret Lore of Magic*, (Frederich Muller, 1967; Abacus, 1972)
Vallée, Jacques, *Passport to Magonia*, (Henry Regnery Co, Chicago, 1969)
Waters, Frank, *The Book of the Hopi*, (Viking, NY, 1963; Ballantine Books, NY, 1969)

4 'VEHICLES OF VITALITY'

Burr, H. S., *Blueprint for Immortality*, (Neville Spearman, London, 1972)
Crookall, Robert, *Ecstasy. The Release of the Soul from the Body*, (Darshana International, India, 1975)
—— 'OBEs and Survival', *Life, Death and Psychical Research*, (Rider, London, 1973)
—— *The Techniques of Astral Projection*, (Aquarian Press, 1964)
Eliade, Mircea, *Shamanism: Archaic Techniques of Ecstasy*, (Princeton University Press, 1964)
Green, Celia, *Out-of-the-Body Experiences*, (Hamish Hamilton, 1968)
Greenhouse, Herbert, *The Astral Journey*, (Doubleday, NY, 1975)
Hoffman, Joseph G., *The Life and Death of Cells*, (Hutchinson, 1954)
Knight, David C., ed, *The ESP Reader*, (Castle Books, NY, 1969)
Merleau-Ponty, Maurice, *Phenomenology of Perception*, (Routledge & Kegan Paul, 1962)
Moss, Thelma, *The Probability of the Impossible*, (Tarcher, Los Angeles, 1974)
Osis, Karlis, *Deathbed Observations of Doctors and Nurses*, (Parapsychology Foundation, NY, 1961)
Ostrander, S., & Schroeder, L., *Psychic Discoveries Behind the Iron Curtain*, (Prentice-Hall, 1971)
Puthoff, H., & Targ, R., *Mind Reach*, (Delacorte Press, NY, 1976)
Russell, Edward W., *Design for Destiny*, (Neville Spearman, London, 1971)
'Yram', *Practical Astral Projection*, (Weiser, NY, 1976; Rider, London, nd)

5 'MIND BEYOND THE END OF ITS TETHER'

Huxley, Laura, *This Timeless Moment*, (Farrar, Straus & Giroux, NY, 1968)
Hyslop, James, *Psychical Research and Survival*, (G. Bell & Sons, 1913)
Johnson, Rayner Co, *Psychical Research*, (English Universities Press, 1955)
Murphy, Gardner, *Challenge of Psychical Research*, (Harper & Row, NY, 1961)
Proceedings of the Society for Psychical Research, Vols XIII and XXXI
Salter, W. H., *Evidence for Survival from Cross-Correspondences*, (Bell, London, 1938)

6 'THE SPACE PEOPLE'

Hoyle, Fred, *The Black Cloud*, (Heinemann, 1957)
Koestler, Arthur, *The Ghost in the Machine*, (Hutchinson, London, 1967)
Lem, Stanislaw, *Solaris*, (Faber & Faber, London, 1970)
Lunan, Duncan, *Man and the Stars*, (Souvenir Press, London 1974; US edition entitled *Interstellar Contact*, Henry Regnery Co, Chicago, 1975)
Monod, Jacques, *Chance and Necessity*, (Collins, London, 1972; Knopf, NY, 1971)
O'Neill, John, *Prodigal Genius: The Life of Nikola Tesla*, (Ives Washburn, Inc, NY, 1944)
Sagan, Carl, ed, *Communication with Extraterrestrial Intelligence*, (MIT Press, 1973)
Shapley, Harlow, *Of Stars and Men*, (Elek, 1978)
Stoneley, Jack, & Lawton, Anthony, *Is Anyone out There?* (Star Books, London, 1975)
Temple, Robert K. G., *The Sirius Mystery*, (Sidgwick & Jackson, London, 1976)

7 'THE UFO PHENOMENON'

Bowen, Charles, ed, *The Humanoids*, (Henry Regnery Co, Chicago, 1969)
Condon, E. U., *et al*, *Scientific Study of Unidentified Flying Objects*, (Bantam Books, NY, 1969)
Fuller, John, *The Interrupted Journey*, (Dell, NY, 1967)
Hynek, Allen, *The UFO Experience*, (Henry Regnery Co, Chicago, 1972)
Jacobs, David, *The UFO Controversy in America*, (Indiana University Press, 1974; Signet Books, 1976)
Keyhoe, Donald E., *Aliens From Space*, (Doubleday, NY, 1973; Signet, 1974)
Klass, Philip J., *UFOs Explained*, (Random House, NY, 1974)

Sagan, Carl, & Page, eds, *UFOs: A Scientific Debate*, (W. W. Norton & Co, NY, 1974)
Sanderson, Ivan, *Uninvited Visitors*, (Neville Spearman, London, 1969)
Vallée, Jacques, *The Invisible College*, (Dutton, NY, 1975; UK edition entitled *UFOs: The Psychic Solution*, Panther, London, 1977)

8 'SUPERMIND'

Bailey, Alice, *The Unfinished Autobiography*, (Lucis Press, 1951)
Eliade, Mircea, *Myths, Dreams and Mysteries*, (Harvill Press, London, 1960)
Hare, Michael M., *The Multiple Universe*, (Julian Press, NY, 1968)
Holroyd, Stuart, *Prelude to the Landing on Planet Earth*, (W. H. Allen, London, 1977, Corgi, 1979)
Keel, John, *The Mothman Prophecies*, (Dutton, NY, 1975; Panther Books, London, 1976)
Lilly, John, *The Centre of the Cyclone*, (Julian Press, NY, 1972; Bantam, 1973)
Roberts, Jane, *The Seth Material*, (Prentice-Hall, Englewood Cliffs, 1970)
—— *Seth Speaks*, (Prentice-Hall, Englewood Cliffs, 19   )
Steiger, Brad, *Revelation: The Divine Fire*, (Prentice-Hall, Englewood Cliffs, 1973)
Toben, Sarfatti & Wolf, *Space-Time and Beyond*, (Dutton, NY, 1975)
Wilson, Robert Anton, *Cosmic Trigger*, (And/Or Press, Berkeley, 1977)

Index

Agrest, Professor: 198, 199
Alien, definition of: 15
Alpers, Anthony: 40
American Society for Psychical
  Research: 106, 107, 111
Ameslan: 25, 28
Ardrey, Robert: 164
Arnold, Kenneth: 94, 188
'Artificial Paranoid' computer
  program: 57, 58, 65
Ashby, Dr Ross: 44
Asimov, Isaac: 46, 68
Assagioli, Roberto: 210, 211
'astral' body: 108, 110, 112

Babbage, Charles: 48
Backster, Cleve: 75
Bailey, Alaice A.: 211, 212
Bergier, Jacques: 170, 173
Berosus: 77
Bertrand, Rev.: 118, 119
Black Cloud, The: 164, 165, 167
Blueprint for Immortality: 123
Blavatsky, Helena: 207, 211, 212
Bracewell, Ronald: 150, 152, 156
Book of the Hopi, The: 78
Book of Mormon: 210, 221
Broad, C.D.: 129
Bronowski, Jacob: 41
Brown, Roger: 27, 28
Browning, Robert: 137, 138
Burr, Professor Harold Saxton: 122, 123,
  124
Byron, Lord George Gordon: 108

Camperdown: 146
Cardan, Facius: 69, 70, 71, 75, 90, 94, 220
Castaneda, Carlos: 110
Centre of the Cyclone, The: 205
'Chaffin Will' Case: 126, 133
Chess: 42, 50, 58
Chimpanzees: 25-28
Chomsky, Noam: 26, 55
CIA: 95, 190, 191
Clarke, Arthur C.: 43, 44, 47, 58, 156
Colby, K.M.: 57, 58, 65
Condon, Edward U.: 192, 193
Convergent evolution: 165-166, 168
Conway, David: 86
'Cosmic Trigger': 267
Coyne, Captain Lawrence: 195, 196
Crawford, Prof. E.: 152
Crookall, Dr. Robert: 110-118, 119, 121,
  124
Crookes, Sir William: 72, 75, 94
Cronin, A.J.: 117
Cross-correspondences: 133-139
Crowley, Aleister: 86, 207
Cummins, Geraldine: 120

Daniken, Erich von: 198, 199
Darwin, Charles: 12, 19, 20, 21, 123
Descartes: 60
Design for Destiny: 123
'Doctor' computer program: 55-56, 65, 66,
  67
Dogon, The: 175, 176, 199
Dole, Stephen: 174
Dolphins: 29, 32-40, 169
Drake, Prof. Frank: 156, 157, 163, 173,
  174

'drop-in communications': 139
Dyson, Freeman: 163

Ectoplasm: 72, 75, 121
Eddington, Sir Arthur: 220
Edison, Thomas: 149
Einstein, Albert: 10, 229
Eiseley, Loren: 21
Eliade, Prof. Mircea: 110, 111, 112, 115,
  223
'energy body': 108, 120
Epsilon Bootis: 151
Evans, Dr. Christopher: 58, 59, 60, 67
Ezekiel: 80

Fatima: 202
Fein, Dr. Louis: 55
'fly-in experiments': 107, 124
Fontes, Dr. Olavo: 89
Fouts, Dr. Roger: 28
Fox, Oliver: 110, 111
Frazer, James: 218
Freud, Sigmund: 218

Gagarin, Yuri: 9
Gardner, Beatrice and Allen: 25, 28
Garrett, Eileen: 105, 106
Gatty, Mrs. Margaret: 145
Gauld, Professor Alan: 139
Geddes, Sir Auckland: 97-99, 100, 112,
  115, 119
Geley, Gustav: 72, 121
Gerhardi, William: 99, 100, 105, 112, 115
Golden Bough, The: 218
Good, I.J.: 59
Goodall, Jane: 25
Gorique, Erkson: 108
Green, Celia: 100, 105, 109
Gurdjieff, George: 207
Gurney, Edmund: 133-139 passim

Haldane, J.B.S.: 161
Hall, Manley P.: 75
Hall, Prescott: 111
Hayflick, L.: 121
Hare, Michael: 224, 225
Hill, Betty and Barney: 177, 178, 179, 186
Hodgson, Richard: 129, 133, 134, 137
Hoffman, Joseph: 122
Holland, Mrs.: 134-138 passim
Home, Daniel Dunglas: 72, 108
Homeostat: 44, 45
'Hopkin's Beast': 45, 47
Hopi Indians: 78, 79
Howe, Margaret: 32, 35, 36
Hoyle, Fred: 164, 167
Huxley, Aldous: 108, 126, 127, 128, 133
Huxley, Thomas: 19, 217
Hynek, Prof. J. Allen: 189, 190, 194, 196,
  198
Hyslop, James: 130, 133

Incubi: 87, 88
Intelligence: definition of: 16-17
Inyushin, Victor: 123

Jacobs, Prof. David: 189, 191, 194, 195
Jacobs, W.W.: 67
Jacobsen, Dr. Thorkhild: 77
James, William: 129, 133, 224
Johnson, Miss Alice: 134, 135

Johnson, Prof. Raynor C: 145
Jung, Carl: 21, 94, 187, 219, 220

Kabbalah: 219
Kachina people: 78, 78
Kant, Immanuel: 9, 15, 217
Kardashev, Nikolai: 152, 155
Keel, John: 95, 208, 209, 216
Keeler, Mrs. 111, 112
Kempelen, Baron Wolfgang von: 42, 50
Keyhoe, Donald E.: 191
Key of Solomon: 83
King, Katie: 72
Kipling, Rudyard: 134
Kirlian, Semyon and Valentina: 120, 124
Klass, Philip J.: 195, 196, 197
Koran: 210, 212
Koestler, Arthur: 169
Kornberg, Arthur: 161, 162
Kortland, Dr. Adrian: 25
Kropatkin, Prince: 20

Lang, Andrew: 218, 219
Lasers: 156
Lawrence, D.H.: 108
Lawton, Anthony: 156, 159
Leary, Dr. Timothy: 207, 208
Lem, Stanislaw: 167
Lemegeton: 83
Leonard, Mrs. Gladys Osborne: 125, 126
LeShan, Lawrence: 93
Levi, Eliphas: 71, 90, 94
'L-field': 122, 123
Lilly, John: 10, 11, 12, 30, 32, 35, 36, 37,
  38, 39, 40, 205
Lincoln, Mary Todd: 140
Locke, John: 16, 26
Lorenz, Konrad: 169
Lunan, Duncan: 150, 152

Maerth, Osker: 164
Magic: 71, 86
Marais, Eugene: 21-25
Massachusetts Institute of Technology: 26,
  46, 47, 55, 160
Masse, Maurice: 179, 180, 186
Materialisation: 72, 75, 202
Maupassant, Guy de: 108
McDonald, Dr. James: 193, 196
McIntyre, Joan: 40
McVittie, Prof. G.C.: 152
Mediums: 72, 125, 130, 206
Melville, Herman: 30
'men in black': 94, 95
Merleau-Ponty, Maurice: 116
Michel, Aime: 180
Michel, John: 173
Mind of the Dolphins, The: 32
Mind-Reach: 106
Misraki, Paul: 199
Monod, Jacques: 162
Morrison, Philip: 160
Moss, Dr. Thelma: 120, 123
Mothman Prophecies, The: 208
Mowat, Farley: 31
Muhammed: 210, 211
Muldoon, Sylvan: 110, 111, 112
Multiple Personality: 130
Murphy, Prof. Gardner: 138
Muses, Dr. Charles: 76, 77, 78
Myers, F.W.H.: 133-139 passim

Napoleon: 42, 90
NICAP: (National Investigations
  Committee on Aerial Phenomena) 177,
  191
Newburg, Victor: 86
Newbrough, Dr. John: 210
Newell, Allen: 49, 50, 66

Oahpse: 210
Oannes or Oés: 77, 78
OBE: (out-of-the-body-experience): 97,
  106
Oparin, I.A.: 161
Osiris: 78
Osis, Dr. Karlis: 106, 107, 108, 118, 124
Ostrander, Shiela: 120, 121
Our Haunted Planet: 95, 208

Paracelsus: 70, 75, 76, 121
Pascal, Blaise: 9, 149
Pascagoula Fisherman Case: 195
Pauwels, Louis: 170, 173
Piddington, J.G.: 136, 137, 138
Piper, Mrs: 129, 133, 134-138 passim
Poe, Edgar Allan: 42
Prince, Walter Franklin: 130
Project Blue Book: 191
Project Cyclops: 157, 159
Project Grudge: 189
Project Ozma: 157
Project Sign: 188, 189
Puccetti, Roland: 16
Puharich Andrija: 205
Puthoff, Harold: 106, 124
Pythagoras: 216

Quantum Geometrodynamics: 202
Quetzalcoatl: 78

Raphael, Bertram: 53
'remote viewing': 106, 107, 124
Rensberger, Boyce: 28
Rhinehart, Keith Milton: 126, 127, 128
Richet, Charles: 72, 76, 94, 121
Ritchie, George: 119
Roberts, Jane: 205, 212-216
Robertson Panel, The: 199, 191
Rose, Steven: 29
Russell, Bertrand: 119

Russell, Edward W. 123, 124

Sagan, Carl: 35, 36, 38, 57, 67, 155, 161,
  162, 164, 166, 173, 194
Sanderson, Ivan T.: 180, 185
Sarfatti, Jack: 119, 173
Schlemmer, Phyllis: 205
Schroeder, Lynn: 120, 121
Secret Doctrine, The: 211
'Seth' material: 205, 212-216
Shakey: 45, 54, 60, 65
Shamans: 110, 111, 112, 115
Shapley, Harlow: 163
Shelley, P.B.: 108
Sidgwick, Henry: 133-139 passim
Simon, Dr. Benjamin: 177, 178
Sinon, Herbert: 49, 50, 66
Simonton, Joe: 88, 89, 197, 198
Sirag, Saul Paul: 205
Sirius Mystery, The: 174-176, 207
Smith, Joseph: 210, 211
Snell, Joy: 117
Social life of Apes and Monkeys: 20
Society for Psychical research: 106, 133
Socorro Case: 180
Socrates: 70, 83, 206
Soul of the Ape, The: 21-25
Space-Time and Beyond: 119, 222
Stanford Research Institute: 45, 53, 60,
  106, 188
Stapledon, Olaf: 13, 124, 166, 221, 222
Star Maker: 13-15, 166, 221, 222
Steiger, Brad: 197, 209, 216
Strinberg, August: 108
Succubi: 87, 88
Sumerian Civilisation: 77, 78, 176
Szilard, Leo: 29, 30, 31

Talbot, Mrs.: 125, 126
Tanous, Alex: 107, 108
Targ, Russell: 106, 124
'Template hypothesis': 122
Temple, Robert: 174, 175, 176, 207, 216
Tesla, Nikola: 149
'T-Fields': 123-4
Thales of Miletus: 76
Tibetan Book of the Dead: 115, 118
Tiller, Dr. William: 120

Toben, Robert: 119, 222
Tolstoy, Leo: 108
'trace cases': 197
Troitsky, Dr. Vsevolod: 152, 155
Turing, Alan: 65, 67
Tylor, Prof. E.B.: 218

UFO controversy in America: 189
UFO Experience, The: 194
UFOs: 10, 88, 89, 177-203
UIMs (ultra-intelligent machines): 59, 60,
  67

Van de Pol, Prof: 151
Vallée, Jacques: 87, 88, 89, 95, 178, 185,
  186, 194, 203, 225
'Vardoger': 108
Verrall, Helen: 137
Verrall, Mrs.: 134-138 passim
Vietnam War: 67
View over Atlantis: 173
Villas-Boas, Antonio: 89, 178, 179, 186

Walter, W. Gray: 45, 65
Washoe: 25-28
Waters, Frank: 78
Weizembaum, Joseph: 55, 56, 57, 58, 65,
  66, 67, 68
Weldon, John: 202
Wells, H.G.: 12
Whales: 29-31
Whitmore, Sir John: 205
Whritenour, Joan: 197
Wiener, Norbert: 50, 67, 68
Willett, Mrs.: 135, 138
Williams, Mrs. Margo: 139-147
Wilson, Robert Anton: 206, 207, 208, 209,
  216
Winograd, Terry: 46, 48, 58, 65
Wittgenstein, Ludwig: 54
Wohler, Friederich: 161
Wolf, Frank: 119

Yerkes Primate Research Centre: 28
Young, Robert: 147
'Yram': 110, 111, 120

Zamora, Lonnie: 180, 197
Zuckerman, Sir Solly: 20, 22